THE BOOKSELLER
OF HAY

THE BOOKSELLER
OF HAY

James Hanning

corsair

CORSAIR

First published in Great Britain in 2025 by Corsair

1 3 5 7 9 10 8 6 4 2

Map by Barking Dog Art

A CIP catalogue record for this book
is available from the British Library.

ISBN 978-1-4721-5978-6

Typeset in Garamond by M Rules
Printed and bound in Great Britain by Clays Ltd, Elcograf S.p.A.

Papers used by Corsair are from well-managed forests
and other responsible sources.

MIX
Paper | Supporting
responsible forestry
FSC
www.fsc.org
FSC® C104740

Corsair
An imprint of
Little, Brown Book Group
Carmelite House
50 Victoria Embankment
London EC4Y 0DZ

The authorised representative
in the EEA is
Hachette Ireland
8 Castlecourt Centre
Dublin 15, D15 XTP3, Ireland
(email: info@hbgi.ie)

An Hachette UK Company
www.hachette.co.uk

www.littlebrown.co.uk

To dear Ru, without whom going to the
Blue Boar will never be quite the same

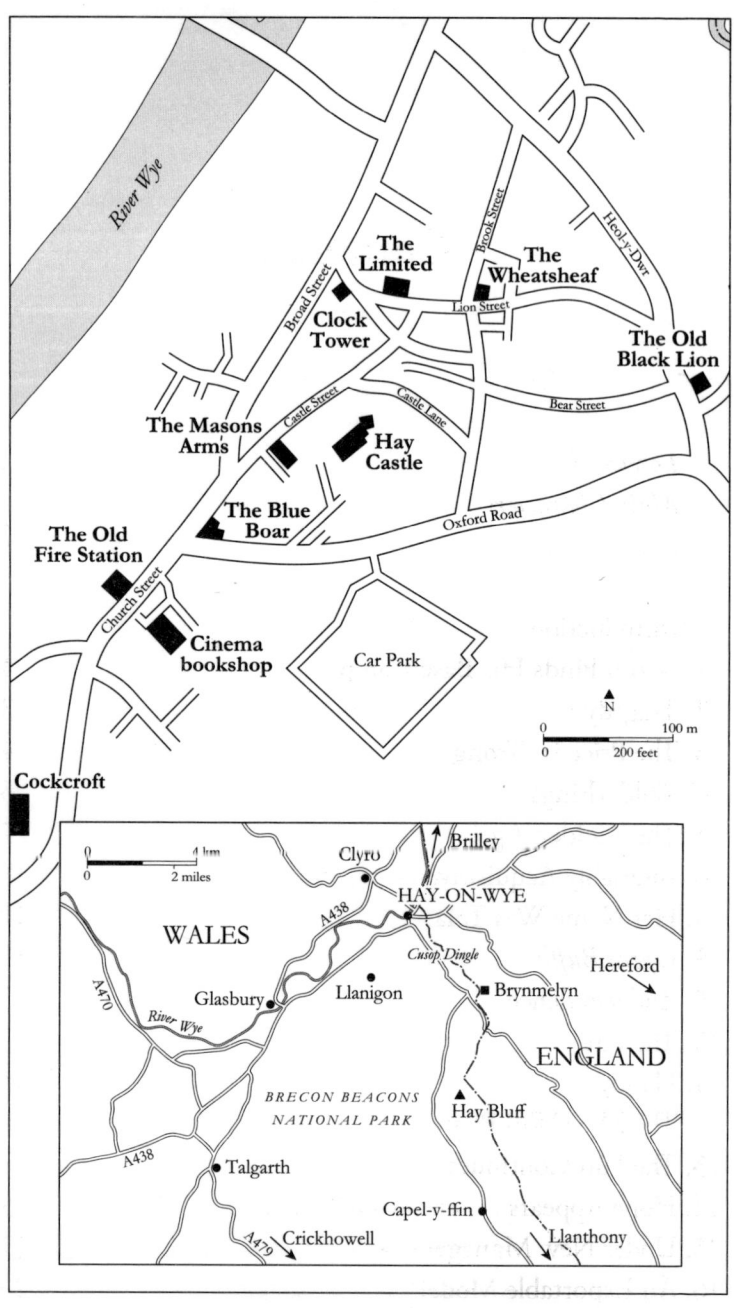

Hay-on-Wye and the Surrounding Area

Contents

Foreword		*ix*
Main Characters		*xv*
Places		*xvii*
Introduction		1
1. Booth Finds His Base Camp		19
2. Tragedy		36
3. The Price is Wrong		43
4. Wild Things		58
5. The 'Golden Age'		75
6. Insatiably Acquisitive in America		86
7. Her Name Was Tola		101
8. *Opera Buffa*		123
9. Independence		132
10. The Fire		149
11. Halloy		156
12. The Mice Will Play . . .		167
13. The Fun Continues . . .		181
14. Hope Appears . . . and Morelli Arrives		193
15. Under New Management		215
16. An Exportable Model?		232
17. The Open Road		247

Epilogue   263

Acknowledgements   *279*

Foreword

Hay-on-Wye is the brand leader among literary festivals. It has been going for over thirty-five years. It attracts over two hundred thousand people every year to a town of fifteen hundred inhabitants on the border between England and Wales. With more than twenty bookshops, if any town in Britain is synonymous with the world of books, this is it.

But why Hay? Other festivals are older. It is a difficult place to reach by public transport from Manchester, Birmingham, London or Cardiff, and not particularly easy by car. It is notably lacking in large hotels and the conventional manifestations of a media hub. Nor does its longstanding agricultural heritage make it the likeliest fulcrum of the written word. It is true that the possibilities for a festival in Hay were developed with exceptional entrepreneurial verve in the late 1980s and subsequently, but the answer to the 'Why Hay?' question is the extraordinary Richard Booth. It was his force of personality that transformed an obscure border town making an uncertain living into an international phenomenon.

Booth set up his first shop in 1962. By the early 1970s, in a development that would have been as laughable as it was unpredictable, other bookshops were beginning to appear. Some were direct competitors, some were offshoots of Booth's original and some simply sensed an opening. Booth himself was selling around two thousand books a week at that point. By the end of the decade, he was selling ten times that number. The 1978 *Guinness Book of Records* acknowledged Booth's as the world's largest second-hand bookseller, with shelves running to 8.12 miles and a stock of about a million books. There were around twenty other bookshops in the town and the growth seemed unstoppable. By 1986, no fewer than forty bookshops were represented in Hay, employing some 150 people – a tenth of the town's population. The bookshop explosion was outlandish, but genuine.

If setting up a shop that also sold books and antiques was a whim, it is clear that Booth was soon seized with a wish to make bookselling the town's unique selling point. He had an extraordinary singlemindedness, drive and determination to bring to Hay – in the 1960s more than ever a backwater in the international marketplace – sustainable prosperity. And the thousands who came to buy books testify to his success, and to what an extraordinary place it became within a few years of the first shop opening. That success later spawned imitations across the globe as 'book towns' became a new 'ideal type' for those with an interest in rural revival.

The launching and subsequent success of the Hay literary festival in 1988 took place despite *and* because of Richard Booth. He opposed the organisers' plans for the festival, yet he had created the terrain in which it could flourish. The literary cred was there, and it was cleverly enhanced and nurtured by first Norman Florence and then his son Peter, in concert with countless people in Hay. But it was Booth who put the town on the map, and the aim of this book is to offer an account of how he did so.

It is not exactly a biography and doesn't seek to detail every dusty book deal that Booth ever did. It lacks a specialist's knowledge of the book trade. It also offers no judgement on where Booth's theories on rural economic prosperity stand in the academic literature. It *does* aspire to present a readable account of how an eccentric, maddening, shambolic, hard-living businessman of innumerable contradictions managed, with a largely loyal staff, a ramshackle approach to recruitment, a flair for publicity and an extraordinary degree of determination, to create a world-famous phenomenon.

Richard Booth was a divisive figure. Beyond the briefest of encounters in the street, I never really met him. What follows is based on written material and the recollections of others. And among those, often there is little consensus. To some he was a benign, paternal, swashbuckling advocate for what his father's generation would have called 'the common man'. To others he was a shambolic, egotistical, capricious, unreliable spendthrift. That divisive quality – the fact that there is little agreement among those who knew him – makes the accurate depiction of the facts all the more important, and makes this book as much one of reporting as of analysis. If the reader is able to draw more settled conclusions than I am about a highly idiosyncratic figure, I am delighted.

Booth's contribution to Hay, though, is not in doubt. He was not everyone's favourite person, but if I had a pound for every time I heard the words 'but he did a lot for the town', I would be able to buy nearly as many drinks as he did in the Mason's Arms and Blue Boar pubs. Hay and its countryside is nearly unrecognisable from the town I, then at school, first visited in 1966 when my parents bought a cottage a mile from its centre. I spent most of my school holidays there, escaping from London, and for most of my life, as now, it has felt more like home than anywhere else.

Not that that makes me any more than a blow-in, of which Hay has many. How long a person has been spending time in Hay can become competitive, such is Hay's pride in itself, its attractiveness to outsiders and the regrettable waning of much of 'old Hay'. (It is inadvisable for those who think, after a few years, that they are beginning to settle in to ask one distinguished lady in Hay how long her family has been in the area: the answer, which she is generally too well-mannered to utter, is 'since the crusades'.)

I have had connections there long enough and have sufficient childhood memories, though, for it, and neighbouring Llanthony, to remain a very special, almost magical place. I remember walking to the farm down the road to collect the milk, which was still cow-warm when poured on my cereal. In summer the car's windscreen could do with being hosed down halfway to Hereford, so spattered was it with insects. Watch the River Wye for a few minutes in summer and I'd see copious fat salmon – about the length of a car bumper, I used to think – crash back into the water after some prodigious feat of fly-catching. The sheep and cattle used to stop what little traffic there was as they were walked through the streets to Russell, Baldwin & Bright's market. There were blacksmiths, basket weavers, dry-stone wallers and fence layers aplenty, and those who lived in the countryside were able to remain unambiguously its yeoman defenders.

Hay still has a lot of bookshops, but the town's success, and the internet, have made it a different place, for better or worse. It is at risk of being famous for being famous, a tourist destination in the middle of still beautiful if denuded countryside, rather than the place of Booth's vision that book buyers felt they needed to visit. Recently, I am told, someone complained about a tractor being driven through the middle of Hay, which delivery vans now treat as their own. It isn't quite what Richard Booth was aspiring to create. The law of unintended consequences has taken a major hand. Many local people have benefited from tourism, but many haven't. What he did want, though, was economic sustainability for the town, and Hay has had that. Without Booth, Hay would be just another border town. His influence remains immense, and his story worth telling.

Main Characters

Anne, Mary and Joanna Booth – Booth's sisters

Philip Booth – Richard's soldier father

Elizabeth Booth – Richard's Yardley heiress mother

Lennox Money – antiques dealer, friend and travelling partner of Booth from Oxford days

Hugh Vickers – opera-organising friend of Booth from Oxford

Lance Hughes – Hay-on-Wye vet and father figure to Booth

Elizabeth Westoll – daughter of Cumbrian farming family who married Booth in 1968

Frank English – carpenter, drinking partner and consigliere to Booth

Cotters (Michael Cottrill) – literature expert and long-serving Booth employee

Greg Coombes – Newport-born Booth employee who still works at the Cinema

Pat Wiggington/Thornton – ultra-loyal Booth PA and employee

Paul and Val Haynes – couple who met and married while working for Booth in the 1970s

April Ashley – one of Britain's best-known transgender
women who moved to Hay in 1975

Leon Morelli – London-based businessman whose move to
Hay in the 1980s brought a fierce rivalry

Norman and Peter Florence – organisers of the Hay Festival

Victoria del Rio (aka Vicky, aka Tola) – high-born Spaniard
who Booth met in Oxford in the late 1950s

Hope Stuart – Booth's widow

Lucia Stuart – daughter of Hope from her first marriage and
co-author of Booth's autobiography

Places

Hay-on-Wye – small border town on the edge of the Brecon Beacons

Brynmelyn – the Booth family home in Cusop, on the edge of Hay

Hay Castle – purchased by Booth in the mid-1960s, used as an office and later a bookshop

Hay Cinema – an ex-cinema which became the largest bookshop, purchased by Booth in the late 1960s

The Limited – large shop in the middle of Hay, the centre of Booth bookselling from the early 1980s

Cockcroft, aka Frank Lewis house – former workhouse, later store and bookshop, on the edge of Hay

Cusop Dingle – small valley on the edge of Hay, above which Brynmelyn was situated

Black Mountains – range of hills to the south of Hay, home of Capel-y-ffin and Llanthony Abbey – a nine-hundred-year-old former Augustinian monastery eleven miles south of Hay

Hay Bluff – mountain on the northern edge of the Black Mountains overlooking Hay

'What you have to understand is that Richard Booth was completely mad.'

Marianne Faithfull

Introduction

In the early 1960s, a visitor driving west from Hereford towards Wales would have been conscious of a heavily agricultural landscape, at that time devoted largely to the rufous Hereford cattle, and of the Black Mountains, dozing splendidly to the left, along the top of which runs Offa's Dyke, the ancient border between England and Wales. Though barely two thousand feet high, they appear larger. As the mid-twentieth-century writer L. T. C. Rolt explains, there are two reasons for this.

> First, their most prominent escarpments face north and east and are therefore nearly always in shadow. Hence they appear to loom over the rich red fields, the pastures and orchards of Herefordshire as darkly menacing as a thunder cloud. Secondly, they have a perfection of outline and symmetry that is incomparably grand. So majestic are the curves by which their projecting bluffs stoop towards the plain below that one is reminded of a succession of great waves, petrified upon the instant of breaking.

The Black Mountains mark the start of the Brecon Beacons, a thinly inhabited, spectacular range which runs east–west an hour's drive north of Newport and Cardiff. The countryside, through which runs the beautiful but currently troubled River Wye, has long attracted those in search of pastoral tranquillity. But the numbers to sustain a railway were no longer there. The line, which ran alongside the westbound road and the Wye, was closed in 1962, further sealing the motor car's late-twentieth-century primacy.

If tourists came, as outsiders they had the old-world agricultural charm of the place to themselves and the locals. They could fish for prosperous salmon, canoe, ride recently broken-in mountain ponies, stride across the hills and enjoy an existence that saw little reason to change. The Welsh–English border runs through Hay, on occasions aping Offa's Dyke, designed to keep the Welsh at bay. The small market town (pop. 1,500) most memorable for its name, Hay, was largely undistinguished from the many other border towns so reliant on agriculture.

If Hay has a distinctive flavour, apart from its Nonconformist heritage, it stems in part from its time as a lawless borderland ruled, after a fashion, by 'Marcher lords' from Anglo-Saxon times into the late Middle Ages. Nearly twenty miles from Hereford, administratively it doesn't feel like an essential part of Herefordshire, but it also lies on the very Anglo-leaning fringe of the Brecon Beacons and doesn't really claim much overlap with Brecon. Both larger towns see it as what it is: on the edge.

Notwithstanding the crippling hard work of its agricultural community, the word 'sleepy', even, would suggest a degree of animation unclaimed by most of Hay's residents of the two decades after the war. It was a timeless place untroubled by 1960s faddishness. Implicitly conservative, people worked diligently and with humility and looked after their neighbours. London, Birmingham and Cardiff were happily remote, and providing the nation's food retained an almost wartime assumption of centrality and moral purpose unsullied by the arrival of cheap processed food.

The town supported fifteen pubs, notably well patronised on Thursdays, market day. Customers, once settled, would take some shifting, taking full advantage of the 10 a.m. until 5 p.m., then 6 p.m. till 10.30, opening hours. 'You couldn't close at five o'clock,' remembers locally born Brian Wilding. 'You could shut the front door or draw the curtains, but closing was out of the question.' Meanwhile, the wives were at home cooking, feeding animals or doing the shopping.

Local history has it that there has been a market in Hay for seven hundred years, and until only recently farmers would bring their sheep and cattle to Russell, Baldwin & Bright's market, often driving them on foot along the road. Buses – 'standing room only and running all day on Thursdays' – came in from the surrounding villages.

Neighbours would sometimes offer horse and cart lifts, until the combustion engine came to the fore. When Tom Morgan, a local farmer, bought a new 'Fergy' (Massey Ferguson) one-seater tractor, he enjoyed showing it off and would be keen to offer anyone a lift. 'It was quite comical,' remembers Wilding. Passengers had to sit awkwardly on the rounded metal mud-guard above the giant rear wheel as they negotiated the untarmacked back roads. 'As Tom bounced along, he used to turn round every forty or fifty yards to see if they'd fallen off.'

Mary Tyler, well into her seventies and living alone, used to go to town on an old bike to buy a big bag of seed for the chickens and make the wobbly three-mile journey home. And the market would allow her a chance to pick up on local news and chat to friends. Rather less dutifully, so the story goes, one farmer from a couple of miles west of Hay used to ride into town for a day in the pub. At the end of the day, he would be strapped across his donkey's back and the dutiful beast would then transport him back up into the hills. The story endures because it is untypical in an area where, for all the pubs (now greatly reduced in number), moderation and the need to earn a crust have long had primacy.

If fashionable London had heard of anybody from Hay, it was probably either of its murderous solicitor Herbert Armstrong, eventually hanged in 1922 for doing away with his belittling wife (or so the court concluded), a tale depicted in *Dandelion Dead*, a 1994 ITV drama. Or it might have heard of Francis Kilvert, a Victorian-age priest who wrote an awestruck, beguiling diary about his walks around the area's parishes. Of one afternoon, when the setting sun illuminated the glistening snow on the mountains, Kilvert wrote: 'One's first involuntary thought in the presence of these magnificent sights is to lift up the heart to God and humbly thank him for having made the earth so beautiful ... I could have cried with the excitement of the overwhelming spectacle ... it seemed to me as if one might never see such a sight again.' Modern audiences familiar with his writings – dramatised in the 1970s by the BBC – can be put off by his idealised yet still questionable longings for chaste local girls, but he offers a vivid historical document.

Few people in those fifteen pubs would have known (rather than known *of*) Colonel Philip Booth who in 1960 moved into Brynmelyn, a six-bedroom Victorian house in Cusop, Hay's closest neighbour, which had previously been owned by his uncle. The house had been in the Booth family on and off since 1903, and it sat on high ground above Cusop Dingle, the home of some of Hay's better-heeled families. In his early sixties Philip Booth moved there from the Home Counties with his wife Elizabeth (the latter somewhat reluctantly), daughters and an adored son, Richard George William Pitt Booth. Philip Booth, a former soldier, was a keen book buyer, and was forever ferreting around Surrey's second-hand shops.

For a long time Philip Booth pursued his enthusiasm as much for the excuse it provided for getting him out of the house as for its own merits. In the early 1950s, though, it sowed a seed in the teenage Richard – the sisters were rarely invited – who developed a youthful taste for Arthur Ransome, Meredith, Gibbon and Macaulay.

While boarding at Bilton Grange preparatory school in Warwickshire, a feeder school for Rugby, the son had shown few leanings towards the arts or literature. He made it into the First XV rugby team – football was regarded as thoroughly déclassé – and otherwise distinguished himself only by throwing a brick at the headmistress's dog. When he did show an interest in music, asking his father if he might learn to play the violin, he was told it was something only girls did.

He was to flout the good fortune of his private secondary education – at Rugby – by cheating in an exam, and was expelled. He recalled later: 'My father looked to education to make his son and was desperate for me to make the right steps on the right ladders at the right time. I am not certain whether I felt more unhappy about my own failure or the misery I was to inflict on him by not achieving the set goals.'

The expulsion capped an undistinguished spell at the school, where he was seen as curiously bookish, though he enjoyed the occasional game of tennis, which he played well. Any thoughts he might have had of excelling at sport were dashed by having only one functioning lung, an affliction that was to spare him military service, a further disappointment to his father. He attended a crammer in Guildford, which he put to good use, paying frequent visits to the town's best-known book dealers.

In one such shop he learned a key secret as to how to make a bookshop more likely to entice browsers. If the shop is large enough, they 'don't have to talk to the owner'.

The crammer and a personal plea from Booth's father enabled him to enter Merton College, Oxford, where he read Modern History and an awful lot else, much of it purchased from a charismatic dealer of books and furniture, and later author, called Kyril Bonfiglioli, whom Booth later described as 'the James Bond of bookselling'. Bonfiglioli was a genius at separating rich undergraduates from their parents' money. Booth used to tell of how 'Bon', on spotting a potential victim sauntering towards his shop, would hurriedly put a red 'sold' dot on the ugliest of pictures and rush out to greet the young man. 'I kept this for you! I knew you'd want it!' And, of course, the sale went through.

At Oxford, Booth made a good friend in Lennox Money, later a distinguished antiques dealer, and cemented his friendship with Rugbeian Hugh Vickers. The trio enjoyed Oxford to the full, allowing a flourishing interest in the arts. Richard Ingrams, a fellow member of the Oxford University Dramatic Society and later editor of *Private Eye*, recalls an obviously wealthy, though unshowy young man. Booth, Ingrams remembers, paid for OUDS to perform at the Edinburgh Festival, putting up the entire cast – led by the young Ken Loach – in hotels. Vickers was also a budding arts entrepreneur, becoming a producer of opera, particularly *opera buffa*, an enthusiasm which long outlasted his undergraduate days.

Booth, though, was not good with money. To the horror of his strait-laced parents, he gambled a good deal, generally with his friend Bonfiglioli, with whom he had a card school.

Friends assume that Booth inherited money from an aunt, and that he was a product of the Booth's gin family. Neither is true. His money came from a generous allowance from his parents, to whom he applied a kind of moral pressure whenever his coffers ran low. 'My mother had this rather false impression that a young man needed money to give him confidence,' recalls his sister Joanna. 'And if he ever misbehaved or did something awful he'd say, "Oh, I'll be good if you give me money." And they did help him out a lot when he overspent.' The sisters also received an allowance, but a much less generous one. 'He was the one they favoured, moneywise, anyway.'

Oxford's most famous bookshop, Blackwell's, was well patronised by Booth and Vickers. They ran up substantial debts, to which Blackwell's understandably took exception. Booth, Vickers et al. found this most unsporting and took revenge by stealing the rubber stamp from the Bodleian Library, which was used to assert ownership of its books. They secretly branded a mass of items on Blackwell's shelves, rendering them unsellable in a shop purporting to sell new books. The row it caused was immense. Booth managed to pay off his Oxford debts, though.

Perhaps in a spell of youthful rebellion – and who can say if that spell ever really ended? – at Rugby Booth had been tempted by the world of public school homosexuality, though he said later that no sexual contact took place. Hugh Vickers had shown comparable leanings and took things further, being said by one longstanding acquaintance to have been the only man he knew who had slept with a man and woman on the same day, but by the time he settled in Oxford, Booth's enthusiasm for female company was well set.

Lennox Money was of similar mind, and the pair took full advantage of the possibilities offered by visiting foreign females at St Clare's, a recently founded college, independent of the university, that, in the words of its prospectus, 'grew out of a willingness to rebuild links between British and European students after the Second World War'.

Just twelve years after the war, St Clare's played host to a number of daughters of former wartime opponents. Booth, though, was delighted to let bygones be bygones. With alacrity he and Money set about making the offspring of the UK's former adversaries feel welcome. Lennox Money recalls the daughters of both German and Danish Nazis being beguiled by Booth. The numerous Spanish girls, who had only been allowed to attend the college because their families had influence in the fascist government of General Franco, were similarly forgiven the sins of their fathers. To Booth and Money, these foreign girls, often a year or two older than they, were hugely sophisticated, and the friendships they made with many of them lasted for decades. Booth was large, bespectacled and shambling, even as a young man, and was some distance from a conventionally silver-tonged smoothie. He was eccentric, inclined to schoolboyish over-excitement and largely gentle natured. He was a genial, humorous, unthreatening, kindly soul, not over-confident of his own appeal, in whose company women naturally felt comfortable.

At Oxford, Booth had two cars, a Jowett Javelin and an Alpine sports car. One day he and Lennox were driving along and their eye was caught by two girls. One in particular was stunningly attractive, they agreed, and they followed her to the gates of St Clare's. The girl in question was a youthful Victoria del Rio, then studying at the college. Her father was a businessman based in Las Palmas in the Canary Islands, and her mother a landed marquesa from a traditional Catholic family. Booth later admitted he was 'obsessed' and 'besotted' with young Victoria, but, for all his ardour, he remained uncertain as to whether, or perhaps for how long, she might reciprocate.

Though studious when his mind was engaged, Booth was spirited, without direction and keen to have a good time.

He said later he was 'an awkward, immature and outspoken undergraduate', a trait which did not go down well at Merton, regarded as a comparatively serious college. His tutor was Dr J. M. Roberts, described in one obituary as the leading historical mind of his generation, who went on to write *The History of the World* and to TV celebrity. Certainly at the time Booth failed to impress the Warden of Merton, Geoffrey Mure, an awe-inspiring Hegelian philosopher, whose time was spent more profitably with his higher-achieving students. Three years after leaving Oxford, Booth returned one day for a trip down memory lane. In the college bar, he said regretfully to Ron Buckingham, the barman, that he feared he must have caused him a lot of trouble in his day. According to Richard Emeny, another former Merton student who was in the bar at the time, the impeccably mannered barman had to confess that, yes, in fact he had been a bit of a handful. Whereupon Booth said: 'Well, in that case I had better do something to make amends.' By way of apologising, he brought out £100 (the equivalent of approximately £1,800 now) and gave it to the incredulous Buckingham.

The ill-disciplined young Booth left Oxford in the summer of 1961. He spent the few months after he left in London, knocking around with Lennox Money and a wealthy Indian friend, Farouk Bharoucha. Hard to picture though it may be for those who knew Booth in Hay in later life, his days were spent playing the sophisticated man about town, drifting from smart restaurant to gallery to auction house to nightclub. In later years he was famously unconcerned by how he dressed, his trousers sometimes held up with baling string, but in 1961 he confided to his diary: 'I discover to my annoyance that I am wearing green socks with a blue suit.' The diary is full of lines about haircuts in Harrods, tea at the Savoy, lunch at Chez Luba, lunch at Chez Kristoff – 'melon and scampi', 'trout and mushroom at La Speranza and then . . . to the Wallace Collection again', 'talked after dinner at Simpsons – too much boiled cabbage and a garrulous waiter – with Farouk . . . [I] may share a flat with him in Chelsea Cloisters.'

With Farouk and Lennox, Booth travelled to India, staying at some of the country's most agreeable hotels and visiting its most prized sights. It was a voyage of splendid indulgence, and offers no sense that any of the trio had any direction to their future lives. Booth did spend an unfortunate and lengthy spell in hospital, having treatment for a boil on his backside. The ailment, which in other circumstances Booth would surely have found very amusing, turned very nasty. At one point his friend Lennox was seriously concerned that he might not pull through.

Having done little work, he had left Oxford without a degree (thereby emulating Walter Savage Landor by leaving both Rugby and Oxford prematurely). He almost never alluded to the fact – even sometimes claiming to have 'an indifferent Oxford degree' – and almost nobody knew. His father was at a loss as to how best to speak to his son, knowing how the wisdom of fathers can go unrecognised for many years and that guidance from a buttoned-up veteran of two world wars to a feckless young drifter would fall on particularly fallow ground.

He toyed with taking up the law before being offered the sort of traineeship then more easily accessible to the comfortable middle classes – a job with an uncle's accountancy firm. His later difficulties in managing money would have come as no surprise to his colleagues of the time: he lasted three weeks in accountancy. His mind was elsewhere, not least in fast cars. Lennox shared his enthusiasm, and proudly told Booth that he believed his small car, an Austin 25, could go faster than Booth's Sunbeam Alpine. Booth doubted this, despite the

Austin having been in the care of Graham Hill, then on the verge of becoming Formula One World Champion, whose motor repair company had carried out an extensive upgrade. It was agreed there should be a race to London, with Graham Hill, no less, in the Austin and Booth in his Alpine. Booth defeated Hill, and, to his amazement, Lennox actually paid the £500 bet. Thus was born a notion of Booth as a talented driver of fast cars.

The young Booth was at a loose end, his father concerned about what he might do with his life. A family friend was Lance Hughes, the Hay vet, a cultured and benign figure who lived a few hundred yards from Brynmelyn. Philip Booth was unable to exert much influence on his wilful son (or, for a while, even locate him geographically), but Lance Hughes, regarded locally as 'long-headed' (shrewd), was a different matter. Much of Hughes's veterinary work involved listening silently to farmers air their concerns. Hughes performed much the same function with the young Booth, allowing him to offload his hang-ups. Hughes reassured him that nothing that had happened at Oxford need impair his future.

But the booksellers of Woking, Guildford and Oxford had left their mark. As it happened, the Hughes family owned a number of well-positioned shops in Castle Street in the middle of Hay. One of them, the former fire station, might make a very handy berth for Richard to set up in business. In early November, Booth received a telegram from his white knight, Lance Hughes, confirming that he accepted an offer of £750. Five days later, he wrote in his diary: 'Drove from Hay-on-Wye having definately [*sic*] contracted with Lance Hughes to buy the "firestation" – £800. He pulled a fast one about his offer, but I will remember.'

Booth would not admit this at the time, but he later confided to someone close to him that £500 of the purchase price had come from the bet he won from Lennox. Seemingly it strengthened their already close relationship, and was to encourage an attempt at reciprocation by Booth later in life.

A fortnight later, he wrote of 'the opening of Fire Station Antiques, to which I am definately [*sic*] committed ... In books, we will specialise in local history. I will try to get influential local directions. Hughes will be a great help.'

At the age of twenty-three, Booth opened his first shop. The opinion locally was 'Booth won't last three months ... nobody reads books in Hay'. His parents, certainly, thought it pointless and would merely postpone the day of Richard finding a proper career. 'Richard is ruining us,' his mother used to tell people, and he later admitted it was a crazy gamble: 'If cities like Birmingham and Cardiff couldn't support this kind of thing, what chance was there for a remote little Welsh town like this?' But property in Hay was not expensive, and the former fire station provided a platform for his boundless energies.

At that point, Booth wasn't fully committed. He claimed he intended to use the Hay shop as a base for buying antiques and books for his mentor Bonfiglioli to sell in Oxford, but he was still talking to friends about other sorts of job. At one point he and Bonfiglioli also talked of setting up in business in Nottingham. His parents had little faith in his prospects, and continued to suggest he sign up to get a qualification. If Bonfiglioli came up with something, he wrote in his diary, he would be 'in a stronger position to resist the blandishments of my parents – the security of a career. At Brynmelyn three days ago I nearly succumbed.' He wrote gravely of 'grim situations' with his father and mother.

The Hay shop offered him something to do, a form of escape, rather than a determined first step towards anything. One of his very first customers was nine-year-old Haydn Pugh, who now runs one of Hay's record shops, and who remembers buying an old copy of the *Boy's Own* annual for 3d. (three old pennies) early one Saturday morning in 1962. The selling of a second-hand book should not mislead, though. The project, such as it was, was unfocused. 'He had some chain-mail armour and all sorts of artefacts when he first started,' said Pugh.

Some have claimed that he realised a certain clumsiness was an obstacle to him selling antiques – he would be bound to drop them, so he decided to concentrate on books. In fact, he was an accomplished horseman and, as we have seen, a more than adequate tennis player. If there was an apparent lack of coordination, it was probably the result of a short attention span. Rather more likely is that he was again indebted to Lance Hughes, who told him how many of the old libraries in the mining valleys of South Wales were closing down and needed to offload their collections. Maybe there was a business opportunity there, he suggested.

That tip set Booth on a course that guided him for most of his life thereafter, and he accumulated supportive arguments as he went along. By what logic was the book trade solely urban, he demanded. Book buyers as much as anybody would enjoy the beauty of the Brecon Beacons, surely? The events precipitated by the opening of that shop was to transform Hay from a ramshackle, charming and unpretentious market town into, first, Britain's foremost home of second-hand books, then a world-leading 'book town', copied abroad, and finally the home of the world's best-known book festival.

Brian Wilding worked at the Old Fire Station from August 1964. He remembers being paid 25s. a week, much of which went on cider (a shilling a pint) in the Blue Boar pub. Booth's management style was in evidence from the start. 'Sometimes you were lucky if you got your money every week, sometimes you got it two months late, but you'd get it eventually.' Booth was inclined to turn up at the pub and announce that he had a van full of books arriving imminently. 'And we'd be unloading them sometimes till eleven at night. He had no idea of time. Very weird.' That indifference to day or night was to last for decades. He was forever up before the sun on buying trips, initially travelling all over Wales and the West Midlands and latterly all over the UK.

Booth's drive spurred him to expand quickly, buying two sites for storing books and then another shop. If Booth had a gift, it was a commitment to seek out dusty gems on out-of-the-way shelves that somebody might want to buy, ideally at a profit, and a compulsion to acquire them. (Some gems were so dusty that picking them up was like 'touching the fur of a young rabbit', he said.) The world of second-hand books was full of enthusiasts but rather fewer experts, he concluded. The caricature of the venerable, tweedy, even crusty, antiquarian bookseller in half-moon glasses with a generations-old customer list was not far wide of the mark, and in the big cities they seemed to have been there for ever, but Booth brought an extraordinary, almost (in modern parlance) punk zeal and dynamism in pursuing his prey.

Not that he was always an enthusiast for what was contained in the books, unlike some of those employed by him. According to the author Margaret Drabble, who knew Booth in the 1960s and 1970s: 'I don't think we ever talked about literature. Did he ever read books? The books themselves were just the product. I don't think Richard was interested in literature. Richard and I had nothing in common at all.'

It was the deal-making, the buying, that set Booth's pulse racing, and he quickly built on the thrilling expertise of Bonfiglioli and others, finding there was indeed a living to be made.

But surely not in so agricultural a setting? The mayor of Hay, for one, told Booth his shop was destined to fail, but he began attracting book-buying students from Bristol, Birmingham and Oxford. Shops were inexpensive to buy and he was picking up cheap, unwanted books and making a profit from them. So much so that, with the help of family money and that of friends, he acquired a second, third and fourth shop, and before long a house of his own, enabling him to move away from his parents and Brynmelyn. Travelling far and wide to visit old rectories, closing libraries and grieving spouses, he soon found himself buying books by the thousand.

Bookshops continued to spring up in Hay, bringing cash to the town. He had little time for formal education, and was keen to employ those who had suffered at its misguided hands. He said the economy was skewed towards driving the capable away from their countryside homes, leaving the 'stupid people' in charge.

As if to counteract that logic, he also brought in his own intelligentsia, employing a handful of gifted Oxbridge grad-uates to sort the books into some sort of order. They brought a bacchanalian liberal lifestyle that frightened not only the horses but also the sheep, cattle and their conservative, chapel-going owners.

The late-sixties vibe, the lure of magic mushrooms on the hillsides and cheap living created a buzz in a bifurcated town, where farm life carried on, side by side, the wilder crowd con-gregating around the expanding Booth empire. He made it his business to employ a good number of local people, a hallmark of his company, but conservative locals didn't entirely take to Booth and his racy friends (he admitted having 'a disastrous reputation').

Among travel writers, one of the great no-no clichés are the words such-and-such a place 'is a land of contrasts'. With biographers, a comparably tempting truth is that the subject was 'full of contradictions', but with Booth the term is unavoidable. The impression, at least, that he created was of countless paradoxes and differing views, many of those who knew him best disagreeing sharply among themselves, whether it related to his capacity for kindness, his abilities as a driver or his empathy with children.

Some former girlfriends call the thrice-married Booth a deeply sensitive, thwarted romantic; others saw him more as a promiscuous man in a promiscuous age. Was he an out-of-control boozer reliant on pub banter for a sense of validation or a rooted, outgoing and generous charmer (and only moderate drinker, despite the time he spent in pubs) with a flair for gregariousness and putting people at their ease? Was he a thwarted family man who longed for fatherhood, or someone who knew from an early age that children would only restrict him? Was he an inspired businessman with a brilliant, prophetic insight into the potential and pitfalls of the rural economy or an undisciplined, chaotic and childlike spendthrift?

Was he a selfish, out-of-control boor or an ultra-kind and sensitive paternalist with a deeply sincere admiration for artisanal and agricultural labour? Was he an old-school gentleman or an indifferent welsher on debts? Was he an enabler who was pleased to launch countless careers or a controlling autocrat who demanded his own way? Was he unselfconscious to the point of autism, or did a drive for the good opinion of others lie behind much of what he did?

The reader will draw conclusions from what follows, and some less contentious threads can be identified. The word from which few would dissent is 'eccentric', and his idiosyncrasy, at least, was of the most unstudied, spontaneous, unbridled sort.

Dawn Madigan, ostensibly Booth's secretary though the role contained a multitude of duties, remembers: 'When you met him in town, he'd have gravy down his front and look really scruffy but he'd always talk to you. There was a naivety about him. He'd be put on the spectrum now, I think. He was probably autistic, Asperger's but high achieving. He was very strange. He could upset someone and walk away ... and it wouldn't mean anything to him.'

From his shambling, chaotic physical appearance to his feral acquisitiveness in accumulating books to follow his dreams, immediate or longer term, he did his own thing. Where most would hesitate, he would dive in, spluttering inarticulately, barely able to convey his excitement at some new wheeze. Caution and restraint were strangers to him.

His leaps into the dark made for an often thrilling, often exasperating ride for his staff. They would be the ones who had to make his schemes work and deal with the consequences of his financial profligacy.

One of Booth's longest-serving employees says he never grew up, and retained the tastes of a testosterone-fuelled adolescent for most of his life. The childishness and single-mindedness of the pursuit of his goals, as if nothing else mattered, was a wonder to behold, something on occasions to be envied even by 'the sensible'. The childishness had its unattractive side and could result in thoughtlessness and insensitivity. He would cause offence, sack people on a whim, fly into rages and appear indifferent. When people asked, 'How could he be so cruel?', the answer was generally because he didn't realise he was being cruel. Or if he did, in his mind it was done for the greater glory of the people of Hay, for whom he had enormous affection. His public-spiritedness, which his critics would say was a disguised form of egotism, was directed primarily towards helping the town.

But perhaps the most striking characteristic of the life of this businessman was his indifference to money. Among entrepreneurs this is almost unheard of, and it was an attitude that was to cost him dear. Money was never a goal in itself and was deployed only reluctantly to achieve other goals. An empty bank account counted for little if he set his heart on a collection of books. The details would sort themselves out.

Booth Finds His Base Camp

'Richard wanted prestige and to be the centre of things.'
Rob Hughes

'There were a few odd ones in my father's family,' says Joanna Booth, seeking to place her brother as a black sheep of sorts. 'I think there was an inherited eccentricity occasionally. It was something in his blood, the way he turned out . . . in my father's family there were people who were not just eccentric but slightly cavalier towards others.'

The overwhelming sense is of a family inclining towards the conventional, so those who went their own way stuck out all the more. The Booths were a Yorkshire family, living for generations in Brush House, a Queen Anne mansion in Ecclesfield near Sheffield. Most of the men in the family went into the army and stuck assiduously to society's rules and conventions.

Richard Booth's father, Philip, had a prosperous but then unhappy and impecunious upbringing. Philip's own father had been educated at Eton and his parents and three siblings spent time initially in Canada before moving to Argentina. The father, good-looking, amusing and sociable, was part of an expat clique – he established the local polo club – and had a good job as treasurer for a railway line that crossed the Andes, connecting Argentina with Chile, but back at home money was tight and eventually the family had to return.

Even then things did not run smoothly. Not only was his family's return clouded by a shortage of money and the father's mutual loathing for his sister, but the children had to observe the break-up of their parents' marriage. Philip Booth's mother wanted a divorce, but proof of her husband's infidelity was insufficient to secure it, and she was required to collect evidence of his physical aggression towards her.

Despite his philandering, she still loved her husband, and he would not mend his ways. Her efforts to compile sufficient evidence must have been extremely distressing and damaging to family life. She was on the verge of completing the task when her errant husband, by now realising her serious intent and desperate to avoid a scandal, agreed that if she handed over the evidence they would repair their relationship. She agreed, but within days he had disappeared with a girlfriend to Paris, seldom returning in the ensuing twenty-one years. After a while he had little money to live on, and apparently his wife, left with the four children, had even less. 'Our existence was extremely precarious and depended almost entirely on my mother's courage and ingenuity,' wrote one of the children years later.

The Booth grandfather leaving his wife and four children to live in Paris with his girlfriend was not the only example of black sheepery in the family. A family trawl of letters from the Peninsular War (1807–14) reveals that, for all the toeing the line, they didn't always get on. 'I'm afraid it may be a bit of a family trait,' says Joanna.

Philip was born in 1897, the year which marked Queen Victoria's sixtieth on the throne. He served in the First World

War, developing a hatred of Germany compounded by seventeen of his twenty-one fellow officers being killed or injured on the Somme. This hostility was enhanced in the Second World War when as a member of the Royal Pioneer Corps he helped liberate inmates from Belsen. Between the wars he served rather more agreeably in India. There, at the comparatively late age of forty, he met his wife Elizabeth Joanna Pitt, purportedly a descendant of the eighteenth-century politician Pitts, who had gone to the subcontinent as part of what was uncharitably known as 'the fishing fleet' of women in search of husbands. Her father was president of the Institute of Accountants and a director of Yardley cosmetics, which allowed him to leave a respectable private income to each of his twenty-two grandchildren, Richard included. As successive generations of Booths had done, Philip served in the Oxfordshire and Buckinghamshire Light Infantry (which became part of the Green Jackets Brigade), eventually writing a history of it while living a quieter life in the Home Counties.

During leave from the army, Philip would occasionally spend time at the home of his father's cousin. Major W. H. Booth, DSO, OBE, a Boer War veteran with hunting trophies to match, had bought a house called Brynmelyn, in Cusop, a few hundred yards from the River Wye. There he spent much of his time fishing, with notable success. The family retains a stuffed five-foot salmon that he caught on the Wye at Clyro, and the largest pike ever caught on the river, a thirty-seven-pounder, which can now be admired in a museum in Hereford. Though Philip was no fisherman, he enjoyed his time spent with Willie – in truth, something of a substitute parent – and, while living in Surrey, always hankered to return to the border country. Willie died in 1950 at the age of eighty-seven.

During the war Philip and Elizabeth lived initially at the

family home in West Wittering, Sussex, though the beach was
mined and defended with barbed wire, making the sea inaccessible. Booth's father, ever vigilant, would ring home from the
nearby Isle of Wight to warn that the Germans were coming,
though they never materialised. It was decided to move to a
respectable private housing estate called Pyle Hill, near Woking,
which Richard thought boring and suburban. Elizabeth was
quite happy there, but Philip and Richard found Surrey's golfers
and businesspeople irksome – Jews, for example, were banned
from some of the local golf clubs – and the pair would leave
their womenfolk in Surrey for weekends at Brynmelyn where,
though different in character, they formed an at times uneasy
bond. There they enjoyed the hospitality of Willie's dutiful,
churchgoing widow Kit, who encouraged birds to come to her
garden and fed the native red squirrels in the hope of saving
them from the grey invaders.

When she died in 1960, Kit left £500 in her will for the
upkeep of Cusop church. Almost all the rest of the £55,765
estate was to go to the Distressed Gentlefolk's Aid Association
and to the Church of England Pensions Board, for the benefit of
the clergy. If Philip was disappointed not to be a direct beneficiary of the will, he nonetheless saw an opportunity and agreed
with the trustees of the two charities to purchase Brynmelyn,
thereby keeping it in Booth hands. This delighted Richard
who, having savoured life among Oxford's sophisticates, was
finding Surrey tediously comfortable and felt he fitted in with
Hay's less routine social life. 'Richard was delighted and pushed
them as hard as he could, though my father wanted it anyway,'
says Joanna.

Brynmelyn became the base camp for the rest of his life. For
a while he continued to live with his parents, though there was
plenty of friction. 'As children we got on very well,' remembers

Jo, 'but after Oxford, when he met a lot of interesting people, he didn't want very much to do with his family. In a way you expect a young boy to have rows with his mother and say "I hate you" and so on, but you don't expect that in their twenties. He still behaved like that with my parents at times. Richard was in many ways a sort of inverted or intellectual snob . . . He got on better with my eldest sister Mary [two years older than Booth], who didn't criticise him at all. She was very sweet-natured, but he thought the rest of the family were just boring and conventional.'

His mother was not an uncritical admirer of her son – a very different character from herself – but he was favoured none the less, which gave him an anticipation of being able to wheedle whatever he wanted out of his parents. He was not far wrong. 'Our mother adored him and worshipped him, but there were ghastly rows,' says Jo. 'My parents always forgave him.' This was resented by Mary, Jo, two years younger, and Anne, four years younger again. The sense that to him they were staid grew into real resentment at their disapproval of his expansive ways.

Though Booth needed to keep in with his father, he appeared to many quite unrestrained. He would constantly ask his parents for money to help with some new aspect of the bookshops and would generally get it. Philip was a traditionalist and felt the male offspring should be favoured over the daughters in matters of succession, though he had few illusions about his son's waywardness and, to put it generously, inexperience with money. Local people tell a story of how Booth had an argument with his father in Hay's Market Street. 'I want a thou, Pop,' shouted Booth. 'You're not getting any thou out of me,' exclaimed his father, for whom such a public breach of dignity would surely have grated.

A general difference of outlook did not help relations. Anne

Booth had married a soldier, Philip Powell-Jones, and conformed to type. Richard regarded any spare family cash as his almost by right. After his father's death, he assumed he would inherit a family car, but his sisters refused to let him have it. As a result, he refused to give his sister away at her wedding. Years later, when relationships had improved, he had no memory of the episode.

'Booth behaved really badly towards his own family,' says one old acquaintance, and certainly his sisters would get very upset by the heated arguments he provoked. 'I remember Philip [Powell-Jones] marching him out of the house with a shotgun after he had tried to get some money off Anne ... Philip just wasn't having it.'

Philip Booth was of military bearing and above all a believer in hierarchy. One Hay local who knew him well said his son found him 'boring and conventional'. (The son once said the only thing he had in common with his father was an enthusiasm for books.) The father and his family were respected locally ('good people'), though his manner was occasionally taken by shopkeepers for aloofness. On one occasion one of Hay's best established senior businessman, Mr Grant the newsagent, was moved to show protectiveness towards one of his staff after Colonel Booth had picked her up for her manners. The colonel meant well, and would always give the person who delivered his newspaper a generous tip at Christmas.

Richard Booth's attitudes were essentially liberal, libertarian, mischievous and anti-Establishment, the very opposite of his father's. This manifested itself in selfishness and caprice, but notably in him frequently defending what might loosely be called 'working people'. One longstanding Hay-born Booth employee remembers how different Richard was from some of his family: 'He had relations who used to come and stay and they wouldn't even speak to you. If you said good morning to them, they'd look away. You were beneath them. They behaved as if they had it all, with servants and so on. You know, this is your place. He was rebelling against that. When he escaped that, it was like wahey!' This democratic spirit found a particular outlet in Hay's agricultural surroundings.

'He had this enormous respect for country people,' says Greg Coombes, who worked closely with Richard Booth for six years. Booth never had to do anything practical as he was growing up, he says, and had a sense of wonder for those who did. 'If you've never had to mend a hole in the roof or mend your shoes, you have a great respect for people who could do that. He knew that they had to make do and mend because they had nothing, so there was a great toff sense of obligation. And that was compounded by successive agricultural slumps and increased use of technology which was doing people out of work.'

Coombes, who was born in Newport but married into a Hay family, recalls Booth being respectful of the milieu into which he had moved, and the circumstances in which many people less fortunate than himself had to live. 'There's a lovely local word, scrat, which means eking out a living, often by fruit-picking or foraging or whatever was available.' On Merbach Hill near Hay a saffron flower blooms prodigiously ... It would take a certain local knowledge and awareness to know when and where this flower might bloom, but when it did, if harvested in sufficient quantities, and with the key part extracted, an enterprising local could take it to someone in Hay who made clothes so they could make an indigo dye out of it. 'If you're lucky you'd get two bob for it,' remembers Coombes. It was tales such as these, born of poverty, that gave Booth a profound admiration for local skills.

Such an attitude might be thought condescending. He did

indeed see himself as the public-spirited lord of the manor, somehow in touch with local people. The respect he engendered may not always have been for his own personality, more based perhaps on a local appreciation of what he was able to do for the town. Nonetheless, Booth's admiration and fondness for the locality was genuine, and among those who knew him well, which was not everyone, it was reciprocated. It is a mark of his singularity that if he did display snobbishness, it was unconventional – mainly anti-academic and anti-snobbishness itself, though he remained a firm elitist in many respects.

One friend says Booth was incapable of being patronising in a conventional class sense, and he was as good as his word, employing many local people, and outsiders, with few obvious qualifications as booksellers, and few qualifications of any sort. Some saw this as a necessary way of helping his business achieve public support, and to modern ears it might sound a bit *de haut en bas*, but it was entirely sincere, well-meant and enduring. Of a decision to employ twelve agricultural labourers, he told one reporter: 'They have a natural gift for the job. They have no fads or hang-ups like many university educated people. They buy the books, pack them, drive the container lorries, sell them and handle the whole operation without any fuss.'

His commitment to the people of Hay, though initially slight, grew and grew. One underqualified person whom Booth employed was sixteen-year-old Michael Twigge-Molecey. Booth had heard about him having lost his mother and was aware he needed work, and he was employed sorting books, which at that stage mainly meant carrying them to others to do the sifting. His introduction to the world of Booth was typical, to the extent that anyone's was typical. 'I arrived in Hay when Booth had two full-time staff who did all the boxing and collecting and driving,' he says. 'He arrived in Hay at about 3.30 p.m. one day. Richard said "Go and have a look round town. We meet at the Mason's Arms at about seven and have a few drinks there." I walked down the back alley. Someone said, "Hello, Mike, how are you?" I asked, "How do you know my name?" I was told, "You must be Mike, who has come to work with Richard, aren't you?" That's the sort of town it was . . . if there was someone new coming in, people just knew.'

Molecey identified something that persists in Hay to this day, notwithstanding the changes wrought by the bookshops and the festival. 'The feeling was "You're here, you're one of us." As long as you didn't talk down to locals, they treated you as an equal. They were kind to you, accepting of everybody. I wore a suit and tie every day for fifty-five years. To some it might have seemed eccentric, but people accepted it. I cannot emphasise enough how accepting and generous people were, with their time, their willingness to be helpful.' It was an easy-going aura that Booth enjoyed, reciprocated and exploited. He employed people on a whim. Some lasted for days, some for decades. The turnover was prodigious. Rachel Wiggington, daughter of one of Booth's most loyal employees, Pat, was also employed by Booth. 'At sixteen he sent me up to the Castle to sort and price these books. I had no idea what I was doing. He just said, "You'll know what they're worth if you look."'

One figure featured hugely and irresistibly in the Booth story. On arriving at Brynmelyn, Booth's parents had decided they needed someone to look after the garden. In *The Lady* magazine they found someone claiming 'no job too small'. This was Frank English, who had deserted from the army three times and had no time for authority. Philip Booth's idea of a drink, on a good day, would be a modest gin and tonic before dinner. Wine at meals was a rarity, with the odd inherited bottle occasionally appearing for special occasions. English, though, was a prodigious drinker. Richard Booth admitted in his autobiography, *My Kingdom of Books*, that when Frank English arrived his own personality disappeared, and the drunken English became the sort of mentor that few parents would have welcomed for a directionless, nonconforming son.

Booth was a compulsive contrarian and enjoyed surrounding himself with people who went against the grain of his upbringing. These would often be those he happened to like but who to most were untrustworthy. 'He always had dodgy people around him,' remembers his sister Jo, who says his family was forever finding family miniatures and swords and the like had gone missing. Frank English was generally paid in cash, in part to avoid paying tax, though it did him no favours in other respects – he drank his way through his pay pretty quickly. One night English turned up in a pub with a plastic bag. It contained a silver box engraved and presented to Booth's uncle by Field Marshal Montgomery. English, whose loyalty to Booth was only in question when in urgent need of a drink, was trying to sell it.

Booth's family disapproved hugely of many of his associates, but he would usually end up being indulged by his parents, to the continuing frustration of his sisters. One day his exasperated mother told Booth that he was to stop employing English, who was a thoroughly bad influence (whether or not she knew about his theft of the silver box). Booth junior, though, thought him something of a savant. He wanted to keep English, but his mother wouldn't hear of it. She said she would give him £2,000 if he got rid of him. He accepted the offer, took the money and still refused to get rid of his drinking partner. English was later sacked after one of his cigarettes caused a fire, but Richard Booth continued to give him work.

English introduced Booth to the earthier pubs of Hay, and

quickly Booth 'was moving in a peasant society where all pride was in manual work', as he wrote reverentially many years later. In truth, Booth's attitude in his earliest days was some way from respectful. One evening in the Mason's Arms, after a few drinks, he found himself arguing disdainfully with Bill Cooke, a local lorry driver, who felt the recent arrival from Oxford was getting above himself. Cooke did not appreciate being talked down to and stood his ground. Booth, the worse for wear and riled by such insolence, told him he could put him down. (Despite his size, the idea is laughable.) Cooke suggested they go outside to see if that was true. There was only ever going to be one winner. The humiliated (if not humbled) Booth became a close friend of Cooke, in time employing both him and his son Andy.

English was said to drink all day and build shelves all night, the extent of his drunkenness discernible by the shade of magenta on his beak-like nose. When living at Brynmelyn, one of Booth's colleagues, who owned an MG Roadster soft top, used to drive home up the hill. More than once she saw a pair of legs sticking out of the bushes. 'It would be Frank, who hadn't quite made it home from the pub,' says Lyndy, former wife of Andy Cooke. 'I used to stop and stand him up, leaning him against the side of the car and tip him in ... and he'd fall in, legs akimbo ...'

He certainly gave Booth's wildness some sort of validation, and his wit and ill-concealed bile to those he didn't like gave rise to no end of stories. English would go through occasional dry periods and spells when he and Booth were not speaking, but they were few and far between. 'It was nothing for Frank to get in the car at 4 p.m. and by the time we got to London he'd finished a bottle of whisky,' says Booth's driver Ron Smart, 'but to look at him you'd think he hadn't had a drink.' Even on a good day, English was inclined to smell of garlic and whisky. Smart, though fond of him, always drove him with the window down.

A local antiques dealer, Brian Wigginton, liked fishing very much and would sometimes head off early to dip his rod in the river. English, though as short of ready cash as his boss, nonetheless found sufficient funds to pay local scallies to throw rocks in the river to scare off the fish. 'Frank was a sort of hatchet man,' remembers Greg Coombes. 'If you saw Frank twice in a day, it meant you were for the chop.' Gerard Brookes, another Booth long-timer, remembers English as a deeply unpleasant man. 'English would come up to me and say, "I'm going to ruin you, boy". He held out his hand to me and swayed badly, and he accused me of stealing books, which I hadn't, and I was threatened by one of his friends. He hated me, and I don't know why. He was awful, a horrid man.'

Booth and English had a bond. 'Richard was amused by his anarchic free-thinking mindset,' says former Hay shopkeeper Martin Dearden. 'English opened Richard's eyes a bit and they laughed a lot together. He disdained everybody and everything. He hated the stuffy middle-class denizens of Hay-on-Wye. He sounded middle class and was an educated man, but he had dropped out of the system.'

English's unforgiving edge could be inflicted on anyone. Coombes, one of Booth's most capable employees, who came from Newport, spoke with a South Walian accent which, as a keen-to-impress young man, he modified in order to fit in. English made no pretence of not noticing Coombes's discomfort. He told Coombes: 'I'm terribly sorry, but I just can't bear your provincial accent.'

Even English's drunkenness was an asset on occasion. Booth got wind that a country house near Hay wanted to sell its books, but also that Quaritch, a highly reputable book dealer, was better placed to snap up the collection, having already arranged an appointment to size it up. English decided to intervene. With a six-pint lunch adding to his customary looseness, he turned up at the house in question. He rang the bell and hiccupped, 'Hello. I'm from Quaritch. Can I have a piss?' In truth this plan probably never materialised: if it didn't, it would not have been through bashfulness.

English's fondness for drink was all part of the amiable chaos that Booth so enjoyed. The drink, though, tended to bring out treachery. Gerard Brookes recalls driving with Booth, English and a very drunken Hugh Vickers to Heathrow airport. 'I noticed English taking the opportunity of removing Booth's wallet from his jacket, which was hanging over the front seat. After a while Vickers woke up to find Frank asleep, at which point Vickers stole the wallet from English – and these two were his two best friends. Somehow Richard got the wallet back in the end.' When questioned whether two such close associates would really steal Booth's wallet, rather than simply do so for a lark, Brookes replied: 'Good God yes!'

One of the grievances that Booth's sisters held against him was that after his parents died he did not look after Brynmelyn, where treasured items would go missing, notably military portraits and swords. Some have no doubt that English was responsible, and other candidates have been suggested, though Jo Booth won't go so far. 'I don't know who took the stuff from the house.'

Yet for Sue Jenkins, daughter of the owners of Booth's favourite pub, the Mason's Arms, English was a sweetheart when she was growing up. For one thing, he could blow cigarette smoke out of his ears. 'He taught me how to play chess, he taught me how to speak properly, he taught me so much,' she says. She remembers sitting in the Mason's Arms (now Spar) in Hay, looking in the shop window across the road at a Space Hopper, a giant rubber ball that children used to enjoy riding, using its ears as reins. English looked across the road and, thinking it was a giant balloon, offered to buy it for her. 'When he realised it would cost probably ten times what he had expected, he still bought it for me,' she says. She kept it for so long her own children played with it. 'He used to buy us sweets, give us money to go to the sweet shop, buy us Christmas presents. We had other customers like that. It was a real community back then.'

His kindness could be adapted to those he liked nearer his own age. Lyndy Cooke, when living at Brynmelyn, recalls feeling nauseous one morning when English happened to be visiting. He suggested she might be pregnant – quite possible, she said – and if so she should make sure to have something to eat. In typical English style he sensitively dished out a large bowl of cornflakes, topping it off with a hefty slug of whisky. Even more recklessly, one evening in the Mason's Arms, the father of the pub's landlord Ken Jenkins was looking after his three-year-old grandson, Kelvyn. When he went to the toilet, English encouraged little Kelvyn to drink some of his grandfather's whisky, which he did. When he returned, the grandfather was furious and there was nearly a fight. 'It was his idea,' protested English, pointing at the three-year-old.

Booth's bug for buying books had taken him over and become an obsession. He once said he would much rather sell a million books for one pound than one book for a million pounds. Soon it was not untypical for him to buy a couple of hundred thousand books from the United States and ship them over to the UK. 'Even a bad book about the First World War has a buyer somewhere,' he used to say. Property in Hay was still cheap, and so was the space to store all those books.

Among his regular customers was on old friend from Oxford,

Harold Landry, who started selling books at the same time as Booth and who went on to specialise in literary periodicals. He became a frequent visitor to Hay, often with his then girlfriend, Margaret Drabble, who was married at the time. The couple would visit for weekends, Landry trawling Booth's multiplying shelves for odd numbers to help him buy magazines, for example, while Drabble would look for the odd bargain. 'I remember the excitement of discovering bargains and wondering if the seller was going to realise before you bought them,' she says. She became bored, though, and would take herself off for walks along the river. 'Hay is so beautiful and, in those days, even more beautiful. It was to me a very innocent and delightful time.'

Harold Landry and Booth worked hard and played hard. 'There was very much a Liberty Hall atmosphere which was quite fun for me because I had three small children and led a very regular life, so a little escape to Hay was always fun. It was a very attractive place in the sixties and seventies.'

Landry was a serious collector. 'He just was addicted to collecting and wanted to complete runs of magazines. I think Richard probably had the same kind of attitude towards business ... that you build up your run, your empire, and it was a business model that worked for him. The books themselves were just the product to sell.'

Drabble did not gel with Booth, though, who in this period was at his least restrained. She recalls an occasion when Booth was excited about something, clearly wanting to show it off. 'I do remember being slightly offended when Richard showed me a pornographic eighteenth-century Regency print and I didn't like it and thought he shouldn't have shown it to me. I didn't think it was very funny. It was a very mild bit of pornography, and I was a bit priggish in those days, but I didn't really like it being shown to me, and I thought, There's an awful lot more where that came from, I'm sure. I didn't really like Richard or know him very well.'

As to whether Booth was embarrassed at having misjudged the moment, she says: 'I don't think he cared very much about my reaction.'

Drabble was in Hay because of Landry's work and friendship with Booth. 'I didn't really take much interest in Richard, he was just there. He was certainly odd.'

From the earliest days of his first bookshop, Booth had claims to grandiosity. Having found a living by providing shelf space for unwanted books, which cost him very little in the remote border country, he aspired to bigger things. It was a tendency that Lance Hughes had noticed, and again Booth was to be the beneficiary of his help.

The Castle in Hay dates to the 1100s, when the Normans built it to keep the locals in order. In the seventeenth century it had a large private house attached to it, but it never quite acquired the status to which it aspired. Author Kate Clarke reports that in the mid-1960s it was 'filled with antiques and defunct fairground artefacts – there were suits of armour, fruit machines and brightly painted carousel horses. The interior was in good condition, with wonderful oak floors, panelled rooms, four-poster beds and a magnificent staircase.'

Its owner, Edward Vernon Tuson, who was married to a circus heiress, decided he wanted it off his hands. In its dilapidated state, it was the ultimate drain on resources and, ideally, it required a benefactor for whom money was no object. Tuson offered to sell it to Lance Hughes for £7,000. Hughes decided it was in too poor a condition and in any case its layout was quite unsuited for a vet's practice. But he told Tuson he knew someone who might jump at the chance and encouraged Booth to take up the challenge. 'My father saw this as an opportunity for Richard that he shouldn't miss,' remembers Hughes's son Rob. 'He knew Richard wanted prestige and to be the centre of things. Richard wanted a bookselling space and by buying the Castle – which was an underutilised space – Richard was enabled to mythologise about himself. He couldn't have done everything he did without the Castle.'

Tuson raised the price to £10,000, and some believe Lance Hughes loaned Booth money to help him buy it. In any event, buying the Castle was Booth's big announcement to the world. He had truly arrived. He could now call himself a successful local businessman, with a stage from which to project it.

2

Tragedy

'In those days it was a sleepy one-dog town and Booth
meant something to people. If it had been me they would
have cut my balls off ... but Booth being Booth, he
seemed to have a lot more clout.'

Hay resident

Billy Morgans was nothing if not public-spirited – and distinguished, too. In the war he served as a radio officer in the
Merchant Navy, which played such a dangerous and crucial role
in ensuring that Britain's Atlantic lifeline kept Britain fed. His
facility in sending and receiving Morse code messages at high
speed caught the attention of MI6, who recruited him to be a
'listener', a role he played with impressive discretion from his
front room in a terraced house in Hay. His occupation, when he
returned from his day job, was, with the help of a large antenna
next to a bunker in his back garden (given the codename
'Station Wye'), to spend the evening listening in to German
U-boat traffic. His findings were then collected by motorbike
and taken to Bletchley Park for analysis.

Not that his day job was a breeze. He was a surveyor by

training, but his wartime role included responsibilities for Air Raid Precautions (ARP), tending to evacuees from the cities and the distribution of food rations.

In the 1930s, he and his wife Edith had lost two children in infancy, one to spina bifida and the other to croup. But by the time the war ended, happily the couple's hands were full. They now had two sons, David, born in 1938, and Michael, born three years later. Within two years of the war's end, they were able to welcome a third son, Robert, and David returned to a life of low-key civic orthodoxy, advising locals on their planning applications and the like. In 1962, while working for Hay council, he helped the young Richard Booth set up his first bookshop, attaching a fireman's helmet above the door of the Old Fire Station.

Robert, his youngest son, grew up quickly, and on Thursday 26 March 1964 he found himself marooned in Crickhowell, an agreeable town separated from Hay by the picturesque Black Mountains, but connected by a circuitous thirty-minute drive. The friends with whom he had begun the evening had teamed up with two local girls, but Robbie, going steady with a girl from further west, needed a lift home that night. He was due at work at the Hay accountancy firm of Hughie Lewis the following morning. As luck would have it, he ran into Frank English, then living in Crickhowell. To Robbie's relief, English told him that Richard Booth also happened to be in town, visiting a warehouse where he stored books, though that evening he was in a pub. Booth was planning to open a bookshop in the town – an extension of the growing Hay berth – and was due to drive home to Hay that evening. Three months earlier Booth had bought a red two-seater Volvo P1600 coupé, similar to the sort driven by Simon Templar in *The Saint*, a TV series of the time, and Robbie was pleased to accept a lift with Booth.

At around eleven that night PC Stan Austin had the task of knocking on the door of the family home and breaking the news to Billy Morgans that his son Robbie had been badly injured in a motor accident. Richard Booth's car had hit a stationary lorry parked half on the road, half on the verge outside the Hollybush pub three miles from Hay. Soon afterwards came the news that Robbie, having sustained a devastating blow to the head, had died. Booth, whose side of the vehicle took less of the impact, emerged from the accident with cuts to his face but little other damage.

The reason for the crash was not immediately apparent. The night was dry and moonlit. It is a section of road where accidents have occurred, perhaps because, after a series of bends, drivers tend to speed up on it. How much Booth smelled of drink cannot be known, and the breathalyser was still some years off, though the offence of drink-driving, punishable by a ban and up to four months in prison, had been on the statute for nearly four decades. It is unchallenged that Booth had been in one of Crickhowell's pubs during the day. He was known to be familiar with driving fast cars, though others say he was a poor driver – not bothering to concentrate, frequently driving in the wrong gear and so on. His sister Jo says he was a 'terrible' driver. A barrister's initial opinion was sought on behalf of the Morgans family. His view was that Booth was guilty of dangerous driving.

The day after the crash, Robbie's brothers identified the body. After the accident, Booth wanted to have the car repaired, but his father ordered it to be destroyed. In the run-up to the inquest, Robbie's brother David and his wife Val bumped into a local acquaintance, Freddie Griffiths. Talking about the accident, Griffiths said '. . . these modern cars, they just fold up'.

Griffiths was due to attend the hearing, yet here he was

expressing a view before he had even heard the evidence. David found this perplexing, and wondered if the outcome of the inquest had been decided in advance.

The inquest, held in Hay some weeks later, heard that the driver of the lorry, Albert Edward Cooke, known locally as Bill – Booth's Mason's Arms drinking friend – had stopped to get some change to make a phone call. He told the inquest that he had checked that his lights were on. After ten minutes in the pub, the accident outside had become obvious, and he went out to find Booth's car almost perpendicular to the lorry, across the road. He and some of the dozen or so drinkers in the pub helped the passenger, at that point still alive, out of the car. One report suggested that Booth had fled the scene of the crash but was ordered back by the police. This seems unlikely. More credible, though this does not appear to have emerged at the inquest, was that, according to friends of the pub's landlords Dovey and Joyce Lewis, after the crash Booth, though not obviously under the influence, went into the pub with an urgent request for black coffee.

A local resident had been driving in the opposite direction moments before the accident. In his rear-view mirror he did not see the lorry's lights as he passed, and remarked about this to his passenger. Then, in front of him, he saw the lights of a car approaching 'very fast' and 'heeling' close to the road's central white line. At the time the passenger said: 'The wind of it vibrated our car.' The driver heard a bang after he had travelled a further thirty to forty yards after passing the car. He stopped immediately and reversed back to the lorry, where he saw the other car facing across the road.

After giving assistance at the scene of the accident, the driver shouted, 'Where's your lights? You had no lights on.' Contradicting this, a bus driver, also travelling westwards, passed the stationary lorry and said he was 'definite' that the lorry's two rear lights were lit, as required by law for the previous eight years. Booth did mention a lack of lights privately later in life, although the lorry would have had reflectors in any event. The coroner showed little curiosity about the lights. It was treated as an irrelevance.

The focus, understandably, was on the extent of Booth's culpability. Then twenty-six, Booth admitted he had drunk three brandies in Crickhowell and clearly he had been driving very fast. Yet the coroner could scarcely have done more to help Booth, and his remarks to the jury will be jarring to modern ears. The inquest heard a local doctor assert, in response to Mr Booth's inability to recall what happened moments before the impact, that this was not significant. He had been driving for eight, accident-free years, said Booth.

On the issue of the speed of Booth's car, the coroner doubted its significance: 'Was speed in itself enough to make it recklessness?' Possibly not but, bizarrely, of the most obviously compounding factor, Booth's admitted three brandies, he said: 'There is not the slightest evidence that the question of drink arises. You can banish it from your thoughts.' The jury did as it was advised, concluding the death had been the result of an accident, and no blame was apportioned.

'We were absolutely stunned,' says David. 'I remember seeing the insurance chap who was with Booth and he was gleeful, and so was Booth. He shook his hand and then Booth looked over our way and . . . the smile went from their faces when they saw us. I don't understand how they reached their verdict,' says David, now in his mid-eighties. 'I think the police were pretty shocked. This looked to me like small-town politics. Richard Booth was deemed to be of more value to the town than my brother who had gone to grammar school in Brecon.'

The day after the accident, Booth's father Philip wrote a letter of condolence to Robbie's father Billy. Richard himself expressed no apology to the family, nor showed any contrition or offered an explanation beyond asking the coroner to pass on his sympathy. Years later, in conversation with a relation of Robbie, he referred obliquely to a 'tragedy' at the Hollybush, but without acknowledging any responsibility for it. Referring to the incident years later in a single paragraph in his autobiography, he mentioned that he had been tuning the car radio, while also saying he was tired, having been up since 5 a.m. He called it 'a tragedy for which I cannot forgive myself'.

A friend of his family said of Booth: 'He did at the time go completely doolally . . . he just imploded and couldn't cope with it. I saw him then as I had never seen him before.'

Nonetheless he still made no attempt to contact the family, either at the time or later in life. For the Morgans family this was unforgivable. 'He had no conscience,' said Val Morgans, David's wife, who passed away in April 2024. 'Perhaps he thought his father's letter was sufficient.'

Booth's failure to make contact with the family is at odds with his usual habit when bereavement strikes. Booth's silence, says his friend Peter Dance, 'was not because he was heartless, for he was anything but that. If someone died in Hay he was usually the first to send a bunch of flowers and he would often attend the funeral.' (A friend who hurt her back falling on a metal staircase received the biggest quantity of flowers she had ever received.) On this occasion, however, he did not attend the funeral, perhaps assuming he would not be welcome. 'He certainly wouldn't have been,' says David Morgans.

The Morgans family suffered in a number of further ways. Years later Billy had to attend council meetings at which Richard Booth was often present, the stress of losing his youngest son seemingly having given rise to a recurrence of his tuberculosis. 'Dad got through it better than Mum,' says David. 'Mum never got over it.' Others confirm that Mrs Morgans spent protracted periods in bed, and that her grieving husband was also hugely disturbed, not least by the effect it had on his wife. Local people in Hay wrote letters of sympathy to the family, who have hitherto not commented on the matter. As far as is possible, Booth was allowed to move on.

It is striking how few people in Booth's entourage know of the episode. Almost all of the handful who do say he never spoke of it. One decades-long friend says it would be hard to imagine it not having had a huge impact, but what was he expected to do? No words could undo what had happened. What cannot be cured must be endured. One of his closest associates said: 'It didn't change his life or make him get terrible depression, but he certainly didn't take it lightly or try and hide it. It was something awful that had happened.'

Sue Jenkins, daughter of Ken and Vi, owners of the Mason's Arms, says: 'Knowing Richard, I don't think he could have put that behind him. I think he would have lived with that till the day he died.'

3

The Price is Wrong

'No academic I know scrambled over scrap heaps in the rain trying to save books.'

Richard Booth

Booth's manner was engaging – when he chose to deploy it – and it served him well.

Lance Hughes, the family friend who had encouraged the young Booth and become one of his father substitutes, pointed out that many of the working men's libraries in Wales, set up to provide ancillary activities for miners and steelworkers, were closing. Hughes's own father had been a compensation officer in the Welsh coal mining industry and had a particular bond with mining communities. These libraries were rooted in notions of personal betterment and class solidarity, but the industries they stood for were in decline and their appeal waning. Those responsible for the closures had little or no attachment to their contents and wanted the books dispensed with quickly and defensibly. There were fully 250 such libraries, so for an aspiring book magnate bent on acquisition it was a true bonanza. For better or worse, much of their contents made their way to Hay.

Booth also purchased books from cash-strapped universities, his contempt for academic self-importance seeming to provide some sort of intellectual justification. He had little time for the sanctity of a 'collection', and in March 1972 became involved in an argument on the letters page of *The Times* when academics from Worcester College, Oxford, lamented the dispersal on the open market of 'an old, rich and varied collection' from the library of Ely Cathedral. Many of the books, wrote the dons, had been bequeathed by dignitaries of the cathedral and, as a national possession, should remain part of it rather than dispersed. Booth proudly replied that he had bought a number of ecclesiastical libraries, and that they belonged where there was most interest in them. He said it was unrealistic to state that an antiquarian library was 'part of Ely life'. The books, he claimed, would now be of more use in the following year than they had been in the previous two hundred. Booth was showing a 'distressing insensitivity', wrote another correspondent, in failing to understand the corporate value of a library beyond the importance of its individual volumes.

But such collections were his bread and butter. Of the closure of the Bala College Library, seen now as an avoidable travesty from which Booth made money, he wrote in his autobiography much later: 'It was the beginning of the devastation of Wales, but as a young dealer eagerly searching for books, I was not able to see the tragedy as I do now.' He admitted his part in the disappearance of one of 'the proudest intellectual achievements of Wales', but could not resist pointing out that 'no academic I know scrambled over scrap heaps in the rain trying to save books'. The remark illustrates his longstanding disdain for academics as a breed. He regarded them as overrated and unworldly, and few of the ones he employed brought much to the company. Later in life, though, he admitted to guilty feelings over the

Bala closure, and he spoke at length to his friend Jane Flower of his remorse at enriching himself at the expense, ultimately, of the underprivileged mining communities.

His enthusiasm for travelling to make book purchases had become something like a drug. Whereas just a few years earlier he had been a directionless young son of privilege, he was now gripped with a purpose. Inspiration had well and truly struck. He would get up at 4 a.m., have a large breakfast and travel for miles in the hope of further conquests. Soon Wales and England were too small for him, and he went to Scotland and across the Irish Sea, loving the adventure, meeting new people and filling the car – and then larger vehicles – with cheap books. At one point he decided to take up flying lessons at Shobdon Airfield in Herefordshire, believing the aeroplane was the future for fresh purchases near and far. His flying instructor even flew a handful of senior colleagues in a hired plane to Norwich for what was intended as a lightning raid. In the event, they bought just a couple of boxes of undistinguished books which were loaded into a van by a Booth driver and taken back to Hay. Not a venture to impress his accountant, but reportedly an entertaining day out from which lessons were learned. 'Richard was always doing extravagant and strange things like that,' recalls Peter Dance, one of those on board. In the event the trip was not repeated. Booth decided one flying lesson was enough.

The alacrity with which Booth travelled accumulating books – he had an estimated half a million on his shelves in mid-1968 – was making demands on the town. The business's turnover had multiplied fifteen times between 1962 and 1968 and was now topping £100,000 a year. The bookshops were increasing in number, but Booth's buying was outstripping them. Where was all the stock to be kept and displayed?

The answer lay in the Plaza cinema, now disused and

something of a symbol of the town's stagnant economy, owned by Desmond Madigan, a businessman and local councillor who had struggled unsuccessfully to bring trade to Hay. Initially Booth rented the property, which, despite posing briefly as a dance venue and a bingo hall, had done little for local prosperity. Booth brought the sort of optimism that had given rise to the construction of the cinema in the 1950s, but he was constantly in arrears with the rent and Madigan was becoming frustrated at seeing Booth's business expanding while his own coffers suffered.

Madigan offered Booth the chance to buy the cinema. Booth, perhaps sensing that no one else was likely to have a use for a large, warehouse-shaped building in an out-of-the-way country town, played a long game. He told Madigan that he had just ordered a Rolls-Royce, and that he had a difficult choice to make – the car or the cinema? He chose the car, a white Phantom 6, complete with cocktail cabinet and glass screen between passenger and driver – 'I could smoke my cigars contentedly,' he boasted – and made Madigan wait another two years before he agreed to buy the cinema. Even then, he gave Booth extremely favourable terms and 'substantial leeway' in paying the deposit.

The other big event of 1968 was that he decided – 'faced with the insoluble problem of my domestic ineptitude,' he cheerfully admitted – to get married. As so often in Booth's life, Lennox Money played a prominent role. A cousin of Money had married into the Westoll family, well-established Cumbrian farmers, and the couple had taken over the estate from the cousin's mother. The bride's younger sister, Elizabeth, was offered a 'starter job' as an assistant in Money's antiques shop in Pimlico.

Elizabeth Westoll caught the eye of Booth during one of his trips to see Money in London, and he began to meet her in secret. Only after going out together for several weeks did Booth admit to his friend that he was dating one of his shop assistants, which Money found slightly awkward. Booth was approaching thirty and she was only eighteen. The relationship blossomed, and the pair married in Kirkandrews on Esk, Cumberland, in late February 1968, with Lennox Money as his best man.

Elizabeth was universally described as 'lovely' in Hay. Frank English's endorsement was typically freighted: 'She is easily the best wife you are likely to get.' She was young and lively and was, said one family acquaintance, 'the kind of wife Richard's father would have liked him to have', which, over time, may or may not have been a plus in the son's eyes. She acquired an affection for the Castle and used family money to help Booth do it up, a flagship indeed of Hay life. The fact that she drove around in an expensive car, a Porsche, did nothing to undermine her reputation for good grace and thoughtfulness with those less fortunate. Elizabeth opened the Castle to the public twice a year, an admirably democratic and inclusive – if rudimentary – move in a town where thirty years earlier greengrocer Tony Pugh had been summoned to explain himself after failing to doff his cap when the lady of the Castle drove past.

Booth, having married Elizabeth, continued to be obsessed with the growth of the bookshops, and increasingly she felt more bit player than co-star in the Booth drama. 'He came to take her for granted, and was very neglectful of her,' says Lennox Money.

In the end, her mother came to share her disaffection and, it is believed, persuaded Elizabeth to leave him. 'He knew he had neglected her and very much regretted it,' says Money. 'He had been extremely fond of her.' Elizabeth remained in the area, now driving a lime-green Renault 4, and happily started going out with a writer, David Hughes, who was lodging with the Clare family near Crickhowell. In *Running for the Hills*, one of the sons, Horatio, beautifully records how she found her feet, and love, while living under their roof, and how she and David added to the joy and sense of fun in the household as he was growing up, and started their own family. It was a happiness few begrudged her.

Meanwhile, the Booth sense of mission and ambition was unabated, and the purchase of the Cinema provided a major spurt in his expansion. The key figure in the stripping out and revamping of the Cinema was Frank English, who Booth credited with building a total of twenty-five miles of bookshelves during his career, a decent proportion of which, with the help of a newly constructed mezzanine, bore the Cinema's quarter of a million books. The shelves, on Booth's instructions, were to be within easy reach of a 'five-foot-two woman'.

Booth's quest for new sources of books was rapacious. There were shelves to fill and an unnecessarily large workforce to keep busy. In Hay he would task his staff to write letters to people whose names and addresses were found in the local telephone directory. Only those whose addresses did not include a street number were approached. (Those with books were unlikely to live in numbered/terraced houses, he reasoned.) He would look through the deaths and obituary columns and then, after a suitable pause of a few weeks, arrange a seemingly chance contact. Another Booth maxim was: 'There's never any good gear in a house with an illuminated doorbell.' In terms of books purchased, it was remarkably successful. He had the chutzpah to approach potential vendors – usually novices to the book-selling world – to give a sense of knowing what he was doing, of knowing the trade and being able to make a quick valuation. Added to that assurance, he would happily put troubled minds at rest by saying, 'If you've got a lot of books you want dealt with, we'll do it.' And he or one of his people would obligingly say, 'We'll take the lot.'

One Booth ruse, he explained to a trusted recruit after purchasing books from the recently bereaved wife of a professor, was to carefully review the books on offer and then select five or six. For these he would make a generous offer, which would usually be accepted. This would establish the confidence of the seller. He would then apologise for not being able to make an offer for the rest, on which he would look with undisguised disdain. He would then, as a favour, offer to take the rest away for a nominal figure. He would not admit that among 'the rest' were some real gems, worth a good deal more than the original half-dozen.

Back in Hay, the team, with a collective eye roll, would set to work. This is literature, that is biography, that is travel, etc. Booth used to say, 'Never offer too high a price – it arouses the seller's suspicions.' Jan Shivel, an American former employee and friend of Booth, who lives locally, remembers him talking years later about the importance of the first culling. 'He told me if you buy a library of five thousand volumes for, say, £10,000, in that library you're going to find two volumes that will earn you back what you have spent. Anything on top of that – you're laughing. But the going through of that lot, looking for those really precious things, that was the important thing.'

Booth talked a good game, but former colleagues point out that he was no particular expert on the pricing of old books. Some of his staff knew a great deal more than he did, but he knew enough. Not that the extra, less valuable books went to waste, at that stage at least. Kyril Bonfiglioli spent some time in Hay organising 'the by-product' for the sale or rent of yards of heaving bookshelves for film sets.

But very often those charged with doing the sorting simply weren't qualified to do so.

Michael Twigge-Molecey admitted to having been clueless initially: 'I was pretty poorly educated,' he said. 'I'd always been a reader, having started with C. S. Forester, but Richard was prepared to give people a chance, and I helped him sort books. He trusted me enough to sift, between the ones that could go straight on display to the public and the others that needed proper sorting, in which case Richard would then have a look at them.'

Paul Haynes first started working for Booth in the 1970s. 'I remember Richard telling me simply: "Price this lot,"' says Haynes. 'We had a huge collection of Baedekers and other guidebooks. I started pricing them up. I put £1 on Switzerland and £1 on Russia and then realised people were fighting to get the Russia one. You'd learn very quickly from your mistakes and Richard was happy to enable that process.'

Artist Alex Williams, who was to do a lot of publicity work for Booth as well as running the successful print shop, remembers being deployed in the sorting shed at Brynmelyn in the mid-1970s. 'There were a lot of broken books up there and you could pull the plates out of them. One day a German buyer came in. I sold them and then about two years later a book on European woodcuts came out and the picture I had sold was on the cover. You could never be sure what you had.'

Inevitably, given the quantities, Booth relied upon his staff to sort the wheat from the chaff. Prominent among these was the famous 'Cotters', Michael Cottrill, who made Booth's eccentricity look positively amateurish, and who at twenty-three was diverted from librarianship and hired by Booth around 1970 (no one is quite sure). He was to work for Booth for decades, his love and appreciation of English literature and the arts more widely unrivalled on the staff.

Writing in his autobiography, Booth said of Cottrill, 'the service that he gives customers is the best in the country'. He won praise even from the unforgiving Frank English. 'He's an extraordinarily talented boy,' said English.

Yet for all Booth's hopes for a discerning sorting of the books, even Cotters and his well-read colleagues could not be all-seeing. Filmmaker and author Stephen Weeks remembers how, as the number of Booth bookshops increased, so did the visitor's opportunities. He used to collect Ward Lock guides to the counties of England, and one of Booth's shops sold them for just 50p each. At the Cinema bookshop, though, they were on sale at double the price, and they were prepared to buy copies from customers at 75p. 'So every time I visited,' he recalls, 'I would buy a few at the low price, sell them at the higher price and spend my winnings on the guides I needed.'

One day soon after he bought the Cinema, Booth was walking down the aisles, surveying the shelves. He came across a figure who was becoming an increasingly familiar buyer. This was a young and brilliant American student of theology called Tom Loome, who was based in Tübingen, where he was writing his PhD on modernism and the Catholic Church. Booth approached Loome and mentioned that he had seen him around the shop quite a bit. Loome explained who he was, and Booth, impressed with his learning, asked, 'Do we ever make mistakes in pricing books here? Do you find books that are underpriced?'

'Oh, yes,' replied Loome candidly, 'quite a number of times.' Booth asked for an example. 'Well,' said Loome, 'take this book in my hands. It is priced at four pounds. Actually it's worth about a thousand pounds.'

Booth replied in his usual way: 'Would you like to work for me?' Loome said yes, and was soon sent off to evaluate libraries near and far. The pair worked closely for many years, buying and selling from one another long after Loome returned to the States.

Under-pricing was a perennial problem of which all book dealers must beware and an outfit run by Booth was never likely to be watertight. In the mid-1970s, he admitted that one book in particular was underpriced at under £5. It was an early, unauthorised edition of Sir Thomas Browne's *Religio Medici*, published in 1642. Fortunately, a member of staff noticed and upped the price to £800, at which a dealer snapped it up.

Many years later, as late as the 1980s, one of Booth's staff was approached by a couple offering to sell a first edition of *The Satanic Verses*, bound in leather and printed as part of a special run to mark the infamous book's initial publication. This was within days of its author, Salman Rushdie, being made the subject of a fatwa on the grounds of its heretical depiction of the prophet Muhammad. (Curiously, and unknown to almost anyone at the time, Rushdie was hiding in the Llanthony Valley with his police protection team, just a few miles away.) It would not have taken a genius to work out that the book was likely to become extremely valuable, but the man on the desk sucked his teeth and said he was willing to go up to £10, but no higher. The disappointed customers thanked him and moved on to amble carefree through Hay's narrow streets.

Another Hay bookseller, Anne Brichto, got wind of the couple's presence in town, and of their remarkable possession. She tracked them from shop to shop, finally catching up with the pair and offering them £350, which they were happy to accept. She later sold it for £700, and it was eventually resold in London for well over £1,000. This was an occasion that called for Booth's benign paterfamilias demeanour.

He affected a patrician lack of concern, saying he saw such lapses as part of the sport, as helping sustain the visitor's hope for serendipity. Noelle Beales, who worked at one of Booth's shops, says that if he bought a great library that was worth a fortune and he didn't pay a lot for it, he'd be quids in. 'He knew that at the Cinema, there were people who knew what they were looking for, and there were others who were just stacking them up. Richard used to say, "I'm cool with that ... If someone thinks they can come into the shop and just randomly find a great book, brilliant!" He never seemed to be cross about it. I don't remember him ever gnashing his teeth about someone getting a great bargain.'

The success of the Cinema would depend on keeping it well stocked, which chimed with Booth's high-adrenalin purchasing. He rented coaches which would bring students from Oxford. If they spent above a certain figure, the transport was free. Students came flocking on Sundays, rendering the tiny market town incongruously busy. 'No one came to Hay, and very few people lived here, but suddenly there were these busloads ...' remembers one staffer.

Book collector Ian Sanger was a frequent visitor. 'The key to it was that you wouldn't get people to come all the way to Hay if they were going to have to pay London prices,' he says. 'They would come if they thought they were going to get a good deal or stumble on an unrecognised bargain in their field. And that would bring them back again. I imagine Richard's strategy was to make up through a large volume of sales the income he didn't plan to achieve by emulating top dealers' prices.'

So the turnover of stock was essential, both for the amateur book lover and those in the trade, which, says Sanger, was still pyramid-shaped. 'General booksellers would frequently sell on, often at only a small profit, to specialist dealers further up the pyramid and to dealers at the top, many in London. There were also book-runners, who would comb the shops that constituted the broad base (and tended not to send out catalogues) for books that they would then place with dealers higher up the pyramid. Hay would have been full of runners.'

Brian Lake, owner of Jarndyce Bookseller near the British Museum and former author of *Private Eye*'s 'The Worlde of Olde Books' column, on the other hand, was one of those who did his own digging: 'It was a perfect place to go for a day out … I used to get up early, drive down, have breakfast in Ross-on-Wye and spend the whole day in Hay buying books and then drive back in the evening. It was a really good trade source, especially if you wanted books in a particular area. You could guarantee you'd come away with half a dozen boxes. Booth's modus operandi was to keep moving stuff on and it would encourage people to keep going back to Hay for years afterwards. The stuff was churning through so fast that some dealers from twenty or thirty miles away would be going there every day, because being there when a new lot came in was really important.'

Yet there were down times as well, and, contrary to the mythology that it suited everyone to endorse, it was the dealers as much as the readers who kept the business going.

'Somewhere like that,' says Lake, 'you drift along during the week and then if a book dealer comes in at the weekend you might double the take in half an hour. And the chances are that by the time the bookseller had made the effort to drive all the way there, he wanted to buy. The level of trade being done there could never have carried on without dealers going there regularly.'

Winters in Hay could be particularly bleak, and the book trade's down times could be very down indeed. During the quiet months of winter, Frank English used to find better things – or at least other things – to do than wait in the Cinema in the hope of serving a customer. He would leave a note on the front desk advising, 'If you want to buy a book, bring it over to the Blue Boar.' It would be nice to think the cash he received eventually went into the company's coffers. Nice, but possibly naive.

Bruce Robinson, best known as the creator of the film *Withnail and I*, recalls the early years of the Cinema bookshop with fondness. 'I have always been a keen bibliophile – George Cruikshank, the Victorian illustrator, Charlie Dickens, people like that – and I came here a lot for the books in the 1970s,' he says. 'I came here one summer and one year I came and had a drive around ... it's absolutely beautiful.' He recalls excitedly buying a first edition of Henry Miller's *The Air-Conditioned Nightmare* in 1973 for about £1.50. 'Even then there were books for that sort of price that you just can't get now.'

It was still the age of outsmarting the bookseller, and, with huge quantities of books coming through, the casual buyer stood a good chance. 'It used to be your knowledge up against the bookseller's knowledge,' remembers Robinson, 'and if he didn't know this was a rare piece of Dickensiana, well, good for you. Nowadays, when they don't know what it's worth, they look online and if it's £500 in Cape Town you'd knock a bit off. Now it's you against the internet, but in the days when it was you against the dealer, you could find amazing stuff. I bought a first issue of *A Christmas Carol* in a bookshop in Swansea during my acting days, about fifty years ago, from Ralph Books. It had all the right endpapers and so on. Even then it was worth a hundred quid. I went to the counter and said how much is this? The guy said, "Ooh ... Dickens, I don't know ... £5?"

'Somewhat shocked, I said, "£5?"

'The bloke said: "All right, four pound ten."'

'It's now worth several thousand.'

Booth, though regretful of his monomania and loss of the much-admired Elizabeth, reverted to his youthful ways. Monogamy was not a state in which he ever felt entirely at ease. 'He was completely selfish,' remembers his sister Jo. 'He enjoyed food, drink and sex in abundance. He didn't think twice about being unfaithful to a woman.' The marriage had lasted barely a year, and he admitted that his wife had married 'a kind of monster'.

The loss of Liz, like most things, did not change him. He remained the same unapologetically shambolic muddler-through who couldn't imagine why the world should be seen through anyone's eyes but his own. Greg Coombes said of him: 'Richard never matured. He had the same attitude to the opposite sex as a seventeen-year-old schoolboy. That's why he had so much fun ... he had the fame and the money, or the promise of money, that enabled him to do what he wanted. Richard was very much a bachelor boy. There were any number of liaisons but nobody ever moved in.'

His status as the man who put Hay on the map ensured he was a figure of some fascination in the 1970s. 'He was never short of a girlfriend,' says his sister Jo. 'I wouldn't have thought he understood women very well. He always wanted a bit more money from one source or another ... he thought Elizabeth would bail him out but she didn't so the marriage fell apart.'

One story popular in Hay is that Booth, by then in his early thirties, dressed up as a vicar and arrived at Cheltenham Ladies' College in his Rolls-Royce, announcing that he needed to break the news of a (non-existent) family bereavement to his 'niece', and that only when he took off his dog collar, as he was leaving, was the fraud exposed.

The truth of the story is far less racy than the mythologisers would like. Booth was nearby, visiting Gloucester, and invited the young Janet Hughes, daughter of his benefactor Lance, and a friend of hers to tea. After a theatre rehearsal, Janet and her friend dropped into a tearoom in Cheltenham at the appointed time to find Booth wearing a dog collar as a joke. After the customary Booth-inspired laughter, they returned to school at the usual time. Unfortunately, the two girls had been spotted with Booth 'masquerading as a vicar' by a member of the school staff. The girls' parents were called; they were sent home for a week and could only return when they had written letters of apology. Lance Hughes was less than amused. Booth was thoroughly abashed.

4

Wild Things

'If they didn't behave, I'd deflate their bicycle tyres.'

PC David Jones

Booth's Racing Demon approach to book buying did not happen in a bubble. It changed Hay, whether Hay liked it or not, and on occasion the influx of free-living literary 'sophisticates' jarred with local sensibilities. Yet often the high-living at the Castle, for example, was the subject more of speculation locally than well-sourced reporting. Some of the goings-on might have called for the intervention of the law, but traditionally Hay was a home of low-key, community-enforced policing, and what adults did behind closed doors was assumed to be harmless. Some might say Hay was a law unto itself, which certainly suited the Booth narrative, but recourse to the courts was limited.

There was a certain amount of agricultural crime but generally the malefactors were known about and dealt with privately. 'We knew everyone,' remembers Constable David Jones, who was a local copper in Hay. 'I was at school with a lot of them. We used to have a little intelligence book to pass on what was going on ... we knew their fathers and their grandfathers ... They never held it against me. I always tried to avoid making things worse than they are.'

Policing in Hay came straight from the Elysian playbook, in which the lovable local (always male) bobby has a friendly word for everyone, can spot a wrong 'un a mile off – usually an outsider – and spends his days issuing benign 'mind how you go' warnings. It is nowadays a much-derided idyll, but people in the area insist it worked well. David Jones used to give a gentle heads-up to youngsters playing dangerously on bicycles at night. If that didn't work, he would simply deflate their tyres. If they did it again, he would confiscate the valves so that the bikes were unusable. If that didn't work he would inform their parents.

In his youth he had learned the persuasiveness – and utility – of the indulgent turning of a blind eye. At the age of just fifteen, he was spotted early one morning driving his father's car up a lane to milk the cows. The then local constable, leaning stereo-typically on a five-bar gate, saw him drive past, pretending not to notice. A week later, the copper 'dropped by' for a cup of tea with his parents. When the parents were briefly out of the room, he muttered simply, 'You won't do it again, will you?' He didn't.

This is not to say that Hay was some sort of Utopia. It was certainly more *Trumpton* than Trumpian, but there was recognition that with a skeleton staff and the nearest back-up force twenty miles away, the police needed the goodwill of their public. There was no nonsense about targets then. 'We had to have people on our side for the times when something serious happened,' says Jones. When informed that Jones had not had a motorist convicted for over a year, his boss told him: 'Keep up the good work.'

He recalls a night in the height of a baking summer when

the doors of a pub were wide open – to let the air circulate – after closing time. He walked in as the barman was pouring a pint, the customer's money sitting on the counter. It didn't look good. 'Can I get you something to wet your whistle?' asked the barman nervously. There was a long pause.

'Those boys had been hauling bales all day,' remembers Jones. 'Who was I to stop them having a drink on their way home? So I stopped and had a chat and a half of shandy with them. Of course my bosses got to hear about it and I got bollocked for it, but I could live with that. How you treat people is half the job around here.' Others who held his position were reputedly even more committed to this approach. On another occasion, he had taken the steam out of an altercation in a pub when a young drinker had become violent. Instead of bringing charges, Jones let the young man, who he had known for years, off with a warning. Some time later, an angry and drunken driver tried to run someone over after an argument in a pub. None of the bystanders would say anything. The formerly violent drinker, who years earlier had also had the valves on his bike confiscated, let Jones know: 'You're looking for a black American 4x4 vehicle, and he has gone pony trekking.' A quick trawl of the local riding centres led to an arrest. The man was sent to prison.

Few visitors to the area can resist visiting the Llanthony Valley. Poet Walter Savage Landor lived at the ruined abbey there more than two hundred years ago. In the 1920s, sculptor and typographer Eric Gill lived at the monastery at Capel-y-ffin, and with David Jones had one of his most productive spells. J. M. W. Turner, Eric Ravilious and John Piper also painted in the valley. Sociologist Raymond Williams, musician Robert

Plant and writers Horatio Clare and Owen Sheers have all found inspiration there.

Having seen the Abbey, visitors from Hay return by travelling northwards where a gaping view of the Wye Valley awaits them. It is what Stephen Weeks calls 'one of the most remarkable drives imaginable anywhere in Britain'. Woe betide anyone who tries to put pylons or a wind farm here. As Weeks notes, the road

> passes Wales's smallest church at remote Capel-y-ffin and into the Brecon Beacons proper – climbing up and through the bleak and barren Gospel Pass. Then, bursting out into sudden broad vistas over the Vale of Ewyas, all meadows and orchards, with the lane winding down towards the distant prospect of Hay-on-Wye. Wow! And it always seemed the sun had come out just at that moment of taking in this remarkable landscape.

Richard Booth used to go up there a couple of times a week. Artist Jeremy Deller asked for the view as his *Desert Island Discs* luxury. One of the most striking, lingering shots in Stanley Kubrick's *Barry Lyndon* was taken there. The opening of *An American Werewolf in London* was also filmed there. Cliché though it may be, it demands the epithet 'epic' for its top-of-the-world specialness.

It is a place where people – conventional or otherwise – want to spend time, but, because of the weather, often not a lot of time. Where a dozen years earlier Booth's own free-living ways and dissenting spirit were unusual in the early 1970s, half the world was affecting a taste for rebellion and a desire to connect with the great outdoors. Now, on Hay Bluff, the imposing mountain below which Hay's agricultural folk have farmed for hundreds of years, where Welsh mountain ponies and increasing numbers of sheep had had the run of the place, a new species had arrived.

Perhaps influenced by New Jersey's favourite Beat poet, Allen Ginsberg, who wrote his poem 'Wales Visitation' when under the influence of LSD during a visit to Capel-y-ffin in 1967, 'the hippies', as they were readily catalogued, were not popular with the locals. In truth, many were a good deal less peaceable than their collective noun would suggest, and invited the more loaded tag 'traveller'. In any event, here was a test for Hay's softly-softly policing. The local citizenry generally thought itself capable of resolving differences without outside help, but this was new. 'The hippies' were drawn to the area by the beauty of the hills and the hallucinogenic psilocybin mushrooms, widely known as magic mushrooms, which grew plentifully on the slopes (and which provided Hay's more seditious young entre-preneurs with their first local produce to take to London). There dozens of long-haired, dreamy folk with floaty dresses, Afghan coats, flared trousers and implausible aspirations gathered, erecting tents, big and small, to live their lives in harmony with nature's bounty. That, at least, was the theory.

To local farmers and shopkeepers, most of whom belonged to the non-rebellious half of the world that needed to make a reliable living, they were a damned nuisance. Their concept of hygiene was the least of their points of difference, com-pounded by the frequent theft of machinery and farm animals and general sense of unearned entitlement. Hay's shopkeepers as a whole did not share Richard Booth's indulgent live-and-let-live attitude (which after a while even he struggled to sustain, though initially he had seen it as his patrician duty to try and arbitrate between the travelling folk and farmers) and signs appeared in shops stating 'No hippies'. The welcome that Hay normally extends to visitors was suspended, from a sense that these were either straightforward thieves or spoilt rich kids finding a new excuse for taking drugs and doing little of use. (One Christmas Eve a local shopkeeper made the tortuous drive towards Llanthony and swears he saw Rolls-Royces, Rovers and the like parked up there, as concerned parents visited to deliver Christmas presents to their addled, raddled young darlings.)

Hay's beautiful surroundings were continuing to attract second-home owners as well as hippies. A cottage in the hills was a soothing antidote to city life, and unused agricultural buildings were being turned into snug retreats for the middle classes for whom the Cotswolds were too ordinary or too expensive. These houses were empty for much of the year, and towards the end of winter, when city dwellers would return to 'open up the cottage', the police would receive calls reporting break-ins that might have happened months earlier, evidently only some of them by hippy encroachments. One cottage near Hay was broken into 'for the hell of it' by an unhappy young local who urinated on one of the beds, but he made detection that much easier by signing his name on the door that the owners used as a visitors' book. When the police were informed, he was of course known to them. He had apparently been drunk, and no lasting damage had been done. The cottage owner didn't want to cause a fuss, and the matter was dropped.

Often the houses in question were remote and, with the crimes being reported weeks or months after the event, were hard to investigate with much hope of success. Some break-ins seemed to have been a protest at the affluence of outsiders, or simply carried out as a cheap thrill to enliven an evening in one of the country's most sparsely populated areas. With few personnel to call on, the police had to rely on homeowners locking up as much as possible, asking neighbours to be vigilant and hoping for the best.

One person whose unguarded property was ripe for a hippy incursion was the late Jim Capaldi, drummer of the rock band Traffic, whose beautiful house, Cadwgan, sat unsuspected deep in the woods below Hay Bluff, close to the patch occupied by the hippies. Traffic's tour manager lived just outside Hay, and he would invite Capaldi and others down for weekends. 'We used to go and visit when we came off touring,' remembers Jim's widow Anna. 'It is one of my favourite places. It was like Ibiza before anyone went there. Hay was really quiet and really nice. I still go there every year. It is just idyllic, magical. One day it so happened there was a cottage for sale and Jim bought that.'

Other musicians, some of world renown, would also visit. Bob Marley and Joe Cocker had friends in the area, and Mike Oldfield, whose follow-up album to the hugely successful *Tubular Bells* was *Hergest Ridge*, a hill fourteen miles north of Hay, lived on Bradnor Hill outside Kington, affording him a reassuring view of the mighty Hay Bluff.

One evening in the Blue Boar a local walked in and told the guy playing the piano he didn't think much of what he was playing. 'Let somebody get on as can play,' the new arrival insisted. The pianist graciously gave way, allowing the new-comer to have a go, a decidedly inferior one, it turned out. The unseated pianist in question was Oldfield's friend Steve Winwood, keyboard player, vocalist and guitarist with Traffic, at the time more used to playing keyboards with Eric Clapton and Ginger Baker. 'It's true, it could only have happened in Hay,' Winwood confirmed.

Anna and Jim Capaldi would drive to Hay from the Home Counties in their purple Ford Capri and spend weekends at Cadwgan. The couple had a son, Damian, who was born in

1971, but he died in his cot at just three months. The couple split up three years later. Damian is buried on the hill, a stone's throw from the house. 'That's how special that place is for me,' says Anna. 'There was a magical stream where there were evening primroses and lovely hazelnuts growing. You used to hear the thunder and the cottage would shake slightly and the horses would come down off the mountain for shelter.'

The horses were not alone in looking for occasional refuge. 'Jim was very laid back and generous,' remembers his friend and employee Mick Baulch. 'He'd give you his shoes if you needed them, but people would take advantage. Because he had had a bit of success, and they assumed that a musician of that era would share their attitudes, they would wander down the hill and almost regarded it as their right to move in.' As if not to disappoint them, says an associate, he would sometimes reciprocate. 'He once told me there was one tent there with a complete drum kit, set up permanently, and he used to go up and play it.'

But his happy amenability was abused. Baulch remembers arriving to find the back door open and 'people just sitting around everywhere'. Capaldi would talk to them and sometimes allow them to stay one more night as long as they left the next morning.

Capaldi had no enthusiasm for magic mushrooms, but he liked a joint, as did some of his friends. An associate remembers he was rarely the instigator (and had such an active imagination that certain class A drugs would cause him great distress) but he would often partake if others were doing so. Among these was a Birmingham businessman by the name of Don Carless, whose venue The Elbow Room had played host to some of rock music's most successful performers, including Jimi Hendrix and the young Robert Plant. It had been the venue where Capaldi, Steve Winwood and his brother Muff and others had jammed in the early hours of the morning after their gigs with local bands, which eventually resulted in the forming of Traffic. Carless was a popular, disorganised figure with a perhaps overdeveloped, or misguided, entrepreneurial spirit. If there was partying to be done, Carless would be available. And if musicians wanted a contemplative time striding across the hills, he could provide something to help enhance the walk or help them unwind in the evening.

Richard Booth himself was very anti-drugs and had little or no direct contact with Carless. But as we shall see later in the story, Carless was to make his presence felt in spectacular fashion for someone very close to Booth.

Economically the years that followed the louche 1960s in Britain were chaotic. The Conservative government of Edward Heath, elected in 1970, promised membership of the Common Market and economic prosperity under the chancellorship of Anthony Barber. Unfortunately, the great unshackling 'dash for growth' coincided with appallingly inclement circumstances internationally (including oil price rises and war in the Middle East), but the government kept its foot on the accelerator. Only when it was too late was some sort of brake applied. The government was unseated in 1974.

They might have been being advised by Richard Booth. His attitude to bookselling seemed to many, not excluding some of his employees, even more ambitious and unworldly. One of the greatest gifts Booth possessed, from which so much else sprang, was a remarkable lack of self-consciousness, in some respects at least. Though he was to show an acute understanding and flair for publicity, he was indifferent to and possibly unaware of how he came across in person. Many people spoken to for this book said that nowadays he would be 'on the spectrum', such was his apparent imperviousness and seeming failure to register the reaction of those he spoke to.

Booth's friend Ivor Windsor remarked on his insouciance about himself and his louche acolytes offending local chapel sensibilities. In truth there was an unworldliness, an ingenuousness, about the hand he stretched out to the people of Hay: 'There was no edge to him. He'd be in all the pubs and try and buy people drinks, and initially he was greatly misunderstood and mistrusted – this newcomer coming into town and taking over – he was regarded with huge suspicion. But it didn't deter him at all.

'Richard was so irreverent. He just didn't give a damn. He did have these extraordinary rushes of blood to the head, and was a genuine, unaffected eccentric. He just didn't care how he looked or dressed, or about putting on weight. He just ran around with this manic obsession of selling more books … Sometimes he was acute to what was going on but other times, if he was consumed with the making of a coronet or something, he didn't have a clue what was going on around him.'

His indifference to superficial appearances – though not to more profound esteem, to which we shall return – gave him an empathy with the same trait in others. So the multi-talented Dr Frank Lewis, whom he hired in the late 1960s, was entirely at home as a kind of house intellectual in the Booth empire. A description of Lewis is best left to Booth himself:

I beheld a short fat man who was as ugly as a potato. In his youth, Frank had been a champion runner and gained one of the quickest Philosophy Doctorates at Oxford University. After his thesis, on the mediaeval river system of Cologne, he had been offered the Chair of Mediaeval History at

Bonn University by Ribbentrop, Hitler's Foreign Minister. 'I refused on the basis that Wales was a more important country than Germany,' he said. Now, hopelessly unable to look after himself or his interests, a worn and soiled suit documented his decline in the world. Drugs were a problem. On some days he swallowed handfuls of pills as if they were sweets, becoming passionately vindictive towards rivals and once going so far as to urinate into his pint on the Irish ferry, because he said that if he used the public urinal, the head waiter would make homosexual advances. But Frank had a profound impact on the business. His first innovation was to recommend Sunday opening.

Lewis was also a healthy influence on Booth's choice of books, joining Frank English and Cotters in advocating quality above quantity, for both aesthetic and mercantile reasons.

Lewis was responsible for introducing Booth to his favourite bureaucrat – admittedly a small field – Mervyn Jones, who had recently been appointed as head of the Wales Tourist Board. Booth agreed with Lewis that tourism was the policy of the future and Mervyn Jones did everything he could to back Booth, both in terms of publicity and by awarding grants to help Hay's development.

Not that Booth had the slightest intention of relying on others. The early 1970s saw a major growth in his travels, particularly to Australia, whose seventeen universities, some of them recently founded, were proving keen customers, particularly for nineteenth-century authors, of whose work he had loads, he told one local newspaper. He also discovered America, which had entire libraries that he was willing to take off the hands of universities and colleges small and large and ship across the Atlantic. 'Smaller shops cannot offer the service we can,' he explained. 'Most are in large towns and cannot afford to expand. Here we do not have that sort of problem. We have unlimited room for expansion.'

His globetrotting life did not prevent him from broadening his social circle at home. Indeed, at the risk of ruining a metaphor, the spreading of his wings allowed him to envelop yet more people in the Hay fold, one or two of them through his London connection.

Hay-on-Wye is about 150 miles from Thurloe Square in South Kensington, where Viva King lived. Viva was truly a figure from another age, the tag 'society hostess' barely comprehensible to modern ears. It was said that 'if you fired a shotgun at one of Mrs King's parties you would risk peppering half the characters in the novels of Evelyn Waugh and Anthony Powell'. One publisher, struggling to keep tabs on the celebrated names who appeared in her memoirs, said that trying to do so was like trying to read the names of stations from a fast-moving train.

Born in the Victorian era, there was nothing remotely fusty about Viva King. On the contrary. Booth's mother considered her decadent. She was in her youth a figure of some beauty and was friends with Augustus John, Ezra Pound, Norman Douglas (to whom her husband was literary executor) and Ivy Compton-Burnett. Her world was the Bloomsbury set, and her professional existence, such as it was, as a governess, companion and so on, never precluded a vibrant social life in South Kensington even into her eighties. She and her husband Willy, an Etonian ceramics expert with the Victoria & Albert Museum who had been at school with Anthony Powell, enjoyed an aesthetically enquiring existence of privilege decorated by heavy partying. The couple were prototypes of the main characters in Angus Wilson's 1956 novel *Anglo-Saxon Attitudes*. It was said that she and Willy more enjoyed the company of gay young men than of one another. One acquaintance said recently that she had 'lots of affairs'. According to Booth's autobiography, at the age of seventy-seven she had a twenty-six-year-old Māori lover with an unfortunate talent for stealing from her dwindling collection of antiques.

In a letter to *The Times*, her friends complained that an unsympathetic review of her memoirs was a 'fierce personal attack', quite unfair in suggesting that she had driven her husband to drink. They said her 'most conspicuous characteristic was her generosity, which she carried almost to the point of self-destruction'. They also praised her 'warmth and spontaneity' and her 'power of accurate observation'.

Viva King was Richard Booth's father's sister and for him a merciful refuge from the staid world of his parents. (The stays were never completely relaxed. She would correct Booth's driver from Hay if he announced he had 'come to collect Richard'. She would ask sternly: 'Do you mean *Mr* Booth?') Booth spent several months, while working fruitlessly for Trust Houses Forte, staying with his aunt before going to university. While not quite a role model, she proposed a mindset more liberal and closer to his own than anyone else's in the Booth clan. This old-school *grande dame* was an assiduous cultivator of young talent to enliven her parties, and nephew Richard the bookseller fell willingly into that category.

It was at one of her parties in the early 1970s that Booth met Viva's lodger, a tall, striking-looking thirty-five-year-old restaurateur.

Until ten years earlier, Liverpool-born George Jamieson had been seized by a seemingly unachievable desire to become a woman, and suicide seemed to be the only resolution. The health service's response was to prescribe antidepressants, male hormones, sleeping pills, electric treatment and truth drugs – in short, a variety of treatments that belonged to the age of Dr Mengele, said her friend Duncan Fallowell. At the age of twenty-five, Jamieson decided not to submit and, further, went against the gradual approach recommended for the then exceptional practice of gender reassignment, having a six-hour operation in Casablanca, conducted by the same doctor, Georges Burou, as used by writer James (later Jan) Morris. As a woman and with a new name, April Ashley, her past a secret, enjoyed success as a model, being photographed by Lord Snowdon, Terence Donovan and David Bailey. *Vogue* magazine had her modelling underwear, and, because of her height, she was well paid by the big fashion houses to show off their new numbers. She even got into films, most notably feeding marsh-mallows to Bing Crosby in *The Road to Hong Kong*. Then in 1961 the *People* newspaper revealed the truth about her early years and the modelling came to an end: her name was excised from the credits of films and she was shunned as the sort of freak no red-blooded man could be imagined admiring.

Defiantly she carried on as if nothing had happened, rumoured promiscuity adding to her allure and exoticism. Actors Omar Sharif and Peter O'Toole had affairs with her, and evidently with some pride. In 1963 she was persuaded to marry the Hon Arthur Corbett, heir to the 2nd Baron Rowallan, then married with four children. It was a mistake, and when they fell out, he sought an annulment on the grounds that April was a man when they were married. The judge ended the 'so-called marriage', declaring Ashley to be 'a person of the male sex'. So, in 1970 a mortified April walked away with nothing.

But she was not to be sunk. Her resilience came to the fore again, even if she was growing increasingly disenchanted with running her restaurant. A new chapter was in the offing.

One weekend, Booth invited his Aunt Viva to Hay for the

weekend, suggesting she bring April. The visit, Booth recalled later, caused a sensation. 'Breezing into the Blue Boar pub, a coiffured beauty in white denim, she announced, "Must have a slash." On choosing the gents, she was followed by a waft of perfume and several of the locals.'

The early 1970s saw the development of Booth as someone with a flair for public relations, and it was just as well. He came to understand what the newspapers regarded as a good story, and he knew Ashley's presence would also add lustre to the town. He wrote in his diary: '1975 was the first year in which it became apparent there was almost limitless publicity available for the idea of filling a town with second-hand books.' He would need it, being privately worried, his diary reveals, about 'the serious business of avoiding bankruptcy'. Ashley's arrival in Hay that year raised Booth's hopes that she might open a restaurant, but that never materialised. For Ashley, whose star had waned in London after the flurry of publicity in the early 1960s, it was an intriguing new chapter.

Martin Dearden watched Booth operating from close range. 'Getting dear old April Ashley was a masterstroke of a PR stunt,' he says. 'He thought she was exotic, and he was cock-a-hoop that she'd come to live in Hay.' Ashley, by the same token, was grateful for his help when she was short of money, allowing her to do some PR work for in exchange for rent.

The stories of the colour that April brought to Hay are countless. She was a prodigious drinker, for one thing, and, in the tradition of Booth acolytes, rarely constrained by a lack of cash. Geoff Simkins remembers April's regular arrival at the Blue Boar at about 6 p.m. 'If you were willing to buy her a Glenmorangie, you were a friend,' he remembers. She was also inclined to arrive at another Hay venue and demand champagne. 'And who is paying for it?' the bar staff, who knew her well enough, would ask. 'Why, you are!' she would reply. Generally somebody, often Booth himself, would appear and pick up the tab.

Ashley was well aware of her status as a kind of curio and played up to it. Sometimes she would play the Queen of Spite. 'She was all woman, and she needed to be,' says one female victim of her banter. 'Because she was such a bitch.' On mellow occasions it would be April doing the displaying, sometimes performing her highly regarded 'Butterfly Dance' party piece.

Kamma Andersen, one of the many brave souls who tried to get a grip of the Booth finances, also remembers Ashley, who was never more at home than with a drink in front of her in the Blue Boar. 'The first time I met her, she said, "Do you want to see my tits?" and, in a crowded bar, she pulled her jumper up and showed them to me – just for the shock value. She was a very nice woman.'

April's gentler, refined side was much admired. She was often to be found drinking tea and listening to opera with master craftsman Bruce Addyman. But later in the day, with April in town, there was a constant sense of at least low-level partying. She was notably uninhibited sexually, seemingly anxious to prove her femininity, as if, understandably and perhaps admirably, catching up on lost time. In Hay she was acknowledged as 'all woman', though others were not convinced: in August 1980, after being thrown out of Morton's nightclub in London, she was made to spend a night in the cells – the men's cells.

Her daytime demeanour was pure and elegant, but the evenings were generally alcohol-fuelled, drinks cadged from all and sundry, her voice deepening as the evening wore on. Being asked by April for a lift the four hundred yards home, of which she was often in need, carried an assumption as to how the evening would end. Yet despite behaviour that Hay's more conservative circles found debauched, April is regarded locally as kind, classy and lovely.

One of her friends was Chris Fry, publican of the Blue Boar, famed for his love of shooting and fishing, the excellence of his pub's food and the rackety atmosphere that prevailed there. Fry liked to lead his customers by example, and 11 p.m. closing time was treated as more advisory than statutory (which it was at the time). The cider he sold, billed as 'Bulmer's Traditional Cider', was in fact scrumpy made by a very close friend and local cider-maker in Hay, which cost Fry a good deal less. 'One and a half pints of that and they were pissed as handcarts,' says the man in question.

5

The 'Golden Age'

'It was like the daily unfolding chapter of a surreal novel.'

Cotters

Perhaps the figure who added most to the mythology surrounding Richard Booth was Marianne Faithfull, best known – for better or worse – for her singing, her acting, her beauty, for being the former girlfriend of various Rolling Stones and for being a heavy user of alcohol and narcotics. In truth, she was not in Hay for very long, and when she was, it was only sporadically, but the mystique surrounding her was exceptional and enduring.

She came to Hay to escape and had friends in the area before she met Booth. The bookseller admitted that he had been entranced by the 'aesthetic ideal [he] first saw in a glamour photograph, aged sixteen, before her relationship with Mick Jagger'. That cut little ice in Hay. 'Marianne's nails were filthy and her language for a woman was terrible,' pub landlord Ken Jenkins told his children.

The 1970s were not kind to Faithfull and she needed a change. 'I wanted to get out of London,' she said. 'I had had enough.' One of Booth's most loyal lieutenants remembers Faithfull in Hay. 'When she arrived she was in a bad place. I never saw her take drugs, but she'd drink from when she woke up to when she went to bed. She was down on her luck. Richard had a lot of those.' Kelvyn Jenkins and his sister Sue recall Faithfull arriving at a bar in a polka-dot fur coat. 'She asked us both to teach her to speak Welsh, but she fell asleep on the trestle table because Richard had got her so drunk.'

Richard Booth's association with Faithfull was 'aspirational', says someone who knew him well, in that she brought with her undoubted kudos. He offered her a safe port away from the prurient media storm. Her closest friend in Hay was Henrietta Moraes, a former model for, and friend of, Lucian Freud and Francis Bacon, and for a while one or both women were accommodated in one or both of the Booth residences. Booth himself divided his nights between the Castle and Brynmelyn.

This was at a moment when Booth was between wives, and it is tempting to speculate that the troubled, vulnerable Faithfull might have been more than just somebody he felt sorry for. That was certainly the assumption – which he didn't challenge – made by his bookselling associates. One of Booth's drivers, Ron Smart, remembers Faithfull as a kind and friendly figure, though she was, famously and sadly, at the mercy of drink or drugs. He says she was going through a phase of drinking all night and sleeping all day, and remembers seeing her with a bottle of wine at Booth's breakfast table before he and his boss made a typically early start on a book-buying trip.

In his autobiography Booth quotes Faithfull as having said 'I want to be chatelaine of the Castle', and he mentions that he used to sing in the bath about never having promised her a rose garden. The sense among shopkeepers in Hay was that Booth, with his bumbling, curiously shy charm, had done it

again – seduced a high-born beauty – even if his romantic side
was having to cope with the practical realities of love.

'Booth felt he was looking after me, and he was,' she recalled
not long before her death in 2025. 'I've got nothing awful to
say about Richard, but he was mad. I just remember thinking,
a lot, that he was mad.' Many years after leaving Hay, when her
autobiography was published, she referred only briefly to her
time there. She called Booth a 'lunatic' bookseller, which Booth
watchers saw as shattering any thought that the Booth/Faithfull
rapport had been something rather special.

When asked about their association, and the suggestion that
their relationship might have endured, Faithfull said indig-
nantly: 'No! We never went to bed together. For God's sake.
Absolutely not.' To the idea that Booth might have let people
believe she might have become chatelaine of the Castle, she
said: 'Maybe. But it's not true. How dare he? I'm really quite
offended. How dare he?' A friend of Booth says he would have
regarded having an affair with her as aggrandising for him, but
it almost certainly didn't happen. 'It wasn't for lack of trying,
though,' says the friend.

In her memoir *Henrietta*, Henrietta Moraes recounts her
experiences in Hay. The book as a whole is a hardly uplifting
tale of a disappointed thrill-seeker, and her time in Hay depicts
yet another spell in her life when a lack of self-esteem, mitigated
only by a certain self-confidence, led to her being exploited and
humiliated by a series of men. Her former husband, journalist
and poet Dom Moraes, had covered the Eichmann trial in
Jerusalem for *The Times of India* in 1961, and Henrietta had
sat with him in the courtroom. It was later speculated that
this may have provoked the drug-taking from which she never
entirely escaped.

By most standards, Moraes was wild, though Marianne

Faithfull, protective of her friend and former flatmate, says perhaps she was wild only by the standards of 'provincial Wales'. But in a town of considerable wildness, at the time at least, she set her own standards.

Moraes been part of a troupe of languid, alternatively inclined bohemians who made their stately way to Montgomeryshire in the early 1970s. When the ennui became insupportable, they would move on, unable even to sustain their mutual admiration any longer. Moraes turned up in Hay with a recently acquired dog, Den, and landed herself on American Buddhist Kurt Schaffhauser and his wife Maggie, who lived above Llanigon outside Hay.

Moraes had decided to 'give the second-hand book empire at Hay-on-Wye a chance', she wrote later, and called Richard Booth. According to Moraes, Booth said he had a friend of hers staying with him, namely Marianne Faithfull. She walked to Hay with Den and was pleased to sense that the interview was going well, particularly after Faithfull joined them. When Booth asked what sort of pay she was hoping for, she suggested a hefty £40 a week. 'Hen!' said Faithfull disapprovingly, but Booth reassured her, for reasons known only to him. 'Just what I was thinking myself,' he said.

It was a classic Booth encounter. He gave a job to someone with no appropriate qualifications, and found himself providing her with accommodation, putting her up in Cockcroft, the town's enormous former workhouse that he acquired in 1975, tucked away near the Gipsy Castle estate on the edge of Hay. It was just two hundred yards from the Cinema, but hardly on what might ambitiously be called Hay's 'main drag' and thus a development visited only by those in the know with a special reason for going there.

Moraes had expected to be showing off her learning, but

initially was employed shifting books from one container to another – 'the hardest work I have ever done,' she said. She was soon given more responsible work, and had to 'sort, price and shelve a book in one minute', a measure of the speed of turnover in the book empire. Moraes was never going to set the world of second-hand bookselling on fire. Her social activities, though, are vividly recalled in the town.

It can be assumed that someone with experience of LSD and other drugs found plenty to amuse her in late 1970s Hay, and certainly her enthusiasm for amphetamines seems unabated at that time, but it is for her sexual and alcoholic feats that she is chiefly remembered. She spent lunchtimes and evenings drinking with one of Booth's employees, usually in the Blue Boar or the Old Black Lion, doing the *Telegraph* crossword puzzle and playing pool. Her speed at downing a yard of ale is also remembered with admiration. She and April Ashley, who she found camp, witty and very kind, struck up a good friendship, Ashley presumably affecting some of the strength of character that Moraes lacked. Though no stranger to the main chance, her weakness for alcohol and her obliging nature made a victim of her. It is said that on at least one inebriated occasion she took four local young men to bed at once. Locals recall unkindly being able to measure the extent of the previous evening's drinking by the competence with which she applied her make-up.

Moraes's friendship with Marianne Faithfull had helped persuade Booth to hire her, and the pair would attend drunken dinner parties at Brynmelyn with Frank English and others. Moraes remembered English insisting on finishing every bottle in sight, which scandalised even Booth. 'I don't think I was much better, but perhaps not so obvious,' she later recalled.

One of Booth's tall orders was to end unhappily. He had

decided to open Cockcroft, the former workhouse, as a bookshop specialising in American history, the launch of which was to be attended by the American ambassador, Anne Armstrong, a rising star in the Republican party. Through his friend Mervyn Jones, boss of the Wales Tourist Board, Booth had managed to secure a grant of £50,000 that would allow Hay to be Wales's centre of celebrations for 4 July 1976, the 200th anniversary of American independence.

In her memoir, Moraes uses an expression that will ring bells with anyone who worked with Booth: 'A period of madness followed.' (Cotters referred to the place as 'Bedlam', suggesting that work under Booth's management was part of a 'daily unfolding chapter of a surreal novel'.) In the ensuing three weeks a hundred thousand books were to be found, priced and shelved. The people chiefly responsible were Moraes and a kindly baronet from an old Shropshire family, Sir William Ripley, with whom she started a drunken relationship – 'making love in odd corners amidst spiders' webs, and dust and falling plaster' – to allow some escape from the demands of shelf-filling. Ripley was a likeable figure whose benign, comfortable manner carried an implicit suggestion of family wealth. As such, he was the object of particular interest from Booth, who was hoping some of the alleged Ripley cash might find its way in his direction. Sadly for Booth, Ripley's family saw him coming and made sure no such transaction ever took place.

The job of preparing the American bookshop was completed after a fashion. The ambassador, dressed in a pale pink suit and accompanied by a predictable gang of security people, expressed due admiration. A young soprano, Yvonne Kenny no less, sang some American songs and the party moved from Cockcroft to the Castle for tea. Booth's memoir records that Frank English celebrated the day in equally predictable style, firmly telling someone who tried to bar his route towards the ambassador with the words: 'Get out of the way, you little bastard.' The job was completed, though in a distinctively Boothish way.

The following day, though, Booth sacked Moraes, explaining that she was too expensive to employ. This was pure Booth. His friends looking back on the affair accuse Moraes of ripping him off by asking for higher-than-average wages (and presumably drinking and having daytime sex on office premises would not have been part of her job description). Booth, wanting to oblige Moraes, had agreed to her suggested terms. Later on, she had had no inkling that what she felt was her hard work (and some dispute this) was likely soon to be unwanted. He told Marianne Faithfull afterwards that he thought Henrietta was pretty much unemployable. Good at talking but not so good at working was his verdict. He felt he had done her enough of a favour.

Marianne was furious at Booth's dismissal of her friend, saying if he wouldn't employ her, *she* would. Before leaving Hay, Moraes went to Easter Sunday communion at St Mary's, where she bumped into Sir John Betjeman, whose wife Penelope lived nearby, and a disgraced former bishop.

Derek Addyman worked for Booth for many years before setting up on his own. He recalls 1976, one of Britain's hottest for years, as one of exceptional Booth excess. 'He bought eight containers of crap from America,' he recalls. 'We had to handle three-quarters of a million books in one delivery.'

Thus late 1976 was one of many periods of retrenchment. Booth boasted to a reporter that he was selling five thousand books a day and was offering inducements of £100 to anyone who could help him buy a collection of three thousand or more books, but it was a front. Business was 'desperate', he admitted in his diary. The previous year, substantial redundancies had been discussed but shelved. He was not paying even the smallest of bills, yet complained about the grass around the Castle not being cut. Given the reason was that the mowers were not working (as three gardeners stood around idle), his wages clerk Garry Spencer paid to have them serviced. Booth was furious: 'Why did you pay them? Why?' he shouted, slapping the back of his head in his distinctive manner and storming off.

Radical steps could no longer be avoided. In the summer there had been fifty-eight people working for him, many of them brought from the USA by Tom Loome, mostly being paid in cash. By Christmas there were twenty. On Christmas Eve, he dismissed the five directors, the company's highest earners. Marianne and Henrietta left soon afterwards, Henrietta eventually acting as a minder as her friend renewed her singing career on a tour of Ireland.

Nonetheless a core remained, or, in some cases, was hired, around that time. They reflected well on Booth, both because they were well versed in their areas of speciality, well connected in the trade and professional in their outlook, as well as doing credit to his eye for talent. In increasingly trying conditions, these 'stoker' figures contributed hugely to keeping the ship afloat and maintaining the business's credibility to the outside world.

At the Cinema, Paul Haynes was in charge of travel, topography and history, Greg Coombes did art and architecture, Cotters did literature and Derek Addyman ran general and reference books. Chris Powell was still in the print shop. Down the road at Cockcroft House, Val Haynes ran natural history, science and technology. 'It wasn't a normal nine to five, we never really stopped working,' reflects Paul Haynes. 'It was intrinsic to our lives. Though at times it was chaotic, there was more structure than perhaps one might assume. We were very fond of him and we have good memories of those times. Our lives would have taken different paths if we hadn't met him.'

Others who worked with Booth at the time speak of the 1970s as a golden age, the word 'fun' featuring prominently. The staff was characterised by camaraderie, quiet competence and amusement at the unpredictable brilliance of the boss. The *esprit de corps* was maintained by an indulgent warmth towards Booth and a sense that this was a workplace of extraordinary distinction. What Booth was building was exceptional, and the gifts of those who helped build it were indispensable. Ideas, some inspired, some barmy, would sprout in the Booth mind, and the team would be called upon either to enact them or wait quietly until the enthusiasm had passed. While there were times of feeling like galley slaves, the experience, the freedom to show initiative and, simply, the laughter provided ample compensation.

Christmas meant little to Booth, and from as early as 1970 he tended to spend it with the Cooke family. It became a bit of an unmentioned annual ritual that he would be offered a bowl of peanuts in their shells. He would put them on his lap, cracking them open, oblivious to the flaking shells falling onto his clothes. He would not offer them around. He would then stand up, impervious to the shells as they tumbled to the floor while continuing to talk. It was charmingly, uniquely, 'just Richard'.

One of the phrases – we might now call them soundbites – of the type which were doing so much to help with his publicity was that 'Christ should have been crucified at birth'. It is typical Booth iconoclasm, indifferent to (if not delighted by) the upset it might cause, but his antipathy for the established church was well known. The Cooke family indulged him, allowing him to be called on their phone. One Christmas Marianne Faithfull called from Hampstead. On another, one of his staff members, who had a bit of a crush on him, called him to wish him a Happy Christmas. He fired her, there and then, over the phone. As he returned to the table 'he couldn't stop laughing about it,' remembers Adela Cooke. 'He had a mean streak.' None of this had the slightest bearing on the warmth the family felt for him.

If his distracted frame of mind was down to that year's financial difficulties, maybe his spirits were lifted by a post-Christmas visit from two world-famous animal experts, Desmond Morris and David Attenborough. This was not untypical. Celebrities from television, politics and theatre, including Robert Robinson, Jonathan Dimbleby, Patrick Moore, Denis Healey, Ken Dodd (a bibliophile who became a friend) and Dennis Potter, were often to be found, unannounced, among the shelves.

A Booth sacking was sometimes not the end of the story, though. It was often in the eye of the sackee. One employee, Barry Gibbons, remembers: 'On a Wednesday he'd say, "I've had enough of you, bugger off – you're sacked", and then he'd ask where you were on a Thursday morning. Or sometimes you'd go home on the day and if you fancied having a day off the next day, you'd go in on Friday and carry on as normal. But after a couple of those I'd had enough.'

Barry decided to go to college. The Gibbonses are a well-established Hay family: Booth knew well enough who needed looking after and who was dispensable. 'A few got sacked properly but mostly it depended on your temperament. Some treated it as if he meant it, but if he sacked you and you ignored it and turned up the next day, you'd carry on as normal.'

Unlike some, Gibbons was always paid in full and on time by Booth, and was always given expenses when he went away on trips. Another of Booth's regular repairers said, 'Sometimes you had to wait a bit, but he always paid fully in the end – with me, he never forgot.' Boots Bantock, a painter and poet, was one who Booth always paid in full and on time. Indeed, Booth indulged him, waiting fully twenty-five years for a picture Bantock had promised him.

6

Insatiably Acquisitive in America

'I think in his head he wanted to create a kind of Disneyworld in Hay.'

Michael Zubal, Ohio bookseller

In his compulsion to buy, Booth would head off to the United States, often in January, when he would call colleagues in snowbound, at-its-quietest Hay to make requests for what little cash was available. He wanted to conquer new pastures and arrange pantechnicons and containers to transport his bounty back to the UK.

But there was good reason for going to the States. A shift in domestic politics meant many libraries were merging or closing, and Richard Booth was itching to put into practice his 'take the lot' mindset. This called for considerable organisational and logistical skills, not his own strong suits, but Booth had the team to complement his chutzpah.

One of his first purchases, in 1970, had also been one of his biggest. New York's largest bookshop, Stechert-Hafner, which had been largely reliant on academic sales, could no longer afford to stand aloof from the rest of the trade and assume the business would come to them. They saw a great deal of money rolling in from Richard Bach's bestselling *Jonathan Livingston Seagull*, but otherwise had accumulated far too many books to be handled comfortably in Manhattan. A conglomerate had purchased the customer list of Stechert-Hafner, but the inventory, the books themselves, were for sale.

So Booth and six employees pitched up to East 12th Street and set about shipping the contents of its eight floors to the Welsh borders. Booth said he negotiated a rock-bottom price for the books, admitting that no one else was prepared to devote the necessary hours to moving them. Nonetheless, the cost of keeping his staff in New York for several weeks, and of moving the books across the Atlantic, was a huge drain. The trip had been subsidised by his old family friend Lance Hughes. A Hay-based friend from Kentucky, whose family had been early backers of the young boxer Cassius Clay (later Muhammad Ali), had to provide further funds to keep the trip afloat.

The trip was typical both of Booth's fearless quest for growth and of the gimcrack nature of his organisation. He managed to offload some of the books to smaller US outlets, but five forty-foot containers were required to transport half a million books across the Atlantic to Hay.

In *My Kingdom of Books*, Booth exhaustively cites the places all across the States that he visited, offering comparisons between the Victorian private houses of Chicago, the east coast libraries and the west of New York state. He plundered the Peabody libraries and acquired a great many books that chimed with fashionable west coast thinking of the early 1970s, of which British students could then not get enough. He also homed in on Matthew Needle, a distinguished Boston-based antiquarian bookseller specialising in religious books, who opened all sorts of doors and became a good friend. 'Wisely he allowed me little credit,' said Booth with an air of contrition not always evident at the time. Elsewhere he mentions, with some but perhaps insufficient candour, how he initially struggled with this American reluctance to offer credit or assume his financial bona fides. 'Buying in Britain, one could sell books before they were paid for, but America damaged my cash flow because of the time it took for books to cross the Atlantic,' he wrote.

Paul Haynes recalls having been with Booth when he purchased a containerful of books from outside Minneapolis from Melvin McCosh, a well-established bookseller there. 'Booth said, "I'll send the money through as soon as I get back", but he never sent the money, despite a few threats,' remembers Haynes, who went to see McCosh some years later. 'The first thing he did was get his shotgun out,' says Haynes. 'I had to convince him I was now nothing to do with Richard.'

Notwithstanding his uncertain arrangements for paying, Booth's fondness for a deal helped him establish good links with US book dealers wanting to offload their excess stock, despite his payment difficulties. Tom Loome, who left Hay and went to live in Stillwater, Minnesota, in 1979 was a useful contact with an appetite for buying large quantities of bibles. On occasions, Booth, via Andy Cooke or Paul Haynes, would arrange a U-Haul truck – designed for carrying heavy loads – to transport vast quantities of books across the States and/or ultimately to Hay-on-Wye in lorries, or 'galleons' as he sometimes called them.

Those who accompanied Booth on his US trips speak of them with awe, as if they witnessed something extraordinary, bizarre, his tunnel vision adding to the hilarity even to those used to his ways. At that time, it is safe to say, he was buying more second-hand books in the US than any American dealer. He would very occasionally stay in the smartest hotels – including New

York's famous Algonquin, and in April 1979 he flew to New York on Concorde; but, if cash was short, as it generally was, he was unashamed in his skimping.

'In a hotel he wouldn't buy breakfast,' recalls Paul Haynes, who did half a dozen US trips with Booth. 'We would be on the road early, he would stop at some big hotel and march into the breakfast room. When they asked what room he was in, he would pluck a number at random, and use his legendary bluster and a great guffaw of laughter to correct it if necessary. It was a game to him, one he enjoyed playing, with his eccentric Englishman character.'

Haynes also recalls that, in Booth's mind, not putting petrol in the car was saving money. 'So when we went to Heathrow, even if the gauge was on red, he would say we had to keep going, so that if we could get to Heathrow without the car running out, we would be saving money.'

Whatever the reputation of British travellers abroad, Booth lacked both the élan and the wardrobe of the cultivated British globetrotter. He used to be collected from Brynmelyn or the Castle, having thrown a few things into a couple of bags. 'He'd often arrive with no clothes or toiletries. Going through customs, they would ask to go through the suitcases. In one suitcase was a shoe and a dirty pair of trousers ... and in a hotel he would rip out the bookseller pages of the local Yellow Pages, so that's what was in his suitcases – just bits of ripped-up paper. I remember the customs officer thinking, Just let him through.'

He would expect others to be equally ready to jump to it, whatever he had in mind. It was not unusual for his driver to be asked to work very long hours, criss-crossing the country in the search for books, and one of them resorted to amphetamines to sustain Booth's pace. It was not untypical for Booth to ask a driver if he could drive, say, to Edinburgh and back (with a laden van) in a day. ('Sorry, Richard.') Sometimes he took an expert with him, but on occasions he just needed a driver.

One day he called round to see precocious seventeen-year-old Andy Cooke, son of Bill Cooke, his employee and drinking partner. 'What are you doing tomorrow?' asked the bookseller. 'Going to school, I 'spect,' said Cooke. Booth said he needed a driver and asked him if he fancied going to Boston with him. He wasn't sure, thinking that perhaps a tricky drive across the heart of England to Lincolnshire might be ill-advised on a school day. Booth, of course, meant Boston, Massachusetts. 'I remember him running like mad to get him a passport and a visa and all that . . . but we got him on the plane,' recalls his sister Adela.

Years later Lyndy Cooke remembers accompanying Andy, by then her husband, on one of Booth's US trips. 'Andy had to go somewhere and Richard and I went off together, buying. Richard told Andy, "We'll be back tonight", but we didn't get back for two weeks. We were just roaring around the place in a Pontiac Firebird.'

And when he arrived he couldn't wait to start buying. 'He was always very uneasy and fidgety,' says Haynes. 'In Miami or somewhere that was lovely and warm, Richard didn't know what to do. I used to say, "Why not sit and enjoy the sun?", but he kept just moving around.' The foreign trips were remembered as fun, but Booth never forgot who he was or why he was there.

Haynes remembers Booth flying out to join him in Miami. 'It was mid-morning as we pulled our cars into an empty car park near the airport outside a dubious looking club to meet up. As we discussed our strategy for the trip, two scantily clad hookers emerged from the club and approached us. Richard's response to their proposition was to launch into his electoral pitch and tell them about his plan to abolish the Welsh Development Agency and rotten bureaucracy in Brecon and Radnor. They were completely bemused. Richard was totally oblivious to their motive. He thought they were just two women who might be interested.'

During one US trip in the mid-1970s, Booth decided his business needed more financial discipline. He realised, in his mind at least, that his own behaviour was not conducive to good housekeeping and that somebody needed to get a grip. Georganne Young had recommended a nurse she knew called Kamma Andersen, who happened to be in Birmingham, Alabama, at the time. Having been reassured she had a 'good sense of order', Booth decided that Kamma, to whom he may have ascribed a matron's firmness of purpose, was what he needed. He called from New York asking her to meet him there, and offered her a job. They stayed at the Algonquin and went to see *The Texas Chainsaw Massacre*, then showing on 42nd Street. 'Booth was giggling all the way through,' Kamma remembers, uncomprehendingly. They then went to Long Island and stayed at a motel owned by singer Jack Jones.

They had separate rooms and had to share the adjoining bathroom. At the end of the evening, Kamma went back to her room. 'Suddenly,' she says, 'this whale of a bloke in a string vest came in and threw me on the bed. He was huge. I went, "Get off me, Richard." He said, "Sorry, sorry." Over dinner I said, "I don't mind working for you and working hard, but I'm not sleeping with you and I'm not in the market for that."'

Not for the first time, Booth had overstepped the mark, the schoolboy evidently needing someone to tell him what was acceptable and what wasn't. Subsequently, he was entirely gentlemanly and respectful towards Kamma, abashed by his presumption. (Back in Hay, he was happy to give her free accommodation at Brynmelyn when her commute was no longer practical, though he did not appreciate her tiresome insistence on putting cash from the till in the company safe, which rather spoiled his fun.)

Booth's trips, home and abroad, frequently impromptu and always eventful, often provided a life-changing opportunity for others, for which they continue to express great thanks. 'It truly opened Andy's eyes,' says Adela. 'He'd never seen anything so wonderful in his life.'

Yes and no. Most of Booth's US bookseller contacts were admirably law-abiding and respectable. Andy Cooke was alarmed to find, though, when he and Booth arrived at Boston airport, a man called Jim Rizek and his light blue Cadillac were at the airport waiting for him. Rizek had company. 'They all had guns. Andrew was sitting in the back with these guys with padded shoulders. It was really scary,' Adela said.

This was 1974, the year of *Chinatown* and *The Godfather Part II*, and the demeanour of Rizek's associates offered compelling evidence of their no-frills approach to business. These guys were not fresh out of business school. Rizek sold Booth a book of rare birds put together by the Victorian John Gould, offering 'almost limitless credit'. He charged Booth a fairly reasonable £10,000. The modesty of the price was striking.

Rizek seems to have charmed Booth, who was perhaps amused by his host's incongruous past as a Princeton theological seminary student. Rizek took him to expensive Lebanese restaurants in Brooklyn, catering abundantly for Booth's enthusiasm for tales of shady characters and their time in prison. And the deals were good, or so it seemed. As far as Booth was concerned, their relationship was smooth, even if he was struggling to keep up the payments on a number of books bearing

New York Public Library labels, by now on sale to readers in Herefordshire. These had arrived courtesy of his friend Rizek, the deal oiled with the gift of a few Macanudo cigars.

Rizek didn't just talk the talk. Omitted from Booth's memoir and diaries, perhaps understandably, was the fact that the entertaining Rizek was not merely a bit naughty – which might be said of one or two others in his trade – but a career con man. First convicted of embezzling $139,000 and forgery in 1957 (approximately $1.5 million today), he had a further conviction for theft in 1969.

In 1971 he hired a team to break into the ill-protected library of Union College, Schenectady, in New York state, to steal a single volume of naturalist John James Audubon's extraordinarily prized *The Birds of America*, one of the highest profile thefts in recent US history. The full story behind the theft remains murky. It seems Rizek had arranged a buyer for the book before the theft took place – effectively stealing it to order – but there was a mishap and a feud followed. It later emerged that the putative buyer was, or became, an FBI informant.

Rizek was a master of complicated schemes, sometimes involving microfilm copies of newspapers, welshing on loans, selling goods he didn't own, fictitious flood damage and corrupt librarians. One comparatively minor wheeze of his was to make a down payment of, say, 5 per cent on the total agreed price on a collection of books, saying he would come back and pay the rest later. He would then take a few of the books away with him (obscuring them among worthless ones), and not come back later, having taken the only ones worth anything. He also advised one dealer how to steal individual books from university libraries, telling him to carry them out on a cart, spine side inwards, to avoid pastoral interventions from helpful passing professors, let alone dutiful librarians.

One of Rizek's specialities was getting on the inside track of institutional libraries. Michael Zinman, a distinguished New York-based collector, says these libraries are particularly prone to items going missing. 'Books have a way of disappearing and showing up,' he says. 'The handmaiden to the disappearance of so many books are the libraries of universities and colleges that are indifferent to the possibility of prosecuting those who took the books.' In other words, those who should care most about looking after the books are the least inclined to do so.

'It's a very strange situation,' says Zinman. 'I bought a book for a good deal of money that had a very reputable university's plate but no release stamp, which is normally the case. I called them up and asked, "Have you got rid of it?" The librarian told me, "You don't have the book, it's still on the shelves." It wasn't, I had it with me. He just didn't want to stir himself sufficiently to go and look on the shelf.'

It was the sort of shortcoming of which Rizek had become profitably aware. In chatting to one book dealer, he was open about how he secured a highly valuable book collection from a seminary on the brink of closure. Chatting quietly to a librarian one day, Rizek said that if he had to make a formal offer to the board who ran the seminary, he would have to offer, say, $10,000 and complete a lot of tedious form-filling. But if he made a more straightforward offer of $3,000 plus a further $2,000 going directly to the person in charge of the physical handing over of the books, things would be that much simpler. 'It was a straightforward bribe,' remembers one familiar with Rizek's working methods. 'Many a seminary librarian said, "Thanks very much, Mr Rizek".'

Given Rizek's record in this field, the following story may suggest bravado. It is certainly a reminder of the US's status as the land of possibilities, as well as a sense of victimism among some of its practitioners. On one occasion, Booth was being given the opportunity to view some books Rizek was selling. Booth made complimentary noises about the quality of the material on offer, for which Rizek thanked him, saying the sale was a small consolation because, as it happened, he had recently narrowly missed out on buying a much bigger collection. Holding his thumb and forefinger a centimetre apart, Rizek explained: 'I was *this* close to getting the fucking Vatican Library, but they changed the pope on me.' This was in 1978, months after the mysterious death of Pope John Paul I.

Rizek was not a man to get on the wrong side of. So it was disconcerting when one day a large limousine pulled up outside the Cinema bookshop in Hay and out stepped Jim Rizek himself, a man about whom what little was known in Hay was not favourable, demanding to speak to the boss. (Booth was never the most physically courageous of people. One staffer remembers how, when money came in, unless he had an immediate need for it, he would put it to one side and tell Garry Spencer, 'That can go towards whoever happens to be demanding it most.' He remembers one particularly aggrieved creditor standing angrily at the front desk of the Cinema. 'Richard would have given him anything, his newborn, just to get rid of him. He was a bit of a coward.')

One Booth employee explains: 'The books had been coming out of the back door of the New York library, and of course Richard couldn't keep up the payments, and Rizek wanted his money.'

Few people in Hay knew who Rizek was, but they knew enough from his demeanour, and from Booth's reaction to him, that this was not a man to be trifled with. 'Get me a Fresca,' demanded Rizek. The order 'get me' an anything would have jarred horribly in a town where passing the time of day and empathetic small talk assume a shamanistic importance. The full phrase 'Get me a Fresca' would have been not far short of apocalyptic. (A Fresca is a grapefruit-flavoured fizzy soft drink, popular in Brooklyn but, at the time of writing, yet to make an impression in the Welsh borders.) For all the menace Rizek brought, he had to be satisfied with a 7 Up. But there was still business to be done. He wanted his money. After some vintage Booth flannel, somehow he managed to pacify his visitor, including in the deal an offer for Rizek's New York-based nephew to spend time working in one of Booth's shops.

Soon afterwards the good-looking, clean-cut college boy came to spend a few months as an intern, staying in a flat at Cockcroft House. He was likeable, innocent and not short on self-esteem, to which April Ashley quickly tumbled. Val Haynes remembers taking the macho young visitor to the Blue Boar one evening and introducing him to this tall and beautiful woman. Val recalls, 'April turned to me and asked me with a wink: "Do you fancy a little arm-wrestle, darling?" April and I had played this game before: a lure to entice a dupe. April allowed me to beat her, despite her superior strength. She then offered to take on the American boy and after a second of false hesitation she smashed his arm down on the table. He was in complete shock. Then she reached across the table, grabbed his lapels, pulled him over and gave him a great big kiss on the lips.' For the stunned boy from New York, this was Hay's version of a walk on the wild side.

At one low point during Booth's financial troubles, it seemed an angel might be on the horizon to rescue his finances. That was the good news. The bad news was that it was to be organised by Jim Rizek and his brother Ernest. In 1957, they had been in business together when Jim was running a Ponzi scheme from which he trousered half a million dollars.

Booth noted excitedly in his diary that the plan was for Ernest to raise $50 million – to put into books – from investors disenchanted with the New York Stock Exchange. Ernest apparently felt this would be no problem and he felt 'absolute contempt for the people who would put up the dough', which was apparently an advantage. The idea was to buy various buildings in Hay, though to keep property in the town separate from the rest of the enterprise, and then involve 'the best non-profit organisation in New York' to manage the thing. Unsurprisingly the Rizek brothers were keen for the plan to remain a secret. Mercifully nothing came of it.

Jim Rizek returned to New York, but he did not have a happy ending. His past caught up with him. Those who knew him say he 'got in too deep' and owed money to too many dangerous people. When compared with the heavy hitters of the US crime scene, librarian-bribing Jim Rizek was no Don Corleone, but he was bad enough to meet a premature end in the Arizona desert, apparently having pushed his luck too far with his organised-crime bosses.

Rizek could turn his hand to most things, and Booth's preference was for quantity. Michael Zinman, an expert in the top end of the market, said: 'They liked him and admired what he was doing, but the antiquarian dealers that I knew dealt with expensive items. They did not tend to deal with Richard, who would come in and buy twenty or thirty thousand books. People who dealt in those numbers were businessmen as much as book men. The book was a product, and they were very happy to accommodate Richard, but most of the antique book people I knew did not operate at that level.'

This was not to say that Booth would turn down a valuable antiquarian or rare book, and colleagues back in Hay would have been disappointed had he done so, but his enthusiasm – some would say megalomania – was for bulk, and for the vast containers that enabled him to move them with more ease than previously. 'He didn't strike me as really a book person,' says the venerable Maureen Rodgers, who has been selling books at the Book Barn in Hillsdale, New York state, since 1972. 'He was not very selective.'

Someone who helped Booth with the shipping of those large quantities back to Hay was the late John Zubal, a bookseller in Cleveland, Ohio. Zubal, though a buttoned-down, staid and conservative man, liked Booth and was taken by the rockstar persona. 'When Richard arrived in Ohio with flourish and bombast and with a black British woman, my parents were mildly scandalised,' remembers his son Michael. 'But they always managed to do business together.'

Zubal senior, like Booth, was always optimistic that a pile of books could bring a profit. 'My old man would imagine value in almost anything. He would get all glassy-eyed when he was presented with fifty thousand books in a warehouse. Without even delving into them he would get really excited . . . and I'd say to my dad, "Due diligence! We're not taking it on until we've seen what's there" . . . but Richard had that trait tenfold. He would waltz in, wave a hand and do the deal. He was indiscriminate when buying books from my father. He would look at the top of a Gaylord box [containing between six and eight hundred books] and act like he was assessing it and the next thing you knew he was agreeing to the terms. That's not the way I do business . . . I don't buy pigs in a poke. He really didn't dig through them carefully, and then he'd be on his way. I think in his head he wanted to create a kind of Disneyworld in Hay. Regardless of quality, quantity was going to impress people.'

Booth's charm and willingness to do a deal had won them over, so much so that one year Zubal overcame his wife's scepticism and decided to visit Booth in Hay. They had underestimated Booth's disdain for domestic comfort. 'They were looking forward to spending a night or two in his castle. And they got there and found there was no heat and no hot water. So the bubble was burst. They didn't stay long,' remembers Michael.

One source of copious books was the US's Books for Libraries scheme. Booth managed to befriend a man called Arno Zohn, a former US Army Air Corps bomber pilot who had made millions from reprinting previously published, out-of-print reference books, many of which featured on the reading lists of American colleges. Zohn did exceptionally well out of these deals, but not all these books – as many as two warehouses full – were in demand for as long as Zohn had hoped. By 1980, his former cash cow had become a positive burden, and after flying to see the heaving warehouses in Florida, Richard Booth was delighted to take the excess off his hands.

Paul Haynes was charged with moving the books from Miami to Hay-on-Wye. He hired local staff in Florida to fill four containers with about a quarter of a million books.

Though he paid a proportion of the price, Booth left a large chunk of the bill – $80,000 – unpaid for some years, despite Arno Press's attempts to get him to pay.

Booth's willingness to 'take the lot', while displaying a cavalier mindset, was often counter-productive. Sometimes 'the lot' was a collection that some dealers would have paid to get rid of, including up to two thousand copies of the same book, but the desire to accumulate never dimmed. On occasions, as he was coming to the end of a buying trip, he would say: 'I must get something for Chris', as if remembering that he needed to buy a souvenir for someone back home.

In such a case, he would be referring, to invent an example, to an atlas for which he might pay, say, $5,000. He would take it back to Chris Powell in the print shop in Hay, where the plates would be removed, mounted and sometimes framed for sale. The pattern, though, says Paul Haynes, was that Booth would return to Hay and hand it over to Powell, without admitting the price he had paid. 'By that stage things were muddied about what Richard had spent or not spent ... because he'd like to come back to Hay from America and to say, "Haven't I done well?"'

Given Booth's proclivity for running up debts, and Jim Rizek's famously hard-nosed approach and Byzantine connections, it is tempting to believe whispers in the States that latterly Booth, in some respects very astute but in others an innocent, was the victim of more than one con by book dealers operating in concert with Rizek. Yet, to speculate still further, Booth's inability to keep tabs on his own spending may mean he would not have been fully cognisant of any such con.

Booth is admired in the States for his can-do attitude, his fearlessness and enterprising spirit, but financially he is less well regarded. On occasions (as we have seen) he simply did not pay his bills. Gary Goodman, who became Tom Loome's partner in Stillwater, tells one story and says there are many others. In Dundas, Minneapolis, says Goodman, Booth had 350,000 books shipped to Britain for which he never paid. It was that sort of record that made Peter Howard, a very well-regarded bookseller in Berkeley, California (who died in 2015), say he simply would not deal with Booth at all.

7

Her Name Was Tola

'If you really wanted to drop out, Hay was the place.'

Naomi Levine

The arrival of the hippies up on the hill did not happen in isolation. The mood among free-thinking individuals in the early 1970s was essentially one of opting out. For most people, of course, this was a dream denied them by having to earn a living, but for the feather-bedded middle classes for whom a career could wait, possibly for ever, the appeal of letting their hair grow, wearing outlandish clothes (within unstated sartorial conventions, of course) and deriding anything staid while sitting around smoking weed were irresistible. As author Ian Marchant deftly puts it: 'The easiest way to live a superficially non-alienated life is just to have lots of money.'

'Word got round that if you really want to drop out, Hay's the place,' remembers Naomi Levine, a Canadian who settled in Hay in 1973, setting up a health food store and becoming a Buddhist soon afterwards. She had moved from Toronto to write her PhD about playwright Arnold Wesker, who had bought a house, Blaendigedi, on the slopes of Hay Bluff in the mid-1960s. Wesker himself had first come to the area when his publisher and close friend Tom Maschler of Jonathan Cape invited him to stay at the house that he and Martha Crewe had bought at Capel-y-ffin, seven miles south of Hay. Like their neighbour Jim Capaldi, who lived a few hundred yards away, both men loved the peace and seclusion that the area offered. It was becoming a new bohemia.

Mark Palmer, a baronet whose mother had been a lady-in-waiting, was a fashion entrepreneur in swinging London in the 1960s. He got to know all London's beautiful people, including Henrietta Moraes and Marianne Faithfull, and newspaper articles refer invariably to his association with the Queen (his godmother), the Rolling Stones and Marc Bolan. In 1972 he opted for a quieter life, buying a house in the hills a few miles north of Hay, travelling to Gloucester to sell the odd horse and occasionally visiting the Blue Boar in Hay. He and his wife, Catherine Tennant, whom he married in 1976, lived the ultimate carefree life, later moving to North Wales and Gloucestershire, an enduring object of fascination for the gossip columns. His name, and that of his Ormsby-Gore friends, who indulged comparable opting-out inclinations, became synonymous with lofty lethargy and free-spiritedness.

A good friend of Palmer, screenwriter Jeremy Sandford, was another well-established figure in the hills around Hay. In 1965, in defiance of the usual Etonian stereotype, he and his wife Nell Dunn bought Wern Watkin, a small, cold hill farm with few comforts and an unreliable water supply in Llangattock, outside Crickhowell, near to where George Melly and his wife Diana had a house. It was around the time that family friend Arnold Wesker – they had marched together on Ban the Bomb marches – bought his house. 'You could ride for several days without going through a gate,' Sandford's son

Roc remembers. The radical author of the TV play *Cathy Come Home* – described in the *Guardian* as 'the most talked-about television play ever', directed by Booth's Oxford friend Ken Loach – had grown up between Leominster and Ludlow, but Hay was his preference. 'My dad loved those Marcher castles along the border,' says Roc, 'but Hay was always special, and you could see it in the distance from his parents' house. He also loved Kilvert. Kilvert's niece or great-niece had given my dad one of Kilvert's original manuscript diaries, so he was really interested in Hay Castle because I think Kilvert used to go there. We'd sometimes have drinks with Richard on the lawn in front of the Castle.' Sandford, though not a heavy drinker and with only a passing interest in drugs, would spend long hours with Booth in Hay's pubs, simply chatting. 'Dad enjoyed the subversiveness of Richard Booth.'

Sandford had no time for status symbols, nor, unlike Booth, for prestige cars. 'My dad used to roar over to see Richard from Wern Watkin to Hay in his VW Beetle which had holes in the floor and no muffler. Me and my brothers would be taken along, too. The car smelt of petrol and exhaust and whenever we went through a puddle, water would squirt up inside.' In 1978, he declared he was 'more interested in spiritual enlightenment [than] social engineering as a solution to the problems of the world', and converted his country house, Hatfield Court, a Jacobean mansion outside Leominster, into a study centre for New Age travellers. Sandford himself spent a lot of time sleeping rough at camps and festivals. 'He was lovely but he was a bit smelly,' says one of Hay's more comfort-inclined citizens.

Similarly, Alexis de la Falaise, a designer by training and a man of implicit good grace, and his wife Louisa (née Ogilvie) moved into a beautiful farm, the Bailey, behind Clyro and Rhosgoch, eight miles north of Hay. His Irish mother Maxime was a model for Elsa Schiaparelli, and his father a French writer, Count Alain de la Falaise. His sister, Loulou (not to be confused with his wife Louisa), a frequent visitor, grew up in London and New York, becoming a writer, model, designer of clothes and accessories and ultimately becoming a muse to Yves Saint Laurent, with whom she was to work for three decades. Saint Laurent said of her: 'Other than her undeniable professional qualities, Loulou de la Falaise's real talent was her charm. Particular. Moving. It was the strange power of a gift for lightness blended with irreproachable acuity and her eye for fashion. Intuitive, innate, particular. Her presence at my side was a dream.'

The rural life of Alexis and Louisa lacked catwalk chic. It also lacked money. They had decided to work on the land, which may have been a surprise to their farming neighbours who had been doing so for generations, much of their slight income coming from farming subsidies. They worked hard and produced and cooked copious vegetables, which inculcated a sense of living off the land in their son Daniel, now a much-admired chef. (Having started under his great-uncle Mark Birley, founder of Annabel's nightclub, he is now 'the most stylish chef in the industry,' according to French *Vogue*.) The parents kept chickens, but were too squeamish to wring their necks for the pot, preferring to shoot them instead. (It was a similar story with their ragtag collection of sheep, gunshot generally shattering Radnorshire's rural serenity as they enjoyed their last meal.) But, in an era when most Britons were still discovering olive oil, their 'terroir' food, garnished with plentiful herbs, was notably delicious, complemented by the more than occasional spliff.

For the family, though conditions were spartan, it was idyllic. Once a week Alexis and Louisa would brave the mud, climb onto their tractor and drive into Hay for market day, two beautiful children in tow (the second of whom, Lucie, was to marry Keith Richards's son Marlon). 'They had no money at that time but they were truly the beautiful people,' says Naomi Levine. 'This could only have happened around Hay. They cut quite a figure . . . they were not particularly sociable, they just grew their vegetables. Everything was like magic around them. Louisa had an amazing eye for decoration. She made little pictures everywhere in every nook and cranny of the house, with flowers and paintings. She was really highly artistic. Hay was a magnet for a lot of beautiful people, despite the cold and wet. They came here for a few years and then they went again, back to Paris.'

Rural life provides a kind of camouflage of classlessness, and nowhere was this more true than Hay. Those with more money than they want to advertise can disguise the fact by 'dressing down', ideally with a spattering of mud, to fit in – or believe themselves to do so. Similarly, the high-born whose family money is waning are less likely to feel exposed, being able to dress in the same scruff's uniform. Dressing smart is not the thing at all. Paris could wait. And it did.

Other members of the de la Falaise clan would visit, as did their friends Frank Ormsby-Gore (later Lord Harlech), Chrissie and Jean Shrimpton, Mick Jagger and others of the beau monde. Booth was a frequent visitor for meals, insisting that Hay must become a metropolis. His free-thinking affinity with the down-wardly mobile upper-middle classes had its limits, though. One evening he went to collect Marianne Faithfull, who had been staying at Brogyntyn Hall in Oswestry, Shropshire, home of Frank Ormsby-Gore. He spent the evening there and he and Faithfull didn't leave until 1.30 a.m. But overstaying his wel-come was not the problem, he later learned. On the contrary. His diary records: 'Very rude apparently to leave then because they always stay up until four.'

Booth asked Maxime, the matriarch of the de la Falaise family, who remained based in France, to write the dedication in his autobiography. She wrote: 'Richard is a man I am delighted to have met in Wales and in Paris. His astonishing optimism comes through in these pages as do his championship of reading itself, his courage and his scholarship, all combined with an energetic and imaginative business sense and, thank God, a lively sense of humour. He lives in a youthfully humorous world of castles and kings, but his real life is still a successful struggle and a passionate adventure.'

Another figure of almost mythical status, among libertarians and bohemians at least, was the tortured anarchist Old Etonian poet, sculptor and naturalist Heathcote Williams, who lived in the Old Vicarage at Brilley, six miles downriver from Hay, which was owned by his wife's cousin, book dealer David Batterham. Williams, who numbered fire-eating among his talents, acquired tabloid newspaper fame when he set light to himself on Jean Shrimpton's doorstep when their relationship ended. (He unwisely used petrol rather than lighter fuel for the trick, though by covering his face he managed to minimise his visible burns, agonising though they apparently were.) He also earned much opprobrium for the way he treated his lovers and son Charlie, born in 1989, who wrote a memoir exploring his father's unwillingness to see him after he walked out on him and his mother, writer Polly Samson, after six months.

Williams's time in Brilley, living with his long-term partner Diana Senior, is remembered locally for its many excesses and eccentricities. The local vicar, the Rev George Worsop-Hyde, was said to be so shocked by what he took to be Williams's self-centredness that he thought he had been possessed by the devil. In fact, troubled by mental health problems, he was far more ingenuous than diabolical, his art fuelled by pure outrage against injustice. He wrote copious and prescient poems about the threat to the natural environment. He believed all property was theft and after he left Brilley set up what was effectively a squatting agency in London called Ruff Tuff and Cream Puff which enabled those in need of a bed to sleep in unoccupied premises. It later became the subject of a musical.

A comparably cultured and eccentric figure was Williams's friend Peter van Praagh, a writer and aspiring filmmaker with an interest in old farming ways. Van Praagh sold his Fulham house and moved to Brilley, where he and Williams found common cause. Van Praagh made a short film of Williams purportedly showing fire running through his entire body. Williams knelt, naked, as he ate fire. The camera then panned down his body to show flames emerging from his bottom. (Heathcote had a firework called 'the mighty Stromboli' tucked by his naked backside.) The film was entered into Amsterdam's Wet Dreams Festival of 1971, the purpose of which was to explore 'the boundaries between art and porn, voyeurism and participation, exploitation and liberation'. It was not among the prize-winners.

Van Praagh had first come to the Hay area to visit his mother – a close friend of Penelope Betjeman – who lived in nearby Glasbury. He fitted in well in these bohemian circles. He had inherited money at the age of eighteen from his father, but had spent most of it. He launched into making a film of Thomas Gray's 'Elegy Written in a Country Churchyard', employing locals as unpaid extras. Cannabis was as prevalent in Brilley as it was in Hay and elsewhere. 'Everyone smoked at the time,' remembers his wife Joanne, who says no one turned a hair, including the local policeman when he came to check the shotgun licences. When the vicar dropped round and saw the exotic plants growing outside the back door, he would sigh happily and say 'Ah, Cannabis sativa', without further comment.

The high cost of making the totally unsuccessful film, *Restless Spirit*, currently held by the British Film Institute, resulted in the bank foreclosing on the home in Brilley, making the family homeless. A gifted, charming and striking looking man, van Praagh fell victim to alcohol and died at thirty-seven in St Neots in 1988. Joanne speaks of Williams's extraordinary and continuing kindness in his support for her and their very young daughter. He travelled up from Cornwall to read Gray's 'Elegy' at the funeral in the City of London.

Hay's appeal for those looking for a counterculture and something more than rat-race ethics attracted a number of Buddhists, among them Maggie Russell, another comfortably-off product of the aristocracy, who bought a farm above Llanigon, just outside Hay, where she and her husband Kurt Schaffhauser set up one of several Buddhist study centres in the area, consecrated by the Karmapa, head of the Karma Kagyu strand of Tibetan Buddhism and one of its most revered figures, in 1974. The Wenallt, as it was called, became a centre of rather more than contemplation, Maggie having bitten off rather more than she expected in marrying Kurt.

Bruce Chatwin, author of *On the Black Hill* – the most famous novel about the area – and a man frequently untroubled by the extent of his welcome, made the Wenallt (more correctly Middle Wenallt) one of his many long-serving berths.

There were several places of serious religious reflection in the area. Some, though, felt the need to round off a day's contemplation of the impenetrability of samsaric existence with a skinful at the Blue Boar. Andrew Brewer, a Buddhist who lives near Hay, spent a lot of his childhood in the area. He remembers two residents of one retreat who would drive the families to spend their evenings in the pub. 'The wife would take over the bar, and at the end of the evening the landlord Chris Fry would come over to us eleven-year-olds and say, "Can any of you drive?", we'd say no, so we'd have to carry my friend's mother over to the car so she could drive us up to the hills. That was kind of normal.'

Brewer continues:

In the pub, there was a weird mix of hippies, bohemians, minor aristocracy and Welsh hill farmers. I try and tell people what Hay was like in the 1970s, and all I can say is that walking into the Blue Boar was like walking into the bar in Star Wars . . . there is nowhere on earth like it, nowhere . . . a sleepy little border village transformed into this bohemian getaway. It was, and still is to some extent, the most bizarre place, and Richard was very much part of that.

The great thing about the Blue Boar is that as long as you were up for the craic, it didn't matter who you were. A lot of the social norms didn't seem to apply in Hay. That was part of the brilliant madness of it all. No one was fawning over the celebrities. Famous people would be walking along the pavement and nobody was bothering them . . . anywhere else they'd get mobbed but in Hay it would be 'Well, who are you?'

One of Booth's later guests recalls going out to dinner in Hay with April Ashley. 'She was extremely elegant and dressed as if she was going on the *Queen Mary*, with jewels and everything – but no one seemed to notice her.'

Penelope Betjeman lived alone a few miles south-east of Hay. She was spoken of universally with awe and affection, her expertise and experience of travelling in India lending her an unusual moral authority. She was also no slouch in the eccentricity stakes, heading her notepaper 'No telephone thank God!' and riding into town on a pony and cart which gave way to pedestrians and cars only *in extremis*. She, too, thrived on frugality, aping the simple life she longed for in the Himalayas.

She and her husband lived separately, he spending much of his time with Lady Elizabeth Cavendish (famously his 'beloved other wife') in London. But John and Penelope were in constant touch by post, to her address near Kulu-on-Wye, as they called it, echoing the name of her favourite place in India, and he would occasionally visit Hay. Cotters would be invited to provide literary conversation while she clattered pots dutifully in the kitchen. He recalls one evening after supper he and Penelope helping the infirm laureate up the stairs to bed. Later in life Betjeman's visits to Hay were limited. Interviewed by his friend Duncan Fallowell for a book published in 1977, he said: 'I used to go and stay there but she [Penelope] has no water or electricity or heating and all the windows are open with the wind whistling through the place – well, I'm rather frightened to go now in case it kills me. But I like Hay very much.'

Penelope Betjeman was befriended by Bruce Chatwin, for whom she acquired an almost maternal importance, and for whom she offered inspiration for an exuberant character in *On the Black Hill*. (Evelyn Waugh is also said to have based a character – the Emperor Constantine's mother in his novel *Helena* – on Penelope.) Having introduced Chatwin to the brothers on whom the book's story is based, she was an early reader of its first draft. After doing so, she admitted to having walked round in a daze all day, believing it as good as anything written by Thomas Hardy.

On her death in 1986, Cotters wrote: 'What always struck me was her sense of humour, her gentleness and generosity, her humanity; behind the eccentric, the adventurer, the survivor, lay a sensitive, vulnerable, religious and very human being. When a remarkable personality departs, the world is left a poorer place.'

Following her death, Chatwin travelled to India and threw Penelope's ashes, along with tulips and pheasant's eye narcissus, into the River Beas at Kulu. Chatwin later told Cotters that he found the loss almost unbearable.

One of the most intriguing and surprising entries in Booth's diaries is the following, from the mid-1970s, when he was in London one evening before attending a book fair. He wrote: 'Went to Harold who was high – with John Betjeman. Smoked large joint.' 'Harold' is Harold Landry, Booth's Oxford associate, who lived in Hampstead. Neither Booth nor Betjeman were known users of cannabis (and assumed not to be), and Booth was notably anti-drugs – certainly hard drugs – for most of his life. His diary reveals that he also felt a striking lack of sympathy when an American girlfriend was threatened with extradition following a 'drugs bust'. Landry's frequent use of cannabis is confirmed by his widow Judith, who says he also liked a drink but that 'he was much more amiable when he had had a smoke'. Of any Betjeman/Booth/Landry 'triad', she says it is surprising: 'But one never knows of course.' This was the mid-1970s, shortly after Betjeman had been diagnosed with Parkinson's disease, from which he died in 1984. Two former friends of Betjeman say the story is news to them – one of them questioning whether he would have been an active participant – but one of his biographers, A. N. Wilson, says: 'I can easily imagine Betj smoking a joint, the bigger the better.' Late in life he was partial to alcohol, says Wilson, and would have welcomed 'other aids to oblivion'.

For years, Booth had been motivated primarily by growing

his bookshops. The effect of this was, naturally, to increase the glory of Richard Booth himself. It must be said that the phrase 'it was all about Richard' has been heard countless times in the preparation of this book. But his critics must accept, too, that his desire to help Hay become sustainably prosperous was genuine. He had a devout, almost romantic fondness for the place and was seriously committed to the protection of old country methods and the provision of rewarding work for its inhabitants. He would sit in pubs talking for hours about, for example, hedging, the protection of endangered species and the squeeze imposed on farmers and on the environment by the destructive demands of 'greater efficiency'.

Domestically he was hopelessly unsuited to fending for himself, and was largely looked after by Charlie and Cathy Gibbons, who took care of matters in the kitchen, garden and beyond. He still liked the idea of having a settled relationship, but opportunities for briefer ones kept presenting themselves. His existence was less than monastic, his status as the man who made Hay famous making him a figure of some fascination. He did, though, have regular 'favourites', including two women who lived across the river who his friends dubbed 'the fillies of Brilley', one of whom he might well have settled down with and who featured in a racy mural at Brynmelyn by the highly regarded painter John Napper, a friend of Booth.

Nevertheless, his open, unforced demeanour allied with an impressive sense of mission made him engaging company, and many women found themselves being charmed by his unorthodox courting. His idea of showing an American visitor a good time, for example, was to invite her to one of Hay's earthier pubs. Rolling out the red carpet meant ringing Violet Jenkins, the landlady of the Mason's Arms, and asking if she'd mind them bringing their fish and chips into the pub later that evening. As ever, he was indulged. Once a relationship was underway, though, he was capable of great generosity.

At Oxford, as we have seen, Booth had been smitten with a Spanish woman called Victoria del Rio, known more usually, to Booth at least, as Vicky. He had been much taken with her spirit and beauty, and his hopes for a future with her continued after he left Oxford in late June 1961. In a diary entry soon after he arrived in London, he chastised himself for failing to make contact with a friend. He continued: 'My mind, however, was really on Vicky for shortly afterwards I went to [the jeweller] Boucheron to find her a present. The £100–£200 range – ornaments in gold – are all dreary and so it will have to be something in the £200–£400 range – diamonds and enamel – which I get her.' Three months later, when abroad, he bought a pair of earrings. 'They are made from rubies and diamonds and I intend to present them to Vicky, but I am not sure why I got them – probably unwise. Nobody could be more dissimilar than Vicky and myself.' A couple of months later, he mentions talking to a friend 'until 1.00 a.m. about Vicky etc.' But evidently, for Vicky at least, the moment had passed and regular contact was discontinued. Following his disappointment in marriage to Elizabeth, he renewed contact.

Vicky was back in Spain and living with her well-heeled parents in Las Palmas, Gran Canaria. The grand Catholic family which produced Vicky – or Tola as she was known to her racier friends – was more protective of her than she liked. Her two sisters had married and the family felt that Vicky, now in her mid-thirties, ought to be settling down. She felt romantically disposed towards England, having studied there and speaking the language, and a family member believes she saw it as an opportunity to escape. Booth knew, though, that if he tried to visit, her parents would seek to defend her honour.

In short, they would allow him little time alone with her. In anticipation of this, Booth paid for a linguist friend to accompany him to Las Palmas. The friend's job was to impress Vicky's mother with talk of fine art, antiques and so on. In short, he was to provide a distraction.

The recollection of the friend, book dealer Peter Dance, is as follows. 'Because I could speak Spanish I could entertain Vicky's mother while he consorted with her daughter. Her mother was something of a show-off, endlessly boasting about her purchases at the salerooms of Sotheby's and Christie's in London. She really annoyed me. There was a limit to what I could pretend to know about certain antiques.'

Dance recalls Vicky arriving at the hotel in Las Palmas. She was accompanied by a lively bunch of friends who, he suspected, had been taking drugs. In Franco's Spain this was risky and frowned upon in so respectable a milieu, but nothing untoward happened. Evidently Booth was with Vicky for long enough for both of them to be convinced they were made for each other. Each was from a respectable middle-class family, but, equally, each was rebellious and riled by convention. Marriage to one another ticked a 'settling-down' box, but in a pleasingly nonconforming manner. She was a bookish and inquiring product of Madrid University. He was a leading, Oxford-educated entrepreneur in the world of books.

Two further issues, God and mammon, needed to be addressed. As a Catholic, Vicky could not marry a man whose first wife was still alive unless the Church issued an annulment. Booth's diary is unclear as to how this was arranged, but in Rome in November 1974 he was reassured that there would be no obstacle to his marrying Vicky.

That year, 1974, had begun with the death of Mary, his favourite sister. He wrote in his diary, 'I do not feel any event will ever affect me so much'. Now he could anticipate a much happier occasion. He returned from Italy and in late November he informed his young girlfriend of the time that he planned to marry Vicky.

The second obstacle is sometimes recycled to the amusement of Booth's detractors. Once again the popular version is wide of the mark, though not by much. Booth's reputation as an admirer of wealthy women preceded him. In the widely held mythical version, his prospective father-in-law confronted him menacingly on the day of the wedding, assuring Booth that if he thought he was going to get his hands on any of the Spanish family's money, he had another think coming.

The truth is slightly more decorous. Some weeks earlier, Booth was presented with papers renouncing any claim on Vicky's family's money. 'Being a gentleman, he signed them,' remembers Dance.

In early February 1975 he was informed by Vicky that the annulment of his first marriage had been recognised in Spain and the couple were free to marry, which they did on 8 March, in Las Palmas. The precise truth of events immediately after the wedding are unclear. In an early draft of his autobiography, Booth says that 'unfortunately I could not stick marriage for 24 hours and left her at Madrid airport'. The published edition was only marginally more gracious: 'It did not take me long to realise that I had made a terrible mistake.'

Booth quickly decided – possibly as quickly as the wedding reception – that on reflection 'till death us do part' was taking things a bit far. He left quickly for the UK, as if no explanation was required, and found Vicky, unaccountably to him, following him to Hay. He felt obliged to accommodate her at Brynmelyn. Unsurprisingly, she felt this at least was her due, though he often stayed at the Castle.

But Booth had decided he wanted no more to do with her. Vicky wanted the relationship to be 'holy and indestructible', whereas he thought the institution 'may be worth a six-month trial'. If he persisted with the marriage, he calculated, 'I would have an extraordinary collection of influential and aristocratic friends in Spain, but wonder how useful this is in terms of the English second-hand book trade.'

Less than six weeks after he married, he was reflecting: 'I hate marriage more than anything in the world . . . Relationships are totally destroyed by marriage.'

It was not as if he had ever shown what might be called a conventional whole-heartedness about matrimony, or this marriage in particular. He had made it clear that he planned to marry Vicky, but at least until the ceremony he had continued to see the young girlfriend and another woman.

His book suggests Vicky spent very little time in Hay. In fact she was there for many months, but he found it impossible to break with the two other women (both still alive) he had been having a relationship with and acknowledged to himself that he had created a tense and most difficult situation.

His diary confirms that Vicky was indeed in Hay, but money remained a problem, both personally and for the business. Vicky's mother was used to having money – at one point she had complained that she 'cannot manage this house' with eight liveried servants – and her attitude had rubbed off on her daughter. Booth complained to his diary: 'I am acutely aware of the problems of the business especially as I am completely out of control with Vicky running up debts all over the place.' He admitted that Vicky's presence was favourable in one sense at least: 'The house looks much nicer with Vicky here, but it is like growing roses on corpses: next time I shall live with a nice quiet English girl, who can talk a bit about books.'

People in Hay were curious to know about the new wife, glamorous in Louis Vuitton and Gucci, but word quickly got round that she was at least as eccentric as Booth. Equally quickly, she realised the occasions for wearing her catwalk clothes in Hay were few and far between. Her mink coat, even in the cold Hay winter, was out of place.

Her dogs were under-exercised and inclined to leave calling cards around the house. Vicky would show a comparable lack of inhibition in her own habits. On one occasion at Brynmelyn the stairs were packed with people and suddenly one of the doors opened on a landing … 'I am de wife, I am de wife!' she shouted, before disappearing behind a closed door again. 'It was like something out of *Jane Eyre*,' says one who was present. 'People were transfixed by it.' On another occasion when Richard annoyed her, she threw a telephone at him.

There were other episodes that set tongues wagging. Vicky remained in Hay, to sometimes cruel amusement, and was more than once seen urinating in the street in broad daylight ('like a horse,' said one local). She was also found naked, smoking a joint, in the middle of the town.

Further tales of excess and indignity are best overlooked. It emerged she was not only highly eccentric and possibly suffering from mental health difficulties, but this was compounded by her continuing use of drugs, notably marijuana, LSD and cocaine. When Booth finally got together with her, he discovered the truth – she was addicted to cocaine and susceptible to almost anything else. At her family's behest she had been spending an extended period in an expensive private hospital in Spain in the hope of releasing her from her demons.

According to one of Booth's oldest, fondest and most admiring friends: 'He was in the dark about the state of her mind, but she was stark staring mad … raving bonkers. It is true he wanted to marry her for her money, but she was palmed off on him.'

Booth himself was thoroughly liberal about how people behaved in private, but personally he had little time for a druggie lifestyle. Certainly what are now referred to as class As were a world apart from his own, so the discovery that he had married a drug addict, and, for example, the casual arrival one day of a heroin dealer at Brynmelyn, would have shaken him. He did not mention Vicky's drug habit in his book, claiming instead that he and she had political disagreements about whether and how to subvert society. Booth wrote: 'Vicky wanted to flout authority. I did not think authority was worth flouting.' The truth was more simple. He wanted her gone.

Yet she had no wish to go back to her strait-laced family in Spain, and in and around Hay she found plenty of interesting and like-minded people. On one occasion she returned to Brynmelyn, which she regarded as her rightful home. Finding some of Marianne Faithfull's clothes and suitcases, she flew into a rage and hurled them out of the house, assuming – as many did – that Marianne and her husband were having an affair. According to a friend of hers, Vicky felt Booth was cruel to her, making no secret that he was seeing other women while she was still hoping to patch things up. Ivor Windsor says the relationship was not complicated: he married her for her money.

'He was carrying on with other women, and continued to do so after the marriage. I don't think he had a conscience like most people . . . he came back from Spain and he didn't exactly give her a right royal welcome when she came. We were a bit surprised and concluded that this was a contractual thing, a deal. She was abandoned and lost at the time, and actually Frank English was very good in helping Vicky. It is what used to happen in the nineteenth century, and by default Richard would have read a bit of history. People get married for mutual advantage and it's a bit of a deal that suits everyone.'

On another occasion, when Booth was away on a buying trip, Vicky – perhaps in revenge for the way Booth had coldly rejected her so swiftly after the wedding – decided to hold a party at Brynmelyn. She invited around thirty of her recently acquired tent-dwelling friends from up on the mountain, and in the breadth of their tastes comfortably matched the excesses that Booth and his friends used to manage. In her case the air was thick with exotic smells as friends made themselves at home, dressing up in the late Colonel Booth's tailcoats and military regalia and drinking his claret.

The merriment was interrupted only when Booth's Rolls-Royce made a surprise late-night return up the Brynmelyn drive. He was furious, not merely at the unlicensed bacchanalia but the disfigurement of the family's history which greeted him, shouting, 'Where's my fucking gun!' A number of guests scarpered, terrified, for the hills, but many stayed, perhaps too out of it to realise how angry he was.

Vicky, though, was unfazed, and continued the mayhem. She locked Booth out of the room where his family's wine was stored and, one by one, started smashing the bottles. Realising his threats would achieve nothing in her drug-addled state, Booth looked through the glass and begged, 'Please, not that one', which just spurred her on to break precisely 'that one'. On another occasion, she grabbed one of Colonel Booth's walking sticks and began smashing windows, causing the impecunious Frank English to laugh hysterically and proclaim: 'At least I'll get some work as a glazier!'

In mid-June of 1975, ten weeks after they were married, Vicky began the legal process towards divorce, but she continued to tell Booth she wanted the marriage to last and that she loved him. He was occasionally amorous towards her, but his mind was made up. In July he wrote: 'Vicky is in a very loving mood: Gonzi [her brother, who had taken a shine to a local girl] is around: they do not seem to realise that I want to be absolutely clear of everything and don't want a marriage or anything else.'

When the frustration with Vicky wore off, Booth, the friend recalls, was 'incredibly sad about this, really very upset ... He was very distressed because she was in such a state.'

Vicky was almost certainly unreachable to anyone wishing for a conventional marriage, but her brief association with Booth was particularly poignant. Booth's emotional immaturity brought extreme discomfort, for both him and his wife. Vicky was quoted as complaining of her husband: 'He's put me in exile because I would not join in sex orgies with women and pop stars at his castle. He promised I would be a queen, but I finished up washing dishes in a café.'

It is sometimes mockingly said that not only did Booth marry Vicky for money, but also that she married him for the same reason, and that both were mistaken in thinking the other had money. Booth's continuing cash-flow problems and the sight of Vicky hanging around in Hay washing dishes showed conclusively how futile any such hope would have been for either. There were eventful parties, including one in the 1970s at which a now senior politician slipped into a tutu at midnight. Local people speak confidently (and unrepeatably) of wild, Roman goings-on attended only by those closest to Booth, but the idea that participation in those might have been a condition of their marriage is far-fetched. Booth, it is now clear, had had enough almost before the marriage had begun. While some close to him applaud his bravery in confronting a difficult truth head-on, others wonder how he had failed to see it coming.

In some respects, the marriage might be thought a close escape for Booth, but it marked him. 'Written all over Richard in the time I knew him was an extreme sadness that he had not been able to get a relationship working properly,' says Sally Bradshaw, another close friend. 'He was feeling lonely and very upset at things having not gone right. That seemed to me a leitmotif ... feeling and worrying about things that had gone wrong and that they had been his fault.'

Other friends were concerned at his apparent decline. Another former girlfriend wrote to him, saying: 'You sounded so sad. I was very worried. People who upset you are such scum. You must ignore them and keep remembering you are a genius.'

The wrangling by their lawyers was predictably unpleasant, with almost every point being disputed. Booth accused Vicky of taking no responsibility for her actions, and her side made claims based on the entitlement bestowed not so much by the marriage vows but by her class. Meanwhile, her behaviour in Hay was as unruly as ever. After a dispute about money in late 1975, he records matter-of-factly: 'Vicky smashed eight windows in the Castle.'

'He was truly sorry that here she was in this Welsh town and he had no capacity to handle it. He had never encountered anyone who was round the bend,' remembers a friend.

After a while, he managed to persuade Vicky to move out of Brynmelyn, and he put her up in a first-floor flat on Lion Street in Hay, where she continued to take drugs and indulge in outlandish behaviour – even for the times – often in the company of New Age travellers attracted to Hay by the magic mushrooms. A friend remembers her leaving her front door open in the middle of one of Hay's bitingly cold winters, telling him to come up and join her. She was smoking a joint in the bath. That same visitor recalls her complaining that the electricity supply kept tripping. 'She had all the elements on the electric cooker running – the rings, the grill, the oven, to keep her warm. No wonder.'

The couple were eventually granted a divorce by a court in Hereford in 1977. Booth said later that Vicky was too aristocratic to listen to her lawyer's advice, so that when she confirmed to the judge that she liked smoking joints in the company of adulterous hippies, any prospect she might have had of a financial settlement went out of the window. In fact in his diary he seems to have accepted his lawyer's advice to pay her off with £1,000.

Asked if Vicky's parents didn't feel let down by Booth failing to stick with his new bride, a relation said they were more worried about Vicky's state of mind. Besides, as we shall see later, if life with Booth had been a roller coaster, she had seen nothing yet.

8

Opera Buffa

'The soprano may have to have a cold bath.'

Anon

It was typical of Booth's flamboyant and incautious entrepreneurial spirit that he decided, in homage to tradition, to play host to a series of operas to be staged by Hugh Vickers. Booth's old Oxford friend had been spending time in Venice and was now running his own company, using gifted but relatively unknown singers.

As ever, the fanfare accorded to news of the intended production drowned out any sceptical voices. Vickers was a brilliant, charming and enthusiastic figure, but he was not best equipped to run the sort of tight ship that these productions require. He was the indulged only son from the second marriage of Sir Geoffrey Vickers VC, an extraordinarily distinguished civil servant, and Ethel Ellen, an heir to the Twinings tea company. The family lived comfortably in Carlyle Square, the young Hugh sent to play in the Harrods toy department when he could not be otherwise entertained.

Nicholas McGegan, a harpsichordist and specialist in early

music who collaborated with Vickers on several projects, remembers him fondly. 'Hugh was full of bounding enthusiasm and everything was terribly important. He'd wag his tail and knock over the furniture, and then be terribly sorry about it. You knew you had to keep your distance, and with him a lot of facts were often very negotiable. He was slightly Bunteresque, in that his foibles were so obviously on display and you couldn't help liking him.'

Soon after leaving Oxford he produced a number of *succès d'estime* operas in private houses and at the Lycée in South Kensington. At the height of the summer of 1964, for example, he organised a performance of Mozart's *Il Seraglio* in Campden Hill Square in west London, for local residents Lady Antonia and Sir Hugh Fraser. (Hugh was air minister at the time, so happily there was no problem about aircraft noise spoiling the audience's enjoyment: he simply arranged for the planes to be diverted.) This event, though a huge triumph artistically, was not a success financially.

Similarly, his next production, even more ambitious, was an open-air London Philharmonic Orchestra performance of *The Magic Flute* in Belgrave Square. The evening was a disaster, having been set for late September, not a reassuring moment in the calendar for prospective ticket-buyers.

Friends had chipped in with contributions to putting on the production, but film producer John Sutro, who had underwritten the event, trusting Vickers to do his sums correctly come what may, lost out most of all and had a breakdown as a result. It was only conscientious after-the-event raising of cash by Vickers's wife Jane – through a Cambridge fellow, John Procope (a schoolfriend of Hugh and a King's College Cambridge classicist) – that saved any sort of face. Vickers himself fled to Venice in embarrassment. Ultimately Sir Geoffrey Vickers and his wife had to make up the shortfall.

The model that Vickers deployed was unimpressive, wonderful though the productions were agreed to be. Ostensibly any profits from these productions were to go to charity, but Vickers's own fondness for lavish expenditure and entertaining generally ensured there were no profits. Jane Flower, Vickers's former wife, was appalled at his modus operandi: 'This was money people thought was going to charity. That sort of dishonesty among friends is totally unacceptable, leaving other friends to clear up the mess. Richard and others perfectly understood what was going on. You just don't take money like that. That was why I left the marriage. It was horrifying to find the money was being spent taking five or ten people to expensive restaurants, living the high life. In hindsight, it was fraudulent and dishonest, though that only became apparent later.'

The best interpretation of Booth's willingness to stage Vickers's productions is that he believed he could do them on the cheap. These mini-operas required just three singers and at most four musicians. The venue, Brynmelyn, was his own, though it was hardly luxurious. At one point the words 'the soprano may have to have a cold bath' could be heard. The tiering was put together by Bruce Addyman, a master of most building skills, and the food provided by willing locals. Whether that would be sufficient, while paying impressive up-and-coming performers, would become apparent.

The first production was Pergolesi's *La serva padrona* in 1975, the audience the aesthetically appreciative of Hay-on-Wye and beyond. Beneath the mounted wildebeest trophies that still adorned Brynmelyn, the hallway was treated to a scintillating performance by Yvonne Kenny, who went on to global fame, accompanied by harpsichord, flute and violin. Though not without the odd hiccup (few things in Booth's life were), the performance excited him and a series of further occasions followed, calling on Vickers's specialisation of *opere buffe*. In 1976 he put on *La Zingara* by Rinaldo da Capua and Haydn's *Lo Speziale* in 1978.

Kate Hadley, a friend and former lover of Booth, remembers how pleased he was to play host. 'He could always generate a good number of people,' she said. 'If there was something he could claim was excellent, he was delighted.'

The attraction for the performers – apart from being paid – was certainly not global celebrity. Hay could offer no such thing, but it provided fun and warm memories on which to look back. 'It was a very eighteenth-century experience, in that you went to a nobleman's house and performed,' remembers Nicholas McGegan. 'They were always nicely costumed,' recalls Sally Bradshaw, another singer who was to achieve widespread prominence. 'The cast all stayed at Brynmelyn. It was a most eccentric time. I think there were a lot of empty rooms, dusty carpets and a degree of chaos – and often no food. It was as if we were living out *Ariadne auf Naxos*.'

There was plenty of chaos offstage. Yvonne Kenny had to resist a badly staged late-night seduction attempt by a Spanish guest. The excellence of the steak tartare and turkey, cooked by two accomplished locals – 'and the de la Falaises did a pâté' – defied the vagaries of Brynmelyn's antiquated Aga. At the Castle a drunken Hugh Vickers fell thirty foot down the narrowing shaft where the Castle's portcullis was meant to go, and would have fallen further, possibly to his death, had he been less Bunteresque. 'Hugh's life was saved by his enormous stomach,' Booth wrote later.

One of the attractions of Brynmelyn was never knowing who else might attend. Of course, among the forty or fifty guests there were the sophisticated Hay regulars, but others, down from London, would also turn up. Among these the odd MP,

Prince Yuri Galitzine, Paul Jones (of Manfred Mann fame) and Dudley Moore, who Booth knew through Jonathan Miller, a friend of Hugh Vickers, and who seemed to particularly relish the unscripted, amiable mayhem that Booth encouraged. Australian artist Sir Sidney Nolan, who had a studio, the Rodd, north of Kington in Herefordshire, was a compulsive buyer of books, and ran up a large debt to Booth as a result. To Booth's frustration, the debt was never repaid, but a few years before his death in 1992, Nolan gave the Booths a couple of pictures in lieu. At the time, though, they would have welcomed the cash.

'Dudley went a couple of times,' remembers Kate Hadley, who thinks Moore, part of the great satirical *Beyond the Fringe* foursome, found solace in Hay. 'Dudley used to be invited down by Richard to play the piano. He was enormously charming, though inclined to depression about life and I think he always found it fun and sympathetic, because things weren't competitive. Richard was very good at promoting that sense of just letting things develop in a relaxed way, which Dudley enjoyed.'

Sally Bradshaw was also grateful for the relaxed ethos of Brynmelyn. 'He was not one for ceremony. He didn't worry about appearances. It was very liberating and enabling, a really very nice place to be. You could go and lie in a corner and read a book. Nobody had any expectation of you there.'

Nonetheless many of those who attended the *opera buffa* events wore the smartest of outfits, which might be thought to be the embodiment of the complacent privilege that Booth saw himself as challenging. It would have been a difficult balance, had anyone given it much thought. But that was the point – Booth banished any such fretting. This soft subversiveness may also have been part of the appeal for Dudley Moore.

'What Richard didn't like was the structure of hierarchy,' says Kate Hadley. 'He also didn't like ambitious, successful determined Etonians. He couldn't bear that determined pursuit of success. He'd rather arrive at success by falling into it effortlessly. He was a Whigite.' So, while disliking those who took for granted the power and rewards that go with privilege, he also disdained those who *didn't* take them for granted and who worked for their rewards. Or perhaps he simply disliked unreflective Etonians.

He found academics unworldly, cossetted and – when they came to work for him – reluctant to roll up their sleeves and do the necessary lugging of books. For Booth, intellectualism as a whole was to be regarded with suspicion, though he was well read and cultured himself. In 1980, Martin Amis noted the paradox that the 'world's largest bookseller should turn out also to be one of its leading anti-intellectuals'.

The shows were a socially smart extension of the hospitable ethos that Booth so enjoyed at Brynmelyn. He would invite people to stay, invariably leaving unstated how long they were welcome. (The answer was almost always 'indefinitely', and sometimes they would indeed stay for months.) People would turn up, with or without notice, and he would make no demands on them beyond expecting them to make themselves comfortable and tolerate a degree of chaos and, often, cold. He had a hatred of bores, but such people would never get past the front door. By definition those admitted were considered agreeable and entertaining enough to be allowed to stay. Mischievous tongues have suggested that many of the women who stayed had been invited for one reason alone, but that is not the case – he simply enjoyed playing the host, no strings attached.

Kamma Andersen, who lived at Brynmelyn while trying to instil some discipline on the business, was one beneficiary. 'I think I was employed because he was a soft touch. He had a good heart and put us girls up, and we never paid a penny.

He was always very kind. People did rip him off because of his nice nature.'

That said, his capacity for caprice was never far from the surface. At many of Booth's parties, a delicious and potent elderflower wine was available. Sally Bradshaw was a regular performer in the *opere buffe*, and she is credited with beginning what became an annual tradition. She suggested that Booth might enjoy the alcoholic drink with a taste, she told him, comparable to Gewürztraminer. One glass unleashed one of Booth's bouts of over-excitement and he arranged for the early summer flowers to be picked in advance of her frequent visits so she could make large quantities in buckets and plastic barrels. (On one occasion, a mischief-maker laced the drink with a hallucinogenic drug, though the culprit was not identified: it certainly would have not had the approval of Booth or his regular friends.)

One year, all was going well as the wine was brewing. 'Then he did a terribly strange thing to us,' remembers Sally. 'The deal was usually that we would bottle it and take away a certain number of cases and he would have the rest, but then, when we came back one day, he had ordered the thirty dustbins of fermenting wine to be removed by Charlie. There was a lot of bad blood. I think it was retaliation for some perceived slight, or maybe he believed we were taking more than our agreed share. And then, all of a sudden, a couple of hours later, all the wine reappeared and we went home. It seemed he easily believed the worst about people. But I think it was all soon forgotten, by him and by me. It looked like a bit of irrational spite on his part. It was a mad and bad thing to do – extremely childish. I always had a weather eye for him acting badly, so it wasn't a surprise that he should act peculiarly ... because he was peculiar – but in a way that enabled lots of positive things.'

The critical success of the performances was considerable, and Booth was so pleased with the initial production that he arranged a free performance for the people of Hay. As ever in Booth's world, the trifling issue of money was less than transparent, as those familiar with Vickersworld might have expected. The invitation announced the first event, in 1975, which offered a 'champagne buffet' for four nights, as being 'in aid of the National Society for Mentally Handicapped Children (now Mecap). But Booth admitted later that his friend Hugh Vickers 'rapidly embezzled the profits which were supposed to go to some now forgotten charity'. There was no apparent regret at his willingness to indulge his friend's profligacy.

Booth and Vickers were the only male products of marriages between upright, public-spirited and morally committed fathers and similarly strait-laced, comfortably off mothers. Money, when it had the impertinence to intrude on life's merriment, was something to be inherited rather than earned. For Booth, certainly, very often the money was secondary, incidental.

To some, money is the goal. To most of us, money is a means to an end. To him, though, it was often not even that: its lack would be no obstacle. Failing to pay for something was not down to him knowingly intending to con people; he simply believed that somehow things would work out all right, a kind of Marcher lord Micawberism. 'I think P. G. Wodehouse would have turned them into wonderful characters, perhaps the same one,' says Nicholas McGegan. 'I can imagine Richard and Hugh at the equivalent of the Drones Club, where they would have drowned their sorrows at unfortunate romance or lack of money whilst drinking off somebody else's expense account.'

This financial carelessness had consequences for others, of course, though in one facet of life neither man absorbed the message until it was too late. Just as Vickers's unreliability cost him his marriage, Booth's love life also suffered. Kate Hadley, a huge admirer of Booth, found his attitude to money, and his failure to understand how important it was to other people, a major obstacle to their relationship. Booth wanted to marry her, but she turned him down, partly because she could not imagine how she could reconcile her very successful professional life in London with wifeliness in Hay.

But his indifference to making others suffer for his over-spending was also a factor: 'He would not pay his bills. He would stay in his house. People would come to the door with sad expressions, asking for the money he owed them, and he wouldn't answer the door. He had an irritation with other people's need for money. At the *opera buffa* events, the idea was that the audience, many of them pensioners, would put their money into the opera, so effectively Hugh was borrowing money from pensioners, and he knew he'd never give the money back, nor would anything go to charity. Richard and Hugh felt these people were paying for the pleasure of their company. The idea was that the people who paid for the tickets should be grateful for the time they spent with these brilliant people ... And that's dangerous ... that was sailing too close to the edge for me. It was awful. Richard had a pretty dangerous side to him, and it was risky, but that's how he built the town.'

9

Independence

'There are levels of belief. Nobody completely believes in it or disbelieves in it.'

Richard Booth

In April 1977, Booth executed his most brilliant PR coup. He announced that Hay-on-Wye had had enough of being told what to do and taken for granted by big government and faceless bureaucracies. The town was declaring itself independent, and would henceforth be ruled by a king, by the name of Richard Booth. It was an exceptional announcement, based on not the slightest public mandate, but bound to attract coverage from newspapers amused by tales of wackiness and eccentricity.

Booth's preferred version of how he announced his plan for Hay to become independent is that some weeks earlier a journalist from the *Sunday Mirror* arrived having received a tip that Marianne Faithfull was in the town, and that an off-the-cuff Boothism gave rise to an extraordinary PR coup. One notion the journalist was chasing was that Faithfull was having a relationship with Booth's friend Ivor Windsor. Ivor is in truth a major-league toff, and is known as Ivor Windsor-Clive, aka

Viscount Windsor, and now known most formally as the Earl of Plymouth, who still lives an hour north of Hay, outside Ludlow in Shropshire.

It was a story of obvious popular appeal – Mick Jagger's beautiful former girlfriend, who had fallen prey to drink and drugs, was apparently being rescued by a senior member of the nobility. It was known that Booth and Ivor Windsor were friends, so the man from the *Mirror* made his way to Hay to see if he could confirm the truth of the story.

Unsurprisingly, the journalist found Booth in the obvious place, the pub, though in the best Fleet Street tradition it can well be imagined that he might have told his news editor he had managed to 'track him down'. Booth knew the truth, which was that Windsor had indeed had a relationship with Faithfull a couple of years earlier, but it was now over. In any event, ever protective of Marianne (whose presence in Hay was in large part intended precisely to escape press attention), Booth, generally a loyal friend, had no intention of passing on this nugget.

This was the moment Booth had been waiting for. He uttered the words: 'Hay is going independent.' No doubt, as was his wont, he added a bit of a lecture about the monstrous behaviour of local bureaucrats. The bemused journalist asked if the people of Hay supported him. In his book, Booth reports: '"Yes," I replied. "They're all for it." *I had only thought of the idea five minutes before*' (my emphasis).

The journalist suggested a picture might be in order and a photographer arrived the next day and a 'crowd' (mostly bookshop staff) assembled in the Market Square. In one brief conversation, Booth had deflated one story and invented another entirely to his advantage.

The truth is not quite as Booth painted it, his instinct for self-mythologising getting the better of him. In fact, he had been talking about independence with Jeremy Sandford since the previous spring, and a few months later he was having logos designed. There was even a story in the *New York Times*, no less, the previous November, telling of how this 'backwoods P. T. Barnum' was planning Hay's independence. A mis-recollection such as this used to be put down by his supporters not to the mendacity that would apply to anyone else but to 'one of Richard's flourishes'.

Even his detractors admit that claiming independence for Hay was a masterstroke in publicity terms, some even criticising him for not pursuing it far enough. Declaring independence, a folly verging on the Bavarian, had probably the greatest impact of all the unlikely wheezes of Booth's life. Pedants pointed out the obvious impracticality, thereby gratifyingly feeding the joke at the expense of the po-faced. Outside the council offices a message was posted. It read: 'The Hay Town Council wish to make it clear that they have never in any way been associated with Mr Richard Booth's "UDI" proposals, neither have they any intention of doing so in the future.' District councillor Rex Jones was outraged by a plan 'likely to bring local people into ridicule'. Mr David Hughes, chief executive of the local council, replied stolidly: 'It is perfectly obvious that Hay is an integral part of Brecknock Borough under the Local Government Act of 1972. No changes can be made except through Parliament.' For Booth, such bovine humourlessness, with a flat-footed failure to see the world through his eyes, offered joyous vindication. In his mind the upholders of the established order had exposed their own absurdity, and his staff were happy enough to join his chorus.

And where publicity was concerned, Booth won hands down. The *New York Times* followed its original scoop by sending a reporter to interview Booth, who spoke with passion and seriousness about the stifling role of college libraries in the dissemination of culture. 'Books should be cheap,' he said, 'but universities have made them expensive and institutional. They pay more for books, and when books get into universities, they are hardly read.' To a TV interviewer who asked if people seriously believed in his plan, he conceded: 'There are levels of belief. Nobody completely believes in it or disbelieves in it.' The people of Hay, he concluded with his customary broad brush, were 'fairly serious about it'.

Though proud of the jape he inflicted on those not on his wavelength, the seriousness of his politics was central to his purpose. He felt strongly about Hay, and anointed himself its protector, like some 'father of the nation' autocrat. 'Since the First World War, Hay's population has declined from three thousand to fifteen hundred,' he explained. 'And whereas there used to be two hundred shops, now there are about fifty. Central government has ignored us for too long.' Where to most this seemed like the simple operation of market forces, Booth pulled together a handful of opinions based on his foreshortened impression of the town to form a passionate defence of traditional methods of production. Whether his local-leaning outlook adds up to a coherent 'worldview' is debatable. To insensitive modern ears some of his views will seem far from worldly, but many of the opinions he espoused have an undeniable truth and, indeed, prophecy. At the time, though, the publicity did more to highlight his sheer eccentricity than the thrust of his opinions, which will ring many bells with those who lament the march of 'progress' in the countryside. It would be a disservice not to ventilate some of those views here, the words taken from pamphlets and articles written by Booth over a period of years:

On Cusop Dingle, his own backyard:

Fifty years ago these were cider factories, leather workshops, homes, farms, tile, slate, lime, bacon manufacturers, blacksmiths, and many others. Rural depopulation and the drift to the cities have destroyed all but one or two. The population has sunk from 200 to 20.

On intellectuals:

The idea that we're going to solve the problem of rural revival by intellectual effort and building universities is totally finished. There must be a revival, but it's got to be a return to local wisdom. People are still trying to stuff other people's wisdom down our throats. I do think the revival of the rural areas of the world will come through the second-hand, labour-intensive economy.

On the relationship between the media and bureaucrats:

A radical attitude concerning the influence of the media in relation to tourism leads to a radical attitude to the media over food. Sixty per cent of TV revenue comes from food or drink-related products and virtually none of this is from local food production, which is crucial to the survival of rural areas. When the supermarket talks of farm, fresh, country, local products, it is, in fact destroying farm, fresh, country, local products. It seems to me that the media and the media-food of the supermarket have a total self interest in destroying rural Britain. Tourism simply provides the alibi!

On local wisdom:

For me all wisdom is in my local community. I am learning

nothing which I cannot learn in Hay. I need our traditional craft, our traditional culture in my business. If a university graduate offered to give me a good idea, or to clean my car, without a second's hesitation I would want my car cleaned. This is the basis of the manual economy. We need hundreds of people to do hundreds of jobs in a town, we don't need a single university graduate.

On academics ...

I am a romantic. I believe that England was great in the 18th century when academics were regarded as freaks and bores. The tragedy of the nineteenth century was that it gave them dignity.

On supermarkets:

They destroy small shops as surely as if they had been burnt to the ground by their competitors.

On prospects for jobs locally:

The education system seizes on a bright rural child and tells him or her that it is undesirable to work with one's hands or understand the traditions of the local community.

The Youth Employment Officer for Brecon and Radnor will readily admit that there are hardly any local jobs for young graduates, but the educational propaganda continues in the press – 'Start climbing the ladder to success.' Like the government bureaucracies, the Universities conceal their failures by heavy advertising and the endless production of glossy brochures.

On the horse economy:

About a mile outside the town of Hay-on-Wye in Breconshire, Cusop Dingle is an area only reachable by horse. The motor road finishes a mile outside town but eight bridle ways lead up into twenty miles of the most spectacular scenery in the British Isles.

A total success is the horse economy – four hundred people lived and worked there and produced infinite products for the town of Hay. It was a total failure in the tractor economy – the population sank to less than twenty and a few hundred sheep and a large patch of forestry commission.

The products it had manufactured from tiles, stones, slates, lime, to home-cured bacon, home-made cider; every aspect of the craft economy was much higher quality than the industrial economy and, because they were largely for local consumption, contributed considerably to the prosperity of Hay.

An attractive development of the Local Tourist Information Centre for me would be to expose how the horse is still a realistic part of the local economy. From stallions, to the hundreds of horses employed in pony trekking and trotting, to the horse-drawn holidays, it is still there to remind us of the age of wood, iron and leather when integrity sold a product rather than advertising. The trotters at Llanigon show, indeed, are considered the main method of keeping that village together after it has lost its shops, post office etc.

The local Tourist Information Centre will issue a bridle way map which will show all the local producers of organic produce, will cover the entire area covered by the old Borough surveyor on his horse and explain how only ten per cent of the area in the Hay region is seeable by car. From the

Castle we will run horse-drawn vehicles under the slogan of 'support non carbon monoxide tourism'.

My principle argument in favour of the horse is that it performed a vital service within an economy in which everything, from home-baked bread, home-cured bacon and home-raised chickens to stone walls and barns was of higher quality than its modern, mass-produced substitute. When all these things were swept away by an unholy alliance of mechanisation and bureaucracy, hundreds of jobs were lost.

On growing trees:

In our earliest civilisations, the sacred groves constituted the first temples, and when the oak, ash and holly are hacked away to be replaced by the dreary acres of conifers, it is not hard to believe that sacrilege has been committed in the name of profit.

They ignore the beauty and value of our many forest trees in favour of endless ranks of dark pines to be pulped for newsprint or sawn into pit props.

'It takes a hundred acres of forest to produce each issue of the *New York Times*' is a frequently quoted statistic, but no one stops to ask whether country people would prefer a flourishing forest to the ephemeral wads of print, voicing the views and values of the establishment.

'Poor dear, it needs it's daily dose of D.D.T.,' said a friend, referring to an extraordinary tree whose trunk seemed to have collapsed into a sort of U-bend, and Forestry Commission pamphlets proudly show a space-suited figure spraying gallons of chemical fluid between the growing saplings.

The [Cusop] Dingle Forests that are administered by the Commission are not even orderly. As one rides, one sees scores of overgrown paths, roofless ruins, tumbled walls and one is hardly surprised that the Forestry Commission is anxious to drive ordinary people off their property.

On government support:

We must get away from the notion of government help, advice and assistance and do it ourselves.

My idea of a real nightmare is people saying: 'If only the government would give us a grant.'

Grants aren't really giving Hay anything – we're already paying for the bureaucracy. Anyway it's pointless to give grants for sophisticated things to areas that can't handle them.

... What we need is anarchic feudalism. It would be 20 times more efficient than the present system which just misunderstands Hay's needs. You can't organise Hay from an office block in Cardiff. You've got to be there and do it.

On small farms:

At one time, there must have been about ten small farms in Cusop Dingle, some of which have vanished, some of which have been amalgamated, and the principle result has been a startling reduction in the variety of local produce.

Nowadays, it is mainly sheep that roam the acres, and the numbers of beef and dairy cattle, pigs, hens, ducks, geese and goats have been considerably diminished.

The orchards of cider apples and perry pears have either been rooted out or their fruit sold to big manufacturing

The young Richard and his parents,
Colonel Philip Booth and wife Elizabeth

Booth marries Cumbria-born Elizabeth Westoll.
Best man Lennox Money is behind him.

April Ashley, Hay's very own diva – and seen outside the Ladies with Cotte

Neffy Hensher and Ellie Wright, co-founders of
Effie's ever-lively bar and restaurant

With Marianne Faithfull

Booth and Victoria
del Rio, informally
and at the altar

Booth and Hope, indulging a shared interest

Brynmelyn, Cusop, home to Booths for 120 years

Ever the showman, Booth poses for the media at Brynmelyn

Booth at the front desk of the Cinema bookshop
with a colleague, Colonel Bill Beere

Frank English, Booth's right-hand man and shelf-builder

Star line-up for Don

By PAUL COLE

Rock superstar Steve Winwood and some famous friends played a secret Birmingham show — to raise cash for the badly-burned victim of a house fire.

Grammy Award-winning Steve teamed up with mates like Jim Capaldi, Ruby Turner, Steve Gibbons, Trevor Burton and Mike Harrison for the show.

The gig was staged at Aston's Elbow Room club, where an audience of 200 fans watched a line-up more used to playing at giant concert halls.

Proceeds went to Don Carless, who founded the club in the 1960s, but who has been wheelchair-bound since a fire at his Kings Heath home.

Don is pictured (centre) with (from left) club owner Albert Chapman, Jim Capaldi, Ruby Turner and Steve Winwood.

Club-owner Albert Chapman organised the gig in conjunction with former Spooky Tooth drum star Mike Kellie — friends of Don in the 60s.

"It was a great gig," said Albert, "They rehearsed all day and played all night.

"There were solo spots, duets and band performances.

"In the end we raised around £4,300 and I added another £500. It was good of Steve and the guys to give their time to help an old friend."

Don Carless (centre), with (from left) Albert Chapman, Jim Capaldi, Ruby Turner and Steve Winwood in April 1989

The Festival site, off the Brecon Road, with the Wye Valley behind . . .

. . . and a few of the 200,000 loyal readers and buyers

companies like Bulmers, and the direct supply of cider to local pubs is a thing of the past.

Many farmers have been forced to give up their dairy herds because the big lorries of the Milk Marketing Board are unable to negotiate the tiny narrow lanes and cart tracks that approach these small farms. Both locally cured bacon and free-range eggs have become largely uneconomic.

Agricultural authorities talk about efficient and economic farming, but the small farmers in places like Cusop Dingle will have to work twelve-hour days whatever they produce, and their manual labours are augmented by quantities of paperwork and the observance of many complex regulations. It would seem that the sole result of bureaucratic meddling is a sharp reduction in the availability of local produce and the working population of Cusop Dingle The proliferation of office jobs in the Milk Marketing Board and the importing agencies for New Zealand lamb and Danish bacon can hardly provide an answer for the sons of dismissed or ruined farmers.

On quarries:

These quarries made Hay one of the most beautiful towns in the world. In the industrial societies where planners replaced workers it has become slowly vandalised. It is easy for an industrialised business to destroy the craft economy of small communities.

For example, a brick manufacturer sells his mass-produced bricks at a very low price, until he has ruined every small local brickmaker and then the centrally produced, standardised product has to be trucked into rural areas from miles away.

This seems all right until petrol prices increase yet again and the bricks become more expensive too: by the time this happens it is too late and the local competition has gone for ever.

On slaughterhouses:

There are many governmental regulations which seem expressly designed to destroy small businesses, but those governing the slaughter of farm animals for meat must be among the most insidious of them all.

Three small slaughterhouses have closed in Hay alone ... and it seems ironic that the butchers of this town were particularly fond of locally killed meat.

Now our nearest small slaughterman is based in Eardisley and he is in constant despair over the multiplying of regulations and it is impossible to believe that he can survive.*

All the business will soon be conducted in Hereford, and the resulting meat will become more and more expensive as the slaughterhouses become bigger and the surrounding farmers waste more and more petrol as they ferry their animals for greater and greater distances to the nearest slaughterhouse.

Soon local meat will become completely uncompetitive and we will be eating even more frozen New Zealand lamb than we do already.

On the Forestry Commission:

Large parts of the Forestry Commissions land looks like a First World War battlefield.

---

*   Indeed, though it took around twenty years to close.

Nowadays, the Forestry Commission owns a large part of Cusop Dingle, and this body claims to protect rural employment opportunities, but it also boasts that it has efficiently pruned its employees, reducing their number from one man to every seventy acres to one man to every three hundred and fifty acres. It also recognises an allegiance with the Wales Tourist Board by boosting its forests as a tourist attraction, but in the Dingle and elsewhere it has created miles of the most desolate and artificial woodland in the country.

One of Booth's lieutenants, Major Bill Beere, said if Hay was going for a universal declaration of independence – the term UDI had currency at the time, following Rhodesia's unscheduled breaking away from the UK twelve years earlier – Booth surely should be its king and should be known as 'Richard, Coeur de livre'. Tom Coyne of the *Birmingham Post* described Booth as the king with more pages than most. Hay's citizens would need new passports, which would raise revenue for the Exchequer.

'The purpose of independence is prosperity for the town,' Booth told a reporter. 'In 1900 Hay had a population of three thousand and two hundred shops. Now the population has dropped to two thousand and there are only about thirty shops [of which about half were bookshops]. What we feel ought to be established is a town union, rather than a trade union, so we can protect our local shops.'

Booth embraced the independence idea with his characteristic youthful sense of excitement, singlemindedness and unsinkability. His loyal staff, liking it or not, joined in with the joke, offering a lot of hard work. The project required huge quantities of paraphernalia which occupied almost all his time. 'He carried the whole thing along,' remembers Denise

Salmon, who was working in the print shop. Booth had also hired his friend Alex Williams, a talented graphic designer who set up a design studio in the shop with a Grant enlarger. Their job was to produce posters, brochures, leaflets, certificates (for the titles he planned to bestow on his subjects) and so on. Williams also designed a flag, which can still sometimes be seen in Hay. (The original was stolen, but anyone interested is reassured it is in good hands.) Richard, Alex and Denise would go to lunch at the Radnor Arms, across the river in Llowes, then serving excellent food, firing alcohol-fuelled ideas at one another. Another wheeze was the printing of Hay car boot stickers, in the style of the 'GB' ones then used by motorists abroad. These no-frills affairs had an official timbre and helped to spread the message.

Some weeks later, perhaps fittingly on 1 April 1977, independence was declared. Four TV stations sent cameras for the launch, and journalists joined the two hundred or so who filled Market Square beneath the Castle. Booth paraded down the high street, his horse as his prime minister, wearing a crown of paper and tin foil. The more ludicrous it looked, the better it served the cause.

The reception was far from unanimous. Some dismissed it as a glorified gimmick, a stunt aimed solely at boosting the Booth empire. On the Castle's terrace Booth, huge cigar in hand, stood with his artist friend John Napper and a filmmaker from the Central Office of Information, Annabel Olivier-Wright, who became a girlfriend. The crowd's reaction was largely positive, though there were a few boos, too. Some unimpressed shopkeepers produced a placard stapled with cheques from Booth that the bank had refused to honour. Ivor Windsor made a speech, offering congratulations. There was an 'air force' flypast (by a single light aircraft) and the crowd moved down to the river where two Booth acolytes launched the Hay navy's gunboat with a one bang salute, from a crow-scarer.

The party then adjourned to the pub, where Hay passports and Hay edible currency (made of rice paper, so people could 'put their money where their mouth is') went on sale and the King dispensed cabinet posts. He made a stonemason his minister for Scottish affairs (he had a Scottish accent), a telephone engineer ran the Welsh office and Charlie Gibbons, Booth's gardener, was made minister for agriculture. There was to be no arts minister because such a position might encourage posers, but local author Duncan Fallowell was made poet laureate on the grounds, said Booth, that 'you're the only literary person I know'. One local, Norman Ratcliffe, drank so much he couldn't remember if he was foreign secretary or prime minister.

'The enormous advantage of Hay,' observed Booth later, 'is that it is possible to give almost everyone a top government or civil service job. Someone who you met in a pub could five minutes later become home secretary. The minister for social security (having the advantage of being on the dole for six years) was appointed in a second.' He also sold dukedoms (£25), earldoms (£15) and baronetcies (£5). Ivor Windsor reacted with patrician good grace when someone asked how much he had paid Booth for his title. His title, Earl of Plymouth, had been first created more than three hundred years earlier.

There then followed loud celebratory music at the Castle as Booth and his friends toasted the rebirth of Hay's local democracy. In traditional style, an ox was roasted on a spit, intended as a sign of the beneficence of the king towards his people. As might have been guessed in Booth's gimcrack world, professional party organisers with experience of spit-roasting oxen were too expensive. Instead, his apparatchiks relied on the British amateur's ability to make a fist of any job, using an electric spit borrowed from John Napper for the purpose. Recipe books had been consulted at length, and twelve hours was allotted to cook the vast carcass. After about fourteen hours it was still too bloody to be acceptable. Some brave souls decided they couldn't wait and dived in, generally to their regret. Most would not touch it. To cap it all, in a shameful display of ingratitude, small boys with full bladders showed their disrespect as only such small boys might, from up in the battlements down onto the unready ox and its servers below.

Weeks of silliness followed. In fighting back against the large multiple businesses that threatened the town's small shopkeepers, schemes of varying outlandishness were launched, or at least mooted. Booth wanted the town's resources and countryside to be used for the benefit of local people, so Hay would have a 'National Loaf', baked locally, a Hay National Sausage (produced by local butcher Dick Keylock) and a Hay National Ice Cream, endorsed by T-shirts proclaiming 'Balls to Wall's'. He also planned to get rid of the Central Electricity Generating Board and encourage local people to use wind and water to generate their own electricity.

Medieval stocks, equipped with bookrests to allow the malefactors to read, were to be reinstated outside the Castle. Two shadowy organisations with responsibility for domestic security were to be launched, the C. I. Hay and the Hay G. B. 'You wait and see,' he said. 'There are lots of things we can do to make life better for the people of Hay. For one thing, there are too many outsiders fishing in the Wye, paying fees to wealthy landowners, not to the town. We'll cut off their lines,' he claimed. Booth's fondness for half-baked puns was ushering in a new dawn. A fresh era had arrived. 'If I can change, so can Hay,' piped up April Ashley.

The independence stunt was an act of genius, as far as publicity was concerned at least. It brought journalists and tourists to Hay in greater numbers than ever. That year, 1977, was momentous for a second reason, as we shall see shortly, but that summer also brought sadness to Booth's personal life. For one thing – and it was a sadness coloured with relief – was his divorce from Vicky. He now felt no obligations to her any longer, nor was there any threat that she might pursue him for a substantial divorce settlement. Second, his father's elder brother, whom Richard 'absolutely adored', died. Martin Booth, who kicked over the family traces by not only not taking up arms in either world war but also in working in the motor trade (considered a bit déclassé, apparently), for Ford in Cirencester, had been a far more approachable figure to Richard than his father had ever been. At about ten o'clock one evening, he and his nephew were in the sitting room in Brynmelyn drinking brandy and chewing the cud when suddenly and quietly he passed away.

'Uncle Martin died,' Booth told a friend matter-of-factly a day or so later. 'I checked he was dead and put a blanket over him and in the morning I called the doctor.' Asked if Booth hadn't felt an obligation to call the police or a doctor that night, rather than leave a corpse on his sitting room sofa, the friend said: 'Richard was perfectly capable of judging if someone was dead and in an upper-class way he would not consider he needed anybody less upper class than him to verify this. I had the feeling that leaving his uncle under a blanket was rather an act of love or gentleness, leaving him in a place where he was at peace and surrounded by affection and near to Richard . . . For him it would have been a natural act of love and although it might be thought an oddity, it wasn't odd at all but perfectly correct emotionally, proper in Richard's terms . . .

but he was clever enough not to discuss this kind of thing with officialdom as he would have known they would get uncomfortable and regard it as lawless.'

10

The Fire

'He was an accident waiting to happen.'

Booth employee

In late 1977 Booth was having a relationship with a woman called Ellie Wright, a gifted performer and organiser in the arts, at that time running the Welsh National Opera's theatrical department. One evening a friend, Helen, invited her and Booth to stay at a gatehouse in Glamorgan. There they met Helen's boyfriend of the time, an architect and builder named Roger Capps. Capps had been working at Wells Cathedral and was also building a school's art gallery in Glamorgan. He was an expert in stone, had an aesthete's sensibilities and specialised in the restoration of old buildings.

Booth took a liking to him, and, typically, tried to sign him up there and then. He asked Capps if he would come and design a theatre in Hay Castle for Ellie to run.

Capps went to visit but turned down the opportunity, believing a theatre would not be appropriate. 'I said no – I wasn't going to screw up the building,' remembers Capps.

It was Charlie Gibbons's job to ensure that whichever

of Booth's abodes he intended to occupy for the evening – Brynmelyn or the Castle – was warm and welcoming when he returned home from a day's book buying. Gibbons's problem was that Booth would often delay until the last minute his decision as to where to have dinner. This left little time for Gibbons – whose preference was early to bed, early to rise, and was sometimes having at least a lie-down by the time Booth made up his mind – to arrange supper and get a large fire going. (Both buildings were largely reliant on wood fires on cold nights, wood being plentiful and oil expensive.) This was all part of life working for this exceptional man, but on occasions he found it frustrating. Booth would often ask employees who had also been away on long day trips to drop by to report on what they had netted. On occasions Charlie's fires were so fierce and so hot that the returning buyers asked for the meetings to take place outside the sitting room. To those in the know, these were known light-heartedly as 'Charlie's revenge'.

On the evening of 28 November, Charlie had lit a blazing fire at the Castle. Booth had a visitor that evening, Constable David Jones, who had called in about the death of Booth's Uncle Martin. Jones recalls a more than decent fire. 'It was drawing well,' he says. On this occasion, the fire had been built earlier in the day, by Mil, a Serb-born Hay resident at that time working as the Castle's gardener. Booth enjoyed a light-hearted relationship with Mil, admiring his physical strength and willingness to work hard in unloading containers full of books. Less fulsomely, he generally referred to him as the 'Slimy Serb'. Mil reciprocated with 'Privileged Prick'. (The wit was admittedly not of Algonquin standards.) Mil suggested that the height of the Christmas-tree shaped pile of kindling and thick logs favoured by Booth was excessive. It will burn out and fall, Mil told him, and it might be dangerous. Booth replied with banter only marginally more amusing and acceptable then than now: 'Mihailović, I'm fucking paying you. You do what I fucking tell you to do.' (Mil's correct name is Peter Milicevic: Booth larkily preferred to call him by the name of a heroic, Nazi-resisting Serbian general from the Second World War.)

Other versions of the story exist, and one includes the use of a fire guard, but the common wisdom about Booth does not suggest much caution. In the words of one of Booth's closest lieutenants: 'Booth wouldn't have given a thought to having a fender in the way. He was very careless with things like that. He was an accident waiting to happen.'

That, indeed, is what followed, or so it seems. He was woken in the middle of the night by a noise he believed, in his half-slumber, to be the applause of the citizenry of Hay expressing gratitude to their great benefactor. It was nothing of the sort. The irresistible crackling sound was that of Tudor panelling burning. Booth, sleeping on the second floor, leapt from his bed and scuttled out of the blaze, which had quickly spread from the fireplace. His attempts to douse it with a fire extinguisher were like 'putting a water pistol on the back of a jet engine,' he later wrote. Soon the heavily timbered Castle was ablaze, the fire brigade – twenty part-time local firefighters – doing its best to hose down the flames, while also struggling (and failing) to prevent Booth going back into the Castle to save a couple of paintings. Locals were woken and gathered on the grass outside the Castle as burning oak panels, staircases and timber beams lit up the night sky.

By the morning, the oak-panelled drawing room on the first floor and the medieval beams had gone, along with the roof. Though the site of so revered a landmark being crudely denuded was a shock to Hay residents, sceptics were quick to mutter that Booth, whose financial difficulties were becoming well known, might have started the fire intentionally, in order to make an insurance claim. Nowadays few are willing to endorse that view, though questioning voices, feeding on scraps, are occasionally heard.

More credible are suggestions of gilding the lily when the assessors came round, with Booth getting his team to create a 'golden brick' of books which no one wanted, 'on the outside and on the top of which we put the valuable books, supposedly irreparably damaged in the blaze,' said one employee. But even those are open to challenge.

Booth lost little time in thinking about how the Castle might be rebuilt, but it would obviously be a major undertaking. Large parts of the original structure had been destroyed. Further, in trying to put the fire out, firemen had soaked the mortar and plaster ceilings, leaving the stone walls vulnerable. Four-fifths of the building were seriously damaged, and the fire revealed that much of the building spared by the blaze had in any case been undermined by hundreds of years of damp. But once the damp plaster had been removed, many of the earlier features, predating the Georgian and Victorian modifications, became apparent.

Booth's accountant Gareth Jones arrived to reassure him that he was indeed insured. This, in the Booth regime, might have been something of a novelty, and all the more remarkable when cheques were being bounced so frequently. To add to his critics' cause, it emerged that only a few weeks earlier a new insurance policy had been instituted. How very convenient, they said. Further outlandish claims have been made, including that gunpowder, used to deal with unwanted tree stumps at Brynmelyn, was deployed in the basement during the night.

But that is to underestimate Booth's emotional attachment to the Castle, and to ascribe much more cold-blooded cynicism to him than he possessed. Far more likely is that Booth was the recipient of insurance company beneficence in a quite different way. The destruction of the Castle's roof left it open to the elements, which particularly in a Grade I listed building could spell yet more disaster. So the insurers insisted on erecting tarpaulins – and removing books and anything else that was vulnerable – to prevent inclement weather inflicting further damage.

As it happened, some months earlier Richard Booth had let his staff know that he was planning to move much of his more valuable stock from the Castle to Cockcroft house. Knowing that some of the material was valuable, he and Gareth Jones asked the insurers to put a value on the stock he planned to move. The existence of such a letter has been confirmed by those who worked with Booth.

When the fire took place, however, the insurers were embarrassed: they had failed to carry out the valuation. Part of Booth's claim was that because the insurers had not carried out the valuation, he had hesitated to move the material, so it remained in the Castle and was consumed by the fire. Also included in the claim were some very valuable old books of which even someone familiar with the Booth stock was unaware. Booth explained that these hitherto unseen volumes were not part of the business's stock but books from his own rooms in the Castle.

Those familiar with the case say the insurers, having not got round to doing the valuation as requested by their client, and by now anxious to preserve a reputation for fair-dealing and probity, felt honour-bound not to challenge the Booth claim with, for example, the robustness which characterises the modern world of insurance. Someone familiar with the case – not a Booth employee but an admirer – puts it succinctly: 'Richard had a good war.'

In the later 1970s, Booth's zeal for local autonomy was undimmed. He wrote a pamphlet called 'Abolish the Wales Tourist Board', into which he poured considerable built-up anger. 'A number of grants have been totally counter-productive, producing no increase in prosperity and simply creating bad will and envy in poor, neglected areas. The fact that a Board consisting of ex-politicians, a trade unionist and a caravan-park owner, amongst others, should have the power to allocate millions of pounds with the abandon of drunken sailors must be fundamental to the continuing decline of the British Isles.'

Booth's words, and other protestations about the role of entrepreneurs and freedom more generally, preceded the first election victory of Margaret Thatcher in May 1979. The Britain of the 1970s, which began with a 'dash for growth' followed by strikes and high inflation and ended with economic sluggishness and a winter of discontent, was coming to a shuddering halt with the arrival of the most radical government for decades. Booth was too anarchic to align himself with anything as starchy as the Conservative Party, and he certainly disdained the power of big business over small. Two of his most memorable slogans were the aforementioned 'Balls to Wall's' (ice cream) and his protest against industrialised and unhealthy bread production: 'Father died of Mother's Pride'. Where economic growth was concerned they had a lot in common, but where he was radical in some respects he was deeply conservative in others. As we shall see, his politics were as particular as the rest of him. At the time of the 1984 coal miners' strike, a totemic moment for organised labour in Britain, he expressed vigorous support for them, developing a friendship with another 'king' (to his supporters at least), Arthur Scargill, President of the National Union of Mineworkers and a major hate figure of the right, with whom he was to share many merrie evenings at Hay Castle.

His way of dealing with bureaucrats was similarly singular. His attack on the Wales Tourist Board came just two years after it had given him £50,000 for Hay's celebrations to mark the bicentenary of US independence. He had also been given a special grant to convert part of Cockcroft House into self-catering flats lined with books (for sale), chosen according to the tastes of the individual visiting tourists. In the event, no tourist ever stayed in those flats. They were all let locally on the open market.

Mervyn Jones had retired, but if his friend's absence was the problem, this was hardly a diplomatic way of sustaining the relationship. His unworldly sense of personal affront – and mystification when someone disagreed with him – is clear in an interview he gave some years later: 'I got on very well with them. Later I criticised them in a pamphlet. I felt very strongly about it. I found that if you criticised a non-accountable government agency you would be totally excluded from any kind of support. It wasn't whether you were right or wrong, it was that you had criticised them. I thought my criticism was perfectly legitimate.'

11

Halloy

'It was not just the best book deal Richard ever did . . . it was the best book deal *any* book dealer *ever* did.'

Greg Coombes

Richard Booth's impulsive spending was part of his personality, but there was a rationale behind it. Second-hand booksellers agree that the stock needs frequent topping up. The hope of the casual book buyer needs to be sustained by a sense of finding something that wasn't there last time. Similarly, for Booth, for whom cash flow was a constant problem, the prospect of 'the next deal', that would rescue the company from its difficulties, was the sustainer of hope. Like a gambler, he was convinced that riches were just around the corner. After that, the opportunities would be endless.

But too often he was not able to capitalise on the hard work he and his colleagues put in. The early morning starts were impressive, but there was a breathlessness about the whole operation that cried out for calm reflection. Derek Addyman remembers he and a colleague, Austin Wilkes, spending a month painstakingly compiling a catalogue of recently acquired books on magic. One Friday they went to Booth with their handiwork, anticipating some hefty sales to result from its content in the following weeks. 'But by the beginning of the next week he had knocked them out,' says Addyman. 'Knocking' or 'chopping' books out means accepting pretty much the first offer that comes along for the sake of bringing in some cash.

After one of the *opera buffa* productions at Brynmelyn, an article appeared in an abstruse opera magazine, making reference to Booth the bookseller and his singular approach to entertaining. The article happened to be read by a fellow opera fan who lived in Belgium. A letter arrived from the Ardennes, mentioning that a family collection of books would be coming up for sale. Would Booth would be interested in having a look, the letter asked. It was to lead to the most impressive purchase of his career.

The collection at the Château Halloy, near Namur in Belgium, was a treasure trove of a private library, with many books on geology, natural history, Belgian and French history and literature, agriculture and much more. It dated back to the 1600s, long before the establishment in 1830 of Belgium as a separate country, and contained many gems that testified to the extensive learning of its distinguished francophone owners, the de Selys Longchamps family.

For generations the family had added to and cared for the collection. Most recently Charles, an engineer by profession, had devoted his weekends to keeping it in order, though his daughters recall how often he would disappear into the library at the start of a weekend, picking up, say, a history book and not resurfacing for the rest of the weekend. He had performed heroics in tidying the place, which had suffered from neglect and worse during the war and subsequently. (One shelf full of books was later shown to be concealing a row of live grenades.)

But by 1978, when he was in his mid-sixties, Charles hadn't the time to devote to it. Further, and perhaps more significantly, his brother Walter did not share his enthusiasm and he and his offspring made it clear they had other uses for the space that stored the collection.

Parts of the library had already been sold off in a major sale forty years earlier, and at least one household-name auction house which visited a year or so earlier inexplicably felt it had got the best of anything that remained. But there were some sensational goodies still on the shelves. If ever there was an illustration of Richard Booth's drive in pursuit of a deal, this was it. Booth himself went with his driver Ron Smart and appraised the collection initially, seeing enough to convince him. His personal charisma was to work its magic on Charles de Selys Longchamps.

Charles could sense that Booth – with whom he did not share an easily spoken language – possessed a similar willingness to surrender to an enthusiasm. A bond, based on the occasionally inarticulate effusiveness that afflicted Booth in moments of excitement, was formed.

'I don't know what Richard told my dad,' recalls Charles's daughter Pierrette de Selys Longchamps, 'but he certainly per-suaded him [that selling to him] was the right thing to do. My dad didn't ask that much money because he wasn't a salesman at all. He just wanted the books to be in good hands. Out of respect for his ancestors, my dad had put the library in order after the Nazis had been through. But he had other things to do. It was something he knew he had to let go. Maybe he should have given it to a museum . . .' The fact that the financial value was of secondary importance to the family must have delighted Booth.

Greg Coombes, Christine Webber, Booth and Ron Smart

were among those who went in the follow-up team to Halloy, for about ten days. They packed up the contents of the ground and first floors. Booth also contacted a local driver, Graham Lloyd, who drove a forty-foot articulated lorry back to Hay. Another team was sent over to examine what had previously been unconsidered trifles. They were anything but. Mostly diminished, though not irredeemably, by decades of dust and damp, the treasures showed ample evidence of the family's central involvement in the government of France in revolutionary times and later of Belgium, its enthusiasm for natural history and its early grappling with technological advances of the seventeenth and eighteenth centuries.

When Booth's team visited, the château had no electricity, so his team worked while daylight allowed, from 6 a.m. to 6 p.m., snatching breakfast in the château and eating out nearby in the evening. The work was hard, but the sense that they were onto something big unavoidable. Many of the items were wrapped in newspaper from the Napoleonic era. It was an antiquarian's dream.

Greg Coombes, one of those deployed by Booth, remembers the light fading but his boss still revelling, late in the day, in what was being unearthed. 'I was rounding everyone up to go for supper and there was a shadowy figure standing in the corner, who I could hardly see. I said, "Richard, what are you doing? You can't be able to see anything over there." He said, "I can smell 'em."' He was in heaven.

By general agreement the Halloy deal was the best one Booth ever did. Coombes says it was a goldmine. 'Halloy was not just the best book deal Richard ever did ... it was the best book deal *any* book dealer *ever* did. In the family there had been four or five major collectors of books. There were wonderful plate books of natural history. One family member was the only person to survive in the Assemblée right through the French Revolution. At one point I had in my hands the original watercolour design for the tricolour – it was part of the *député*'s collection. There were lists of those destined for the guillotine. It was extraordinary stuff.'

It is likely that Booth bought about 3,500 items from the château, a quantity that may have put off other potential purchasers. Some speak of a first edition of Jean-Jacques Rousseau's *Du contrat social* being part of the collection. There were several sets of books by Georges Buffon, the seventeenth-century scientist considered by some the father of palaeontology and his fellow pretender/successor to that title, Georges Cuvier. He bought other examples of antiquarian natural history, albums, illuminated manuscripts, heraldry, genealogy, French Romance/Chrétien de Troyes/Arthurian legend (in Old French). Omalius d'Halloy, a leading Belgian geologist who made the first geological maps of France, was well represented, as was his son-in-law, entomologist Edmond de Selys Longchamps, from whom the present family descended. There was also a large quantity of pressed botanical specimens of the sort that these days requires an export licence. 'Richard bought the books privately. This wasn't an auction; the team cleared the château and brought the whole lot back to Hay in lorries,' says Val Haynes.

After several weeks of sorting, Ron Smart was sent to Belgium and, a comparative newcomer to driving on the right-hand side of the road, loaded up a seven-and-a-half-ton lorry with a thirty-foot container. A van also accompanied him. Together they managed to bring everything back. In the car park in Hay, as so often, the spoils were split up and delivered in 'tugboat' vehicles around the town for further sorting.

The episode, as so many, is illustrative not only of Booth's drive and enthusiasm, but also his fallibility. By any standards he had struck an extraordinary deal, but two facets of the story show the outfit's engaging, enraging lack of professionalism. Booth returned to Hay full of beans, but with only a vague agreement as to the price. Back in the Cinema bookshop, Booth was chuffed about his conquest. 'It's a fantastic library,' he exclaimed. 'I've got it for sixty thousand!' A sum of £60,000 did indeed sound like an extraordinarily good deal for such gems, but Charlie and Cathy Gibbons urged caution. Booth admitted that the final deal had not been sealed – there was merely a verbal agreement with the very gentlemanly Charles de Selys Longchamps. 'Well, get the buggers out, Richard,' they cried, words that became a catchphrase among Booth's staff. There was concern that Booth's enthusiasm had, not for the first time, got the better of him. The deal needed to be sealed before anyone else got a whiff of it.

In the event, things worked in Booth's favour, and to an almost farcical degree. It was only when the time came time to arrange the method of payment that he realised the family had been talking about US dollars rather than pounds. A pound at that time was worth at least two dollars and for a period a good deal more. He secured the deal for less than half the price – already modest – that he thought he was paying.

Not that a figure of approximately £25,000 was easily within Booth's reach. 'How the hell are we going to pay that?' exclaimed Garry Spencer. The de Selys Longchamps family had been impressed with Booth's manner and apparent success, but they were unaware that such a figure was not easily accessible to him. A series of staggered payments was arranged.

There were further trips some months later. Booth possessed two enormous Datsun estate cars, and on one trip he asked Ron Smart to drive him across to Belgium. Having made some purchases, he and Smart crossed the border into France on the way home. Then, curiously, he asked Smart to go back to Belgium to pick up some other books.

Having collected them, he was stopped by customs as he left Belgium and asked about the books. One book in particular was to be impounded, and Smart was later informed that it wasn't allowed to leave the country without an export licence. The car was also taken and Smart detained in the customs buildings, enduring three interviews (in a language he barely understood) over six hours. Booth by this point, of course, was far away.

After several hours, Smart got fed up. He went outside for a cigarette and to check the car. He noticed a young man was now on duty. 'The chap dealing with it had gone out, and he'd left the book in question on his desk, so I picked it up and hid it under my coat. I waved cheerily at the young bloke and gestured "My car, my car". He put his thumb up, and I just drove off through the barrier. I drove the next forty miles as fast as I've ever driven.'

Eventually he made a rendezvous with Booth in France, who asked him: 'Where the hell have you been?' Smart told him the saga, explaining why he had been held up. Booth said: 'Yes, but where's the book?' When Smart reassured him he had managed to hang on to it, Booth replied, 'Thank God. It's worth about a thousand pounds.'

Smart suggested they scarper as they'd be on a wanted list. 'I'm not on a wanted list, you are!' said Booth. They jumped into the car and headed for Dover. 'I have never been so relieved to get on a ferry in all my life,' says Smart. 'That book was hundreds of years old.'

Belgium was a happy hunting ground for Booth, but not as happy as it should have been. Camille de Selys Longchamps, sister of Pierrette, whose father did the deal with Booth, laments the need to sell. 'They were magnificent, those books,' she says, recalling her family's personal involvement in the production of many of them. 'I know there also had been some incunables, the first books ever printed, although I don't know if they were still there when Richard bought the lot.' No one will ever know, since no proper records were kept.

It is a tribute to Booth that he remained in friendly contact with the de Selys Longchamps family. Michel, a cousin of the sisters, lived in England and would visit him in Hay. The sisters, too, accepted Booth's invitation to enjoy the hospitality of the Castle, despite payment having to be made in smaller chunks than might be expected from a bookseller of Booth's prominence. But Booth had also failed to provide 'a good home' for the books. 'It was a whole history,' says Camille, 'and I must say when I saw Richard's hangars, where everything was mixed up together, that really broke my heart. They had a real sentimental value for us, beyond the financial worth.'

The customary Booth lack of grip on his assets came into play. What is certain is that Booth did nowhere near as well out of the sale of the Halloy treasures as he should have done. A certain laxity was in evidence even before he had returned to the UK. Greg Coombes, still comparatively new to the trade, admits to having been part of Booth's inexpert pricing policy. 'I told Richard this stuff ought to stay together. There were day-to-day accounts from the time of the [French] Revolution of who was going to the guillotine, who was going to safety in Switzerland etc. . . . the lot. It seemed to me that tagging on the foundation of Belgium undermined the Revolution collection.' So some parts belonged on their own and others should be kept as part of a series, yet he was selling stuff in chunks according to whatever he was offered, rather than dictating the pattern.

In the early years of the de Selys Longchamps family, a family member collected the work of one of the best regarded printers of European history. Christophe Plantin was born in France in 1520, moving to Antwerp and becoming an outstanding typographer (and having a typeface named after him). He was a pioneer in the use of copper rather than wood for engravings and printed for a variety of religious and scientific figures. Antwerp was a centre for humanists, scientists, geographers and cartographers, and his business quickly became the most successful in Europe.

Greg Coombes was agog to see the collection of Plantin's work at Halloy, all of it around four hundred years old. 'They had virtually everything Plantin ever printed,' he said. 'In Belgium, in a five-star hotel, we met this industrialist who collected Plantin, and I remember carrying these crumbling and flaking sixteenth-century leather books in and putting them on beautiful linen tablecloths. Richard would look at me, and I'd look at Richard . . . and we'd come up with a figure for what we thought they were worth. And usually this industrialist would not question it and just nod and somebody next to him would write down the figure on a piece of paper. Richard got me to bring another table over . . . "this is the breakfast table, that's the dealing table" . . . I'd carry them out and put them in the bloke's car, and that was it. Given the opportunity, I would never do it in so amateurish a way now.'

Booth's failure to capitalise was partly because, as ever, he was in need of cash to pay for what he had bought, quite apart from keeping the business ticking over. Back in Hay, as at the breakfast table in Belgium, he was inclined to accept a quick turnover rather than maximise prices with patient research and cataloguing. Word had got out in the trade that Booth had snaffled some really valuable material. Val Haynes recalls, 'He was easily persuaded by dealers to accept a lower cash offer. The entire building was inundated with dealers flocking to see what had arrived, rummaging through the unsorted boxes.'

Dealers, who had buyers on tap interested in this sort of material and money to pay for it, saw immediately the potential in Booth's haul, and feasted on it. A returning galleon with this sort of exceptional cargo would arouse *Paint Your Wagon*-style excitement in a trade well aware that Booth needed quick sales. Gerard Brookes said:

> Anyone could have done well out of it. Some of those colour plate books were worth four or five figures. Richard at that time was the largest bookseller in the world and the owners would have been pleased to deal with him, but he wouldn't have maximised on it. He sold it too cheap. There would have been clever dealers there soaking up Booth's mistakes, writing a cheque for fifteen grand just like that, and without that fifteen grand Booth might have gone bust. If that stuff had been marketed properly it would have made someone a millionaire ten times over.

Simply to meet the payments to the de Selys Longchamps family, Booth found himself accepting way below the true value of these treasures. One distinguished bookseller, Tony Laywood, told a friend that his Halloy purchases from Booth set him up for his entire career.

One Hay bookseller and former Booth employee is thought to have done particularly well, selling one item, bought from Booth for a few hundred pounds, for £10,000.

Rumours abound to this day as to where other examples from Halloy might have ended up. Booth's easy-going approach might well have also allowed unscrupulous figures in Hay to offer a temporary home to some of these enviable works – maybe in a domestic garage – before quietly farming them out into appreciative hands further afield. At least one employee lived abroad very comfortably on what former colleagues assume to have been the proceeds, and one of Booth's regular go-to dealers, who handled some of the Halloy haul, later served time in prison for embezzlement, so it would be surprising if some of the jewels didn't spend time in some fairly grasping hands.

Geoff Simkins, who had catalogued a collection of crime writer Edgar Lustgarten writings – amounting to half of his literary output – and who became an expert in early French publishing, working at Liège University and University College Dublin, remembers a French Revolution collection of loose papers and ephemera that ended up in the long room on the upper storey at Cockcroft. 'I was hoping to get my hands on that to do a bit of a catalogue,' he recalls, 'but it never came to anything. I suspect there were universities that would have been very interested in it.' He senses that much of it was stolen. 'I suspect that's what happened to most of the stuff from Halloy. What happened to it all?'

12

The Mice Will Play . . .

'Book dealers knew when he was buying books that he couldn't afford. They knew that was the time to descend upon Hay.'

Anon

In the late 1970s, Booth's breezy, upbeat manner was a façade, though one he believed in. His faith in the business endured, although his diaries admit to his well-concealed concerns about the financial pressures he continued to face. The crown on the great showman's head had worked wonders in boosting publicity for the town and advertising Hay as a place to buy and sell books. The shop had been confirmed by *The Guinness Book of Records* as the world's largest second-hand bookshop, and the offshoot stores it had spawned delighted in the footfall that his name brought to the town.

But underneath, the cracks were widening. His incontinent spending, which his staff had known about for years, was coming to be public knowledge. Too often he was paying a deposit and would then 'forget' to complete the payment. This was not generally intentionally dishonest, to the extent that he thought about it. It was simply that the enthusiasm of the moment would fade and he would move onto the next big thing. Kamma Andersen, who tried to instil some financial discipline and minimise the unpaid bills, when asked if the appearance of creditors at the shop – whether to pay for petrol for his drivers or for more substantial book deals – was a frequent event, replied: 'Not frequent, about twice a week.'

It had gone beyond a joke. Book dealers knew that Booth's willingness to accept rock-bottom offers for books told a story about his cash-flow problems. One of those charged with rescuing the company finances says: 'The book trade was culpable. They knew when he was buying books that he couldn't afford. They knew that was the time to descend upon Hay and they would be allowed access to collections that had just come in, and they were picking over them and paying very little for what they took away … and the good stuff never stayed in Hay. What I understand happened over Halloy is an often-repeated pattern. He had plundered most of the private collections in Wales. There was nowhere you could buy books in Wales. He'd had it all. But there was nothing to show for it.'

There had to be a weekly, sometimes daily, 'blood run' to Abergavenny, when cash would be delivered, perilously close to closing time, to prevent the bank bouncing his cheques, or worse. For a long time, his problems had been the problems that confronted the bank and the town: if the company closed, a lot of people would be thrown out of work, and with so much of Hay's income now derived from the book trade, that would be disastrous.

But that defence was looking threadbare. Increasingly creditors were hearing tales of continued spending on large quantities of overpriced books. Local solicitor Martin Beales, who was handling Booth's legal affairs, would tell close friends:

'I can't believe it. He hasn't just got writs on his desk demanding money, he's actually got *court judgments* demanding payment, but he's still scrabbling away to get money together to buy more books.' With the best will in the world, the bank was prepared to be patient, but Booth persistently failed to show the self-discipline needed to provide reassurance.

Booth's defenders say there was some mitigation. An aspect of his empire that would survive little scrutiny from business-school gurus was his willingness to overlook pilfering by his staff. When the full extent of it became apparent, some sought to ascribe all the company's problems to such leakiness. That would be a mistake, compounded by wagging tongues in Hay, though it played an undeniable part.

The disappearance of books fell into a number of categories, and some context is needed. Booth could be a generous, kind and understanding boss. As we have seen, he would often employ people because he liked them, regardless of their skills or whether he needed them. He would overlook periods of absence due to personal problems, let them borrow his cars when families were in need and was notably helpful when, for example, Noelle Beales's son was in a pram and she was required for work on the till of the Cinema bookshop. Booth was quite happy for her to bring the baby to work. Another mother was allowed considerable flexibility, leaving early to collect children and so on. He would probably have thought it odd to do otherwise, a notably enlightened attitude for the times.

He could also be generous to his more literary colleagues, sometimes intentionally to mitigate his shortcomings as a boss. Cotters, a linchpin of the operation for about forty years and probably his best-read member of staff, bore the brunt of much of the Booth chaos. Sometimes he would spend hours imposing order on a new avalanche of hardbacks, ordering and piling them according to some useful form of taxonomy, when a new delivery would literally be dumped by one of Booth's less painstaking employees onto his handiwork, rendering it futile. Booth referred in his book to how Cotters tolerated his mismanagement, and Cottrill says Booth recognised this at the time: 'He was always very conscious that because of limited finances and knowing how much I loved books and felt I was contributing so much, we had an agreement that sometimes he would give them to me. He was always generous like that. It was a private relationship between us, based, I think, on a degree of mutual respect.'

To some Booth was a generous payer, but overall that is not his reputation in Hay. Indeed, often he was simply unable to pay his staff, such were the cash-flow problems, so his lieutenants might ask which members of staff could go without for a week or two. He could also be annoyingly impulsive and wasteful with valuable books, as well as happily helping himself to the contents of the till before heading off to buy drinks indiscriminately in the pub, of which some took shameless advantage. His generosity in buying drinks extended even to those who would wait for him in a pub, happily accept the offer of a drink before moving on to the next pub in anticipation of his arrival and a repeat dose. So any prevailing ethos of the sanctity of 'the company's money' was limited.

Bookselling is not alone as a market where a professional with superior knowledge can take advantage of an amateur. In law, it is generally accepted that when two professionals (experts, dealers or whatever) discuss a deal, each is entitled to drive as hard a bargain as possible. But when dealing with non-experts, it is considered unfair to exploit a lack of expertise.

One fresh-faced member of staff, recently hired, learned a swift lesson as to how things worked. He and a colleague

were sent to Cardiff to the recently bereaved family of the distinguished art historian and ceramics expert 'Rollo' Charles,
curator of the National Museum Cardiff. They duly came to
an arrangement with his widow Margaret to buy some books,
at which point the family asked the young man's opinion of
an ornate Victorian family album. Scrupulously he expressed
himself unqualified to judge, but said he would take it back to
the shop and get back to them with a valuation. Back in Hay,
he handed it over to Booth. He was shocked to be told by a
more experienced colleague: 'You won't see that again.' And
indeed he didn't. The next day Booth took the album – which
contained a number of treasures including a letter from Alfred,
Lord Tennyson – to London and sold it.

For the next few weeks, the family called, asking what the
album might be worth. When asked, Booth dissembled and
evaded. His colleague – who had learned quickly that this was
not unusual treatment – played for time as the family grew
more exasperated. Eventually one of Booth's money people
came to an arrangement with the family.

Another newly employed staffer recalls being shocked when
confronted with what he later called 'the way things were done'.
A woman badly in need of money came into the shop with a
box of books. A former soldier working for Booth went through
the box: 'Yes, yes, yes . . . nothing of great value here . . . ten
pounds?' They shook hands and he gave her the money. Seconds
later, after she was gone, he shouted, 'Richard, Richard! Come
and have a look. That's got to be worth five hundred quid!'

Mark Westwood, a local collector and later bookseller,
remembers Booth offering him a bound volume of late-
seventeenth-century pamphlets. One of them was a London
printing, from 1693, about incursions by the French into
Iroquois territory in Canada.

Booth asked Westwood £6,000 for them, and wanted a quick sale. Westwood said it was lot of money to shell out, but he knew it was a good buy and that he would try and raise the money quickly. Once he had done so and the deal was completed, Booth admitted he had paid an elderly lady just £100 for them. When he sold them on, Westwood got £25,000 for them. In both buying and selling, for different reasons, it was hardly impressive.

So any idea of his being some sea-green incorruptible would be misplaced. This is not to say that Booth was any more or less scrupulous than others in his profession, but if he led by example, it was a less than saintly one. Michael Twigge-Molecey remembered: 'The very, very first day I worked with him, in the sixties, Richard took me to London in his Roller. The first shop he went into, in Pimlico, he picked up a book and put it in his things. It was just a small book, but probably worth a few bob. That was the way he worked, and it was endemic in the trade.' That was Booth in his early days. His defenders say they would not have found such crass wrongdoing applying to him latterly.

Twigge-Molecey said he never stole from Booth while he was on his staff, but that he did after he stopped working for him for the first time. 'He'd screwed me up financially so much, that I thought right, sod you. I thought, You really have stitched me up big time. I'll get you. He hadn't paid me for so long, and it happened all the time – "Oh, Mike, I haven't got any money on me, but so-and-so owes me twenty quid, why don't you collect it from her?"' 'So-and-so' duly told him where to go. 'When you're single, you can manage that, but when you've got mouths to feed . . .'

So, in 1972, he took some books to a smart bookshop in London. The shop assistant thought he recognised him and asked him to leave them with him for a couple of hours while he conferred with his bosses. He phoned Booth, who called the police.

'I got taken to court,' he remembers, finding slight comfort in a coincidence. 'The magistrate gave me a ten-pound fine and on the same day Richard got a twenty-pound fine for speeding.' Colleagues also remember him in the 1980s cheerily driving through Glasbury, where the limit is now 20 mph, at 60 mph. Given the tragedy of 1964, the fine for speeding is a reminder that it took a lot for Booth to change his ways.

Some – more than a few – might cite the Twigge-Molecey defence, saying the pilfering was, as he said, a way of getting back at the boss. Others regarded it as an unstated perk of the job, a way of making up for perceived underpayment. Alex Williams, whose conscience is credibly clear, says he remembers taking the rubbish out of the back of one of Booth's shops and spotting some nice little prints, by a rural artist, in the bin. Shocked, he alerted Booth. The boss was unsurprised: 'Oh, that's a standard stealing method. They put it in the bin and then collect it later. That way they can say they're stealing from the bin, not from me.'

There is a curiosity in Booth's attitude to some of his staff's light-fingeredness. Many of them say he either must have known or definitely *did* know about it. His tolerance of it is revealing of his character. Jan Shivel, who knew Booth well, says: 'He had an understanding of the wickedness of the human heart, and the greed factor. He'd been around the block, he'd probably done it himself. He got into books through antiquing. They're a scabrous lot. I love them, and they're the most interesting people on the planet, but he wasn't the sort to hugely take against someone who overstepped the mark.' His later re-employment of the convicted Twigge-Molecey is testament of that.

Kate Hadley says: 'He was not judgemental about being

stolen from. I think he thought it needed to be shared.' She doubts it was a tacit admission that he was underpaying them, rather more a reflection of a benign, understanding, patrician outlook. 'He recognised that people had the urge to nick, and he allowed it. People thought he was a fool because he allowed that to happen, and he decided to allow himself to be that fool. He let himself be ripped off.' A disdain for small-mindedness meant he was never going to be wandering around with a clip-board chasing every missing Mills & Boon.

There was a category of theft for which Booth may even have had some admiration. Some of his staff were true book enthusi-asts, romantics who might see a book and feel they must have it, for their own collections. This sort of pilfering on the margins, particularly if committed by someone who was helping keep the company afloat by bringing in other valuable books, while unethical to outsiders' eyes, became almost normal in some cases, the cloak and dagger barely bothered with.

If an employee happened to see an obviously underpriced book on a shelf, they would have no hesitation in paying the low price rather than reporting it to a boss. Such books usually ended up on the thief's shelf or – in the event of an even better edition of the same book being found – made their way sooner or later to another dealer. As one Booth employee put it: 'Such a person might have done it for the books themselves. It wasn't for profit. It was because he or she would have enjoyed having them on their shelf.' For precisely that reason, Booth's staff came to have a sense of which homes they were unlikely to be invited into.

Booth's generally relaxed, expedient attitude had its limits. While initially he had been indulgent, things became more serious when he realised it was becoming systemic. At the end of the 1970s he was hearing stories in pubs of local dealers, often his former employees, coming in to pick up underpriced books from his shelves and selling them at a higher price in their shops. In an impetuous display of zeal, he then banned any of Hay's two dozen or so booksellers from buying from him. Among many, this was one of his least thought-through ideas. The former soldier Philip Powell-Jones, married to Booth's sister Anne, who had taken over the Old Fire Station and was running it as a classics bookshop and with whom he had a mutually beneficial business relationship, was round within moments in a rage to protest. The veto was understandable, though.

Such attempts to assert a greater sense of order caused weary amusement in Hay. Shop owner Paul Golding, a friend and admirer of Booth, remembers: 'Every six months or so through the eighties and nineties a person would come into the shop and very excitedly tell us that he/she was going to be Richard's new PA. We were very non-committal as it usually only took four or five months before they announced he was "impossible to work with" and (usually) they had not been paid, so they were leaving.'

But those in the know were aware of a far bigger problem. Booth was too generous for his own good. Those who have occasionally looked covetously in an office stationery cupboard may see degrees of wrongdoing, and a forgetful few did treat the bookshops as their own private library, but at the other end there were those who leeched off Booth for serious private profit. Slipping a single, fondly regarded tome surreptitiously into a bag was one thing. Serial, systemic thieving quite another. Some of the mice were not only playing: they were getting fat, greedy and streetwise.

Ron Smart recalls being sent out on trips with one of Booth's buyers.

'There was one chap that worked for him who I used to

drive all over the place. When we got back to near his house he'd be loading books into his own garage, and he'd give me £30 to keep quiet, which was a lot of money then. I felt terribly guilty about it, because I felt for Richard. I knew he was ripping Richard off, and so I told Richard. He said, "He thinks I don't know. He thinks I'm dull, but I know what he's up to."'

In Booth's autobiography, he accuses Jim Robson, on whom Booth had come to rely, of one of the most flagrant pieces of theft. He described Robson as having persuasive charm and the looks of a Scandinavian children's book hero. Booth trusted him, allowing him to move into the Castle, sell the Rolls-Royce (claiming a hefty commission) and advise him on the direction of the company. He went on various trips with Booth, concluding – as early as the mid-1970s – that for all Booth's enthusiasm and drive, the business was heading in the wrong direction.

Robson suggested helping Booth refinance the company, starting by offering to buy the Castle. The very idea, let alone Robson's suggested price, was unthinkable. Late one night soon afterwards, Booth wrote in his autobiography, as he was returning from another pub evening he came across Robson filling a van with valuable books. 'I tried to stop him but he sped off, leaving me lying in the road with smashed spectacles and a mouthful of dirt . . . Jim fled to Ireland where he was virtually invulnerable.'

The claim by Booth, who elsewhere calls Robson sneaky and spiteful, is a straight libel if untrue, which Robson's widow Bernadette, now living in Ireland, insists it is. She remembers Booth as quirky, eccentric and fun, but that he became contrary and difficult when several people left at once.

The collective memory of the episode locally is that there was indeed a 'Robson heist'. Booth's version of the episode was accepted by the staff, and Robson's sudden disappearance from the scene was taken as confirming the story. Booth's own diary suggests his trust in Robson had evaporated, and that he feared a power grab by his subordinate.

Someone close to the story – who has no particular reason to defend the Robsons – says it has the hallmark of a Booth relationship – a lot of early enthusiasm tempered later by suspicion. 'Jim and Bernadette were a close couple,' says the associate. 'They entertained Booth together. I do think Richard was paranoid about people trying to steal from him.' Bernadette's Catholic faith would have taken a firm line against wrongdoing, says the source; the roguishness credibly ascribed to her late husband, from whom she later separated, muddies the picture of him.

Robson and his wife were interviewed by the police, to whom Booth had complained about the theft of a white ceramic phrenological head and a book he said had belonged to his father. No action was taken. A few years later the couple visited Hay, when Booth was embarrassed to be asked about the matter. 'When challenged by Jim, Richard laughed, saying the accusation was just a joke,' says Bernadette.

Gerard Brookes, to whom no suspicion is attached, says Booth once accused him of stealing, but satisfied himself he had been wrong. Brookes's tale is a happier variant of the sort of benign relationship he had with those who worked for him.

After a while, Brookes found himself bored. Following a discussion in the Wheatsheaf pub, he and his boss agreed that he should run his own natural history shop in Hay, and Booth agreed to sell him not only the shop, for £10,000, but the books to stock it, for another £10,000. 'The bank could see what a good deal it was and loaned me the money,' recalls Brookes, 'and within a few months I had paid off the ten grand for the stock.' In the back row were two lines of John Murray editions of Charles Darwin's *The Descent of Man* and *On the Origins of Species*. 'It was incredibly generous. He didn't have to do that.' Brookes expresses huge thanks to Booth for setting him up like that, and blames himself for not handling his own autonomy well thereafter.

That was the textbook version of Booth as begetter of the smaller shops that added to Hay's pre-eminence as the UK's home of second-hand books. Derek Addyman was born locally and left school at sixteen, having hated it. But his initiative and an interest in the books that Booth paid him to lug about won the boss's admiration and subsequent promotion. He set up his own shop in 1987, a second one, Murder and Mayhem, special-ising in crime fiction, in 1998, and a third in 2001.

But there were other versions in which shops were set up, in Hay or elsewhere. In some cases, Booth would hand over the deeds of sites in lieu of payment when forced to do so by a lack of cash. The print shop, now Shepherds Parlour in the middle of Hay, was given to its former manager Chris Powell in lieu of wages from Richard.

And one of his leading lieutenants, Andy Cooke, came home from work having not been paid, yet again, by Booth. He was grateful to be able to tell his wife Lyndy, 'No, Richard hasn't got any money this week, but he gave me this great desk instead.' She still owns it.

Booth's control of stock was notoriously vague, so no proof could ever be adduced, but that didn't stop him pointing fingers. During a supposed purge, he would insist that those returning late from buying trips should report to him at the Castle to show him what they had bought, rather than allowing them to stop off for a drink before closing time and arrive back after Booth had gone to bed. 'Richard liked to know that the stuff was back and under lock and key, rather than waiting till the morning, which might have allowed some of it to have fallen into the wrong hands,' said one trusted figure.

In that case, his suspicions were entirely misplaced, but not so with other late-returners. Mick Bullock was every bit as divisive a figure as Booth, for whom he worked. Bullock was known to have an eye for an opening, and Booth became convinced that his employee was ripping him off with the intention of setting up his own bookshop. In any event, Booth's staff were advising him that Bullock might be about to branch out, but nothing could be proved.

Bullock did indeed resign from Booth's employ, having accumulated enough books to set up his own shop. For the moment he lacked his own premises, so he booked the function room of the Swan, Hay's largest hotel, for five days in order to hold a pop-up book sale at knock-down prices. Breakaways from the Booth mothership were to be done on his terms, and this one was particularly unwelcome. Booth decided to scupper the sale, threatening the owner of the Swan that he would take out an injunction on the grounds that Bullock had stolen the books. This was not a risk worth taking so the event was cancelled.

Booth thought no more about it, until the normal peace of Cockcroft House was disturbed when his widely adored and most loyal employee Pat Wiggington announced, 'Mike Bullock's just pulled up.' This induced panic in Booth. Bullock on the warpath was bad news. 'Where's that fucking bastard Booth? I'll kill him this time,' he said.

On hearing the deal was off, Bullock wanted his pound of flesh. Pat Wiggington dissembled heroically. 'He did mention Scotland, I think,' she offered vaguely. 'Or maybe it was somewhere else ...' Bullock didn't want to move but was too angry to realise what was under his nose. Greg Coombes remembers: 'Richard got me and bundled me and himself into a stationery cupboard. He was absolutely terrified, but at the same time he couldn't stop giggling. It was amazing Bullock never realised.'

In time Bullock did indeed open a shop, one which survived his death and thrives to this day. But he was the declared enemy.

Adela Cooke worked in Bullock's bookshop. 'Richard had a terrible jealous streak,' she remembers. 'Mick had women falling at his feet. If Mick had anything good for sale, Richard would ring the police and say we'd stolen them. I don't think he really believed they'd been stolen, he just wanted to cause trouble. The police would come and we'd show them all the receipts. It was just a waste of the police's time. And he probably knew in himself that it was good thing that there were more booksellers in Hay.'

There were several overlapping categories of thief on Booth's staff. There were the straightforward profiteers (who usually sold to dealers beyond Hay) versus the well-read. There were those who took small tokens – worth a packet, or peanuts – and those who took lots. Those who wanted to avenge Booth and those who were simply opportunists. Those who paid cash for books their colleagues had underpriced and those who did the underpricing themselves. Those Booth punished, those he indulged and those he knew couldn't help themselves. Quite who fell into which category is beyond the scope of this book (and probably any other) and its libel readers. But notwithstanding his occasional lapses into paranoia and thrashing about for scapegoats, a number of people owe Richard Booth far, far more than they will ever admit. In the ranks of those who owe him gratitude, and there are many, they – identified or not – should not be forgotten.

13

The Fun Continues ...

'We will oppose everything you do in the future.'
                                    Police warning to Richard Booth

Booth had brought a degree of prosperity to Hay that made it stand out from neighbours like Talgarth, Kington and Presteigne and it had now got used to the large number of book-buying visitors. Other smaller bookshops continued to thrive alongside the mother ship, which now stocked over a million books. Booth's spirit was undimmed, the increasing financial concerns besetting his shops making little apparent impression on him. Agricultural life carried on around the town, supported by Brussels subsidies. Second-home owners brought money in from outside, but continued to nudge local property prices upwards, to the disadvantage of young locals. The number of cottages in the area being burgled continued to increase. In one spell of a few months in the late 1970s, thirty-eight were broken into. This appeared to be comparatively harmless, in that any theft was minor, suggesting youthful over-enthusiasm. Items such as a torch or a pair of gloves or the odd picture would go missing – all in an apparent cocking a snook at authority. It was irksome, and not good for the area's reputation, but hardly calamitous.

A small episode of the Alice in Wonderland lust for expansion concerned a man called Geoffrey Meaden. He was a cerebral former official at the Ministry of Defence in London and he appeared in Hay in about 1977. Richard Booth found himself drawn to the agreeable, amusing Meaden, in part because he sensed the new man had a payoff from the MoD that might be useful for the growth of his business. This would have rung alarm bells for anyone aware of either Booth's prodigious appetite for spending money or his cavalier attitude towards paying debts. Indeed, Meaden had been specifically warned by friends in London that Booth was not to be trusted. Nonetheless, Meaden was reassured by Booth's ingenuousness, and loaned him £20,000.

Meaden was now a Booth disciple, as amused as anyone by the various running gags, including Hay's independence. The first anniversary of its declaration was even more boisterous than the real thing. A host of celebrations during the day culminated in a torch-lit procession through the town, led by a twirling drum majorette from Brooklyn, New York; followed closely by Reg Clark (a former art student, soon to be a close consigliere in the new kingdom) dressed like a potentate from a ludicrous banana republic and beating a large bass drum. Richard gave a speech from the Castle terraces and the evening finished with music and dancing.

In the spring of 1978, Booth had received the insurance money from the Castle fire. 'He'd got the money and he felt like he was rolling in it,' remembers Greg Coombes. 'He wanted to buy more books in the States. "There are barns full of the stuff there," he used to tell me.' And in June 1978, off they went, for the first of half a dozen US trips that year. 'Richard told me I'd be there two or three days, so I took the sort of holdall bag you use for squash. We were there six weeks, and bought back great big containers, each one holding twenty or forty thousand books.'

Booth's crown had been made largely of paper, which, of course, would never do. So later that summer, Reg Clark made him a smart new one out of an old copper water tank bedecked with cheap paste jewels, which Booth loved so much he was loath to take it off. To complete the ensemble, an orb was fashioned out of a copper ballcock from a lavatory cistern and a sceptre from a piece of gas pipe.

Georgie Young produced the first edition of a new newspaper, the *Hay Herald*, effectively a propaganda sheet for the Booth worldview. Its first edition contained a foreshadowing of national events, announcing that Hay had decided to leave the European Union, or its iteration at the time, the EEC, just five years after joining. Also included in the first edition was an exclusive interview with none other than . . . Richard Booth.

The magazine also contained a spoof *Private Eye* cover, in retaliation for the magazine, edited by his Merton contemporary Richard Ingrams, having called him 'Bokassa Booth', after the autocratic dictator of the Central African Republic. In truth it was a nickname with which Booth was delighted.

In August 1978, to keep up the momentum, a national 'Hay Day' was declared. Celebrities such as George Melly and *Monty Python*'s Terry Jones turned up for a day of celebrations in the grounds of Cockcroft, the former workhouse now serving as an off-the-beaten-track bookshop. On the lawns, in between the numerous stalls and tents there were tug-of-war competitions, fortune tellers and jugglers, along with two coachloads of Gujarati dancing girls brought down from Leicester, who entertained the crowds . . .

Three months later, on Bonfire Night in November 1978, came 'Burn a bureaucrat' night, which was the incineration in the Castle grounds of an enormous wooden government bureaucrat that resembled *The Wicker Man*. Amid music, revelry and drinking, at the bonfire's height, to the crowd's delight a large rocket erupted from the 'bureaucrat's' phallus and the massive structure collapsed into a sea of flames.

This was all in defiance of more earthly, hand-to-mouth constraints at home. Mark Westwood recalls going round the Cinema bookshop and filling a box with books from Booth's shelves. He asked Booth how much he wanted for them 'Two hundred quid,' said Booth. Westwood thought they were worth a fraction of that, and decided to go back to the shelves. He returned to Booth, this time with a great many more books. 'Two hundred quid,' said Booth again. Westwood says: 'I soon realised that any pile of books I put together was going to be £200, because he needed £200 that day to pay the staff. So it was clear – if you got a big enough pile you could do a decent deal.' Mutterings about the sustainability of the shops continued to circulate, but Booth had survived so many scrapes in the past that surely this behemoth of a bookshop, one that provided so many jobs locally and brought so many tourists to Hay, was in no danger?

To the outside world at least, there were few signs of it. He upset some of those close to him by selling the stables adjacent to Brynmelyn for Duncan Linklater, who had worked for Booth in the early 1970s, and his wife Sally to live in. He had been desperate to raise some cash and got on well with the Linklaters. The sense of friends doing one another a favour was clear.

Around this time a bistro-style bar was set up next to the Cockcroft bookshop. It was run by Ellie Wright, who Booth had hoped might run a theatre in the Castle, and Neffy

Hensher, two talented and spirited friends drawn to Hay by the Booth buzz. The proprietor allowed them to run the place rent-free, as long as they allowed him to eat and drink champagne free of charge on the premises. The new venue, called Effy's, acquired a legendary status in Hay history, even though it was not open for long. It was the embodiment of loucheness, with crimson velvet seats and bordello decor and put together by Bruno Santini, later a celebrated theatre designer. 'It was very interesting how all the gentlemen of the town come and relax and sit around here in the evenings in a Toulouse-Lautrec kind of way,' said one bemused female customer, carefully choosing not to elaborate.

It was initially seen by the Blue Boar's popular owner Chris Fry as a threat to his livelihood, and he would tear down advertisements for it in the town, though that didn't prevent him turning up as a customer, sometimes abusive and the worse for wear, after closing time at his pub. Open all hours in spring and summer, with the staff often sleeping on the premises' settees 'till it was time to get back in the kitchen', it attracted plenty of tourists and some illustrious (and familiar) clients, including Bruce Chatwin, Seamus Heaney, Penelope Betjeman, Jeremy Sandford, Sidney Nolan and, inevitably, April Ashley. In 1979, Effy's had the shaming distinction of being charged with serving alcohol without a licence after a plain-clothes police officer bought a drink there. 'How ridiculous to be busted for drink,' said one weary sybarite.

The same year, following the Hay Day revelry of the previous August, the 1 April celebrations for the second anniversary of Hay's independence took the usual format, this time centring around an exhibition of Hay Revolutionary Art at Cockcroft House, the unveiling of Reg Clark's Patriotic Machine; followed by music and dancing in a marquee on the bookshop's lawn.

Sadly, the now customary torchlit procession to the Castle was marred at its end by disorder, mainly caused by drunken youths throwing burning torches under police cars in the Market Square. A police officer was knocked over by a noisy gang of revellers. The police had been hoping to breathalyse Booth, at the wheel of a vehicle hugely overladen with supporters, but he drove off before they could do so.

Three days later he was duly summoned and told he would be charged with playing music after hours, Lord's Day obstruction and abusive language, and was warned: 'We will oppose everything you do in the future.' This led to the decision to concentrate on private, invitation-only, events in the future, which were less expensive to put on and easier to control.

Booth had developed an association with a Japanese TV presenter, and in late 1979 this paid dividends. Japan had become a major customer for second-hand books, particularly on education. So it was grist to Booth's mill when the host of Japan's longest running TV show, Rose Kaneatarka, made a film about the King of Hay in which Booth posed at a kissing gate and strode about the hills in lordly fashion. The result was a spectacular spike in the number of Japanese visitors to Hay, many of them demanding to be ennobled by Booth. Rose then flew him first class to Tokyo – allowing him to join the mile-high club with a female air steward, he told a close friend – to mark the twenty-fifth anniversary of her show. Booth enjoyed sampling Japanese culture and brought a large number of kimonos back to Hay, enabling a fashion show to be put on at Effy's in the spring of 1980. He also brought back thousands of copies of a book on Japanese flower arranging, though the book's appeal was limited and most copies ended up being dumped.

The fashion show offered April a chance to dress up, a prospect she never lightly shunned, as well as to display her caustic wit. Neffy, one of the venue's hosts, wore a show-stopping virtually see-through outfit, which is still spoken of with awe. April decided to go on the attack. 'She was very jealous of me,' says Neffy. 'Because I was a woman, and was wearing these clear plastic pants, April said: "Darling, I didn't realise what a huge arse you have." I was so incensed at the time. She was a wonderful bitch, fantastically feminine, great fun and very beautiful, with real chutzpah. Of course, what I should have said was "At least my breasts are real."'

Another character who emerged on the ever-changing Hay scene was a defrocked bishop, Gordon Savage, who had been Bishop of Southwell until the *News of the World* revealed that he had formed an unsuitable liaison. He resigned, reportedly due to ill health. He and his wife separated and he moved to become a chaplain at the Anglican church in Tenerife, where it was agreed he needed a housekeeper. The object of his unsuitable liaison, 'Amanda Lovejoy, [a] 31-year-old former topless dancer', was given the job – a 'private concern', said the church – but continuing publicity put a stop to that. Some years later, Booth stepped in to offer the sixty-four-year-old former bishop a job, hoping he might know of a few libraries which needed to shed some books. Unfortunately Savage was unable to do the heavy lifting the trade requires, and he left to set up the Oxfam Book Service on Oxford Road, Hay. He died in June 1990 at the age of seventy-five.

A common theme among visitors to the Castle and to Brynmelyn is that, in a frequently used phrase, there always used to be 'some girl' in attendance, often standing over a casserole dish and looking after Booth domestically. This gave rise to an idea of Booth as something of a lothario. Depending on the context, he was more than capable of the sort of oafish crudity so prevalent in the 1960s and 1970s, deployed more than once when discussing bodily proportions and functions. But this can be put down to the blokeishness of being in male company and his reputation in some circles seems to have been misleading: he was often bashful and hesitant, as if unsure of his attractiveness (and certainly his idiosyncratic appeal was not to everyone's taste).

Kate Hadley remembers an uncertainty with women that sometimes showed itself:

> When I first stayed with him at the Castle he was always out and I was always reading and enjoyed being there alone. One evening he was out and I was in the flower room at the Castle, and suddenly, there he was in the doorway at 9 p.m., tall and flustered. He was having dinner with a couple of farmers and told them there was this blonde back at the Castle by herself doing the flowers. They said, 'Then what are you doing here? Go back immediately.' So he had rushed off, and returned looking surprised, then blushing. Then he asked, quite shyly, if I minded him coming back early.

In truth, he was anxious to find a partner for life, but as he approached his forties it was proving a struggle. Ron Smart was his driver from 1977 to 1981. He says: 'There seemed to be a different woman every five minutes. Richard had a very kind heart. He was too generous for his own good at times. All these girlfriends who flitted in and out ... it was all to see what they could get out of him. And like a fool he'd give them money. Next week you'd find they'd gone. And then the next week he'd have another one in tow.'

But there were others who did not belong in that category, including a close spiritual soulmate who friends felt was 'the one who got away'. Another object of his affections, Annabel

Olivier-Wright, who was there for independence and provided great service in promoting the Booth brand to the media and on whom Booth was also very keen, had also been and gone. Other associations showed brief but finite promise.

In the late 1970s he started going out with Judy Allen, who had left her family in South Africa to visit the UK, initially planning to stay just three weeks. She had travelled a lot, particularly to India, was a passionate writer and poet and eventually settled with friends near Hay-on-Wye. She was blonde, flamboyantly dressed and bejewelled (when not wearing wellies), wore bright red lipstick and soon found herself working as Booth's PA. They shared an interest in books, parties and good food.

The relationship seemed likely to endure. 'In a previous life she had probably enjoyed a lavish lifestyle before eventually becoming destitute,' said a friend. 'She was a warm, generous and stylish person, and had a taste for grandeur, so would have loved to have lived in the Castle with Richard.'

But it did not last. After nearly two years together, Booth was madly in love and asked Judy to marry him. To his surprise she turned him down. Friends spoke of a fundamental intimate incompatibility, though there were other considerations, too, such as her realising 'how much he basically needed looking after', says a friend. Judy moved to London and began working in the House of Lords for David Ennals in the field of human rights. She was a dedicated Buddhist and she and Ennals campaigned doggedly for Tibetan independence. Richard, meanwhile, did not take another rejection well, though they were able to stay friends and in contact after her move to London in the early 1980s.

Judy had been taken with Booth's kindness, but he was undoubtedly a handful. Ron Smart says:

He was eccentric, and living with him was probably a novelty at first, but after a while it was . . . oh God. He always struck me as a schoolboy who had never grown up. Little things would tickle him . . . like schoolboy humour. But it wasn't for everyone. There were these girls who seemed to drift in and out. They'd be there a couple of weeks and then be gone. They couldn't last the pace.

One of the more colourful bit-part players in Booth's life, though only for a year or so, was Paddy, an Irish veteran of the Normandy beaches whom his boss described gently as 'unable to adjust to the subtleties of civilian life'. Booth describes the police coming to the door of Brynmelyn to be met by Paddy wielding a carving knife with such menace that the officer simply ran away. He was, wrote Booth, a conscientious housekeeper and a limited cook whose philosophy was 'don't get involved with any women'. It was a message that failed to constrain either man.

Booth's memory of Paddy in his autobiography paints only a partial picture, though a charitable one. Paddy had served time in prison for some unspecified deed and was believed to be volatile. An early intimation of this came when he punched the skirting board at the Blue Boar. On another occasion a lavish dinner party was taking place at a long table at Brynmelyn:

Paddy came back drunk and walked in mid-meal. He shouted: 'What the hell is going on? It'll be me who is expected to tidy all this mess up in the morning, so let's make a bit more mess.' He overturned the whole table, sending plates, dishes, glasses and cutlery crashing to the floor. 'Richard was hosting,' remembers one eyewitness. 'He wasn't happy, but he wouldn't go up against Paddy in a roaring temper.'

Booth's caution was well placed. Master and employee parted company after the pair had an argument which ended with Paddy trying to kill Booth with an axe. One of Booth's employees received a call to come and help. He came round in a lorry – a locally famous one whose gears could only be changed by hitting the gearstick with a brick – to be met by Booth running down the road from Brynmelyn in terror.

A day or two after Paddy's departure, Booth walked into the shop carrying a box of food shopping. 'He was so excited,' says a staff member. '"Look at this," he said. "Bread, butter, marmalade! Look, with the bacon I got from Charlie Gibbons, I can make my own breakfast!" He had never shopped for groceries in his life before.'

Up on Hay Bluff, the hippies were eventually moved on, but not before more damage was done. Jim Capaldi had moved to Brazil and visited his cottage only occasionally. John Taylor, Capaldi's friend and manager, remembers Capaldi opening his front door to someone who just assumed he could walk straight in. 'Jim barred the way and the guy said, "I live here." Jim had to explain that actually *he* was the owner.'

So badly protected was the house in Capaldi's absence that, one winter, the travelling folk having failed even to shut the front door, a cow made its way into the house and up the stairs. Its wanderings were abruptly curtailed when its hooves went through the floorboards and could be seen from the sitting room below.

At least Hay's supposed 'crime wave' had been resolved. Late one bitterly cold night about three miles west of Hay a car had taken a bend too fast and skidded into another. There were no fatalities but ambulances had been called. The police realised that approaching vehicles needed to be warned that an accident was blocking the road.

A PC stood ahead of the turn and flagged down an approaching motorcyclist. 'The chap took his helmet off and burst into tears,' remembers David Jones. 'He thought we were stopping him to question him about the burglaries, so he coughed to all the break-ins into all the cottages on the mountain, and agreed to hand back all the recoverable stuff from the thirty-eight sites he had broken into.' This was no Moriarty. He was just a kid, doing it for kicks.

Booth himself suffered from a mysterious episode around this time. His friend Boots Bantock was invited to give a poetry reading in Chelsea Town Hall at midday one Saturday. Booth insisted he would give Boots a lift to London as he was due to go there himself around that time, and would be happy to get to Chelsea by midday. As Boots feared, Booth completely forgot the urgency, forcing the poet to make his own way, scrambling madly by public transport and eventually arriving just twenty minutes late at the King's Road venue. Several days later Boots didn't bother raising Booth's oversight. He should never have expected Booth's departure time to accommodate Bantock's need. But a week later he bumped into Booth, mentioning the word 'London' without animus. 'Ah, London!' said Booth, as the light dawned, failing even to mention the poetry reading, let alone apologise. 'That's where my car is.'

Booth had been without his car in Hay for several days. He had taken the train back from London, having forgotten having driven there. Once back in Hay, he was confused as to why his car was nowhere to be seen. 'He was the vaguest man who ever lived,' says Bantock.

14

Hope Appears ... and Morelli Arrives

'His natural arrogance was incompatible with a trade in which knowledge is more important than wealth.'

Richard Booth on his chief rival

The start of the 1980s was a harsh time for an ailing company. The Thatcher government, elected in 1979, was the most radical Britain had seen for decades. It was anxious to make the point that the state-funded feather-bedding from which many companies had benefited was to come to an end. Previous prime ministers had used robust language in the past, but had lost their nerve in the face of threatened job losses. Margaret Thatcher, in her 'the lady's not for turning' speech of October 1980, had made it clear she meant what she said. A new rigour based on sound money was the creed of the day in no-nonsense Britain. Booth's money was anything but sound. And, though he had had the insurance money, he still had to complete the repairs to the burned-out Castle.

As far as possible, Booth wanted to restore the Castle using traditional methods, and he knew immediately who he wanted for the job. The morning after the fire, just four days after their first meeting, Booth had called Roger Capps, announcing, 'It's gone.'

'What's gone? What are you talking about?' replied Capps.

'The Castle burned down last night,' replied Booth.

Capps drove straight to Hay, where the ruined Castle was still smoking, with firemen still trying to mitigate the damage. 'He asked me to rebuild it. I said I would, but I still wasn't going to put in a theatre.' Capps, though, had also been captivated by the Castle's potential.

He and Booth got on famously for a while. Booth's personal diary is full of references to 'lunch with Capps', 'drink with Capps', 'Capps thinks . . .' etc., but Booth's impracticality was quickly obvious to Capps, who had to stiffen Booth's resolve in dealing with the insurers. Booth was proud to reassure Capps that the insurance would cover the cost of the repairs, and that the loss adjusters had offered £50,000. Capps told him: 'For God's sake don't accept.' That would not be anything like sufficient. He called in a quantity surveyor he knew, who Capps said would be able to get several multiples of what had originally been offered. Capps believes Booth received around £250,000. Others say the final figure was nearer £120,000. In any event, it would never be sufficient.

Capps moved into the Castle and began the repairs. Initially everything went well. After a while he learned that Booth was continuing his spending, using the money from the fire insurance to buy more books. Capps, who has an impressive reputation as a restorer of old buildings, was and still is well connected in that world. He was able to secure a grant from the newly formed Cadw, the agency that looks after Wales's historic monuments.

'I liked him, he had a good sense of humour,' says Capps. A couple of times a week they would ride up to and around the Black Mountains, he on his Arab cross, Glenmorangie, which set the pace, and Booth on his dun cob, Goldie. (The accounts of both suggest a degree of blokeish competitiveness.) 'I told my accountant that I needed to be friends with Booth, so can the horse be tax-deductible,' says Capps. The answer was no, but at Capps's insistence the local tax inspector agreed to letting him have 50 per cent.

There is enough history on the repairs to the Castle to fill several doctoral theses. It might also keep a team of libel lawyers busy. At the start there seemed to be plenty of money to pay for the repairs, and Capps has fond memories of how Booth gave him carte blanche to repair the Castle as he saw fit. But the two fell out badly, largely over Booth's subsequent inability to keep up the payments for the repairs. For some time, Booth resorted to his own currency, books, as a form of payment, with Capps, having consulted one of Booth's own experts, agreeing to accept various highly valuable tomes in lieu of cash. 'I picked up a few incunabula, but I had half a dozen guys working there and couldn't pay the staff in books,' remembers Capps.

There was a breach in their relations and Capps had to go to court to force Booth to catch up on his payments. Capps was then persuaded to return following assurances of better treatment. But a second dispute emerged, stemming from the need to do further specialist work on a chimney. Capps was asked to apply to Cadw for a grant, which he did, and he erected the scaffolding to carry out the extra work. But then a different team was called in to do the work at a lower price, Booth having decided he was being overcharged. This caused embarrassment with Cadw, from which Capps had acquired the funding and which assumed Capps would be carrying out the work.

Capps says the quantity surveyor who did crucial work for him was never paid by Booth, money he badly needed. 'It was only years later that I learned he never paid the QS ... Booth got an extra three hundred grand because of me and him, but he never paid him.' Capps was bemused by Booth's attitude to money, remembering how Booth would open one of his tills, grabbing five and ten pound notes indiscriminately with a claw-like hand, jump into his car with as many people as could fit and take everyone out for dinner. It was his way of confirming his control. There was a huge generosity but also a recklessness that was asking for trouble, he says.

'He didn't give a shit about anything. If you're taking money from the till and not paying the taxman, it becomes a free-for-all. Booth was a rich boy. He never really had to work, but he worked very hard, often going off and screwing people. He was terrible, but clever. On the other hand, I was young and he gave me a huge opportunity to work on the Castle, where I learned a huge amount. He indulged me like hell, and I am very grateful for that. I have quite a lot of admiration for him even though he ripped me off.'

A mark of the mounting concern as to the state of the Booth business was a picture story that appeared in *The Times* in March 1981. It showed Booth semi-buried against a vast pile of books. The caption read: 'Mr Richard Booth, a bookseller, of Hay-on-Wye, Powys, with some of the 100 tons of second-hand books he is offering for sale for burning at £1.50 a car load. He has 1.5m books, occupying 11 miles of shelves.' There was also an item on the BBC's *Six O'Clock News*.

To traditionalists, the burning of books is a heresy evocative of ignorance and political extremism. The admission of a practical need by Booth illustrated both his defiance for convention, his desperate straits financially and his capacity to drum up publicity. He skirted round a basic problem – that books don't burn well – trying to show insouciance, in telling a reporter: 'I burn only academic books, things like theology and legal stuff mainly. Considering the standard of most academic work these days, I consider I'm doing them a favour ... Five hundred PhDs couldn't build Notre-Dame. It was achieved by simple men with their hands.'

But the excess 'by-product' had long been a problem. What do you do with the chaff once the best bits of a new collection had been identified? For years Booth had been able to assume he had infinite space in which to store and shelve his purchases, however thin their value. But in that respect, he was a victim of his own success. His available storage space no longer appeared infinite. An honesty bookshop, where books were left outdoors on shelves to take their chances with the weather, provided pitifully little respite. For years, one of Booth's guilty secrets was that books were ending up on a de facto landfill site between Hay and Clyro. Now, by going public in *The Times*, no less, part of this difficult truth was being admitted.

Sometimes plain logistics meant too many books were a bad thing. On one buying trip in the north of England, Booth identified four boxes of books that he wanted, but the library from which he was buying them insisted on him taking the lot. His driver Andy Cooke spent three hours loading the lorry before they set off for the next stop. 'Just as it was getting dark,' remembers a friend of Cooke, 'Richard saw an empty car park and he told Andy to go down and dump them.' They needed an empty lorry for the next stop. In the event, it all took so long they missed the appointment.

The beast needed feeding, and the buying had to go on, to

sustain the bargain-hunter's interest. But the more valuable, resellable material was not coming in. 'Richard was buying absolute crud from America, which was the only place he could get stuff,' says Greg Coombes. 'Most of us were being paid weekly, or not till the following Wednesday, and no sooner was there cash in the till than Richard was in for it. It really was hand-to-mouth.' To Martin Beales, Booth's solicitor whose wife Noelle worked for Booth and who was friendly with many members of his staff, the writing had been on the wall for a long time. In 1981 he told Greg Coombes that preparations needed to be made for some sort of transition. The boss had run out of miracles.

Beales knew how chaotically the company had been run, but equally the amount of stock, the properties and Hay's global reputation as a home of second-hand books meant that bookselling ought to be able to continue. 'I remember Martin saying, "It could go at any time, just like that. He should not be trading, he's finished already, and when it goes, it could go for nothing. You need to get a company together."' And so, in the expectation that one day very soon the company would go bust, Greg Coombes registered the name 'Hay Cinema Bookshop Ltd'. A plan was hatched to split off the art department, but in the end it was deemed unworkable.

If many old companies went out of business in the early Thatcher years, some new ones flourished, if briefly, in that period. As if preordained, Booth became enthusiastic friends with a businessman called Colin Stone soon after he moved into the area. As was inclined to happen, a couple of years later Stone was added to the list of people Booth had fallen out with.

Stone was a very successful manufacturer of garden gnomes whose business received a shot in the arm when a cult of guerrilla gnome-swapping hit the UK. Overnight, gnomes with, say, fishing rods, would be replaced in people's gardens by a gnome with a spade, or maybe a laughing gnome. Stone met his Waterloo, though, when he tried to extend the gnome fad to continental Europe, ending up with more than he could handle.

But he was hired by his friend Jack Earwacker to take responsibility for transforming Clyro Court, a grand residence outside Hay, into a luxury hotel. It lacked the pomp and kudos of his gnome magnate days, but a lot of money was spent and initially the scheme worked well. Stone was a colourful figure. He was a close friend of Vivian MacKerrell, on whom the Withnail character in the film *Withnail and I* was based, and they used to go on wild trips together. MacKerrell died in 1995.

In a further blow to his friend's dignity, Stone was to go to prison on four counts of fraudulent trading. By that time he had long fallen out with Booth, who used to encourage his staff members to go over to Clyro Court, have a few drinks in the bar, use the pool and sauna and tell the barman to charge it all to 'Mr Booth's tab'. Mr Booth had no intention of paying, and didn't.

This period saw huge change on other fronts in Booth's life as well. First, he met a photographer called Hope Stuart, née Barrie, who came from a long line of Scottish judges. On her mother's side she was descended from Robert Louis Stevenson and from *Peter Pan* author J. M. Barrie on her father's side. She showed early signs of being the figure Booth had both been looking for and needing for most of his adult life. Indeed, had she appeared on the scene a decade or so earlier, the course of the Booth bookshops would probably have been very different.

At the time she was married to Rob Stuart, an alumnus of Downside public school who ran the Langton Gallery in Chelsea, and she was working as a photographer when they met. She spent much of her time living in a hunting lodge in

Northamptonshire. Her enthusiasm was for animals (mostly black), and had little time for the London socialising that her husband enjoyed.

A mutual friend, Boots Bantock, at one time Booth's 'poet laureate', told her she simply must meet this character: he was an interesting figure. Loulou de la Falaise was also convinced that she and Booth would get on, knowing of their shared interest in horses, the countryside and hatred of bureaucracy. Hope was completely uninterested. To a friend she mentioned 'that boastful man who calls himself a king'. Her father referred to Hay as 'the place that awful man lives'. When they did meet at Brynmelyn, though (thanks to the persistence of Boots Bantock), she was first struck by his lack of social polish – 'like an Etonian Eric Morecambe', she told a friend – and by how natural and unaffected he seemed. She left more impressed than she had expected, and began reading some of the pamphlets – on rural economies, the countryside, traditional methods and so on – that were so central to his commitment to Hay.

Booth and Hope teamed up for an initial piece of work together, a guide to Rhayader, twenty-two miles north of Hay. The guide, which in most people's hands would have been informative but workaday at best, managed to inflame the Welsh Development Board, whose activities were heavily criticised in it. As a result, many shops in Rhayader refused to stock the guide, thereby defeating the intention. It was to be the first of many common causes on which the couple worked. From small acorns . . .

A romantic turn for the better did little, at that stage at least, for Booth's financial problems. Creditors continued to clamour at his door. Geoffrey Meaden had grown impatient and taken legal action to get his £20,000 loan back. During that process, with Meaden's anger growing, he nearly levitated with rage when Booth, by way of explanation, announced: 'But I *never* repay my loans.' In this case, though, he had to. Meaden drove a hard bargain. Eventually Booth sold him a prime site in Hay at a favourable price minus the value of the loan. Even so, Meaden was not pacified, and would curse Booth until the end of his days.

The end of 1981 brought the coldest winter Britain had seen for years. Booth was taken to work on a tractor, the only available vehicle capable of overcoming the thick ice on Cusop Dingle. Winter was never a good period for the bookseller, and he claimed the weather destroyed 90 per cent of sales, pushing bank managers yet further up against their limits. What brought a new sense of desperation was a £53,000 tax bill.

An antiquarian law book dealer called John Rees happened to be in Hay at the time. He was working for Leon Morelli, a wealthy London-based businessman with an interest in expanding his own bookshop interests. A meeting was arranged, during which it became obvious that Morelli could take advantage of the company's parlous state. As it happened, Booth owed Rees money. Seeing an opportunity to put pressure on Booth, Morelli bought the debt from Rees.

Morelli claimed later that Booth offered to sell the entire business, but that he declined. He did suggest, though, that Booth's debts could be wiped out if he was to sell him the Cinema, the only one of Booth's bookshops that was making money. At one point Morelli offered instead to swap the recently acquired Swan Hotel, at that point unused and rat-infested, for the Cinema (both being valued at around six figures), but Booth refused. Morelli had expanded his Pharos International distribution business – he had made a lot of money in collaboration with the Post Office – and needed bigger premises. Eventually a deal was agreed, with the pretender knocking £10,000 off at the last minute (requiring all the paperwork to be retyped), making the final price £100,000.

'My position was so bad I had to agree to everything,' wrote Booth later, and the alternative staff buyout plan bit the dust. 'Morelli blasted us out of the water,' remembers Coombes. 'When moneybags comes along in his Bentley, numberplate LKM1, we thought, OK, we'll take a job with this bloke, and a couple of us did.' The name Hay Cinema Bookshop Ltd, shrewdly purchased by Coombes in anticipation of some sort of meltdown, was sold to Morelli for £100. 'He was quite impressed,' laughs Coombes. 'He thought this bloke is marginally a cut above the rest of the drunks.'

The sale of the Cinema, in 1982, would have sunk many in Booth's position, so symbolically important was it to his business. Certainly it was a major change. Book collector Ian Sanger recalls it at its peak: 'People came into the Cinema seven days a week from anywhere in the area or further afield with books to sell. These books, coming from private individuals, generally bore no library stamps ... the Cinema became an essential asset: they bought an oil well. Whether as sellers or buyers, I don't think the public registered it was no longer Richard Booth's; but it lost its former glory. When it had been his there may have been masses of drab books, but there would always be something interesting as well, whatever your field. Serendipity would strike sooner or later.'

In a typical display of fortitude and persistence, Booth refused to buckle, and retreated to a rather more attractive building known as 'the Limited' in the well-visited middle of Hay. It was so called because its former owner, Robert Williams, owned the first company, manufacturers of farm machinery and tools, in Hay to become a limited company. The building itself, on three floors (and said to house a quarter of a million books), dated from the Victorian age, and is distinguished by its wood, glass and tile façade. The relocation of Booth's main shop was psychologically a major step for those of his staff who stayed with him, but they showed a striking loyalty and dedication in confronting the task. 'It was as if we had to start up the business all over again,' sighed one.

Booth did very well on the purchase of the Limited. Initially he rented the building, valued at £60,000, from the Likes, a long-established Hay family, at a cost of £175 a week. The Likes told him if he kept up the payments for two and half years, he could buy the building for its initial value – £60,000. When the time came, Booth had the place valued for himself – at £120,000. At a time when banks would have as little to do with him as possible, on this occasion, having been satisfied that Booth was up to date with the rent, the bank manager Mr Davies was happy to lend him the £60,000.

There was still not a lot of spare cash about. The shelves were taken from Cockcroft to the Limited, but there weren't nearly enough, so beer crates were broken up and converted into shelves. Cockcroft's radiators were sold for scrap, bringing in a useful £2,000, and another large building was denuded of all its fluorescent bulbs to light the aisles at the Limited, leaving one solitary bulb in the middle of the room.

The sale of Cockcroft was another inevitability. Booth had been attracted by the sheer size of the former workhouse, but it never fulfilled its promise and its situation in the town put it off the beaten track for the casual book buyer. A price of £60,000 was agreed with the family of local businessman Jim Morris. Typically, Booth asked for £1,000 of the total to be paid in cash 'for pocket money', said a friend. Morris managed to create twenty dwelling units for his £60,000. 'It was the best buy I've ever done,' he told a friend later.

Much as Booth sought to deprecate Morelli, his adversary was no fly-by-night. He had plenty of money, and decided to go toe to toe with Booth, competing with him in almost every respect. Booth was reported to have understood they had agreed to compete in different areas of the market, but that did not materialise, and there was no gentlemanly rivalry to see who was the stronger.

Morelli's presence brought self-reflection in Booth. 'After twenty years I believe I am bad at making money,' he wrote in his diary, '. . . I have now this opportunity to put my affairs in order but if I do not do it right I will never be able to pursue my political objectives.'

'Richard mounted a kind of terrorist campaign for a while,' remembers one of his staffers. 'There was a kind of cold war for about twenty years. Richard was not a good businessman like Morelli, but people knew what he had done for Hay and where his heart lay, and regardless of what had gone before, that provoked a certain loyalty to him.'

Around February 1983, about six months after the Cinema had been taken over by Leon Morelli, Greg Coombes got a call in his office, asking him to come downstairs where, he was told, 'there's a guy going ballistic in the foyer'. Coombes went down, to be treated to a stream of foul-mouthed invective about Booth. When he calmed down, the man in question, who had some expertise in accountancy, explained that not long previously Booth had employed him to perform some questionable financial wizardry, involving the moving of assets and so on, that would help keep the bailiffs at bay. The man in question had obliged, and had also agreed to help Booth secure the latest in a string of deals that were supposedly destined to save the company.

The purchase in question was of the library of Norman Wood,

a retired teacher at Kings Norton School in Birmingham, who had a considerable collection of, among others, natural history books. Booth needed someone to go with him to provide financial bottom and to reassure the ageing Wood, a quiet, scholarly figure, that even though the pair could not manage a down payment of any sort, the cost of the library, £12,000, would reach him, in instalments, over the next few months. The accountancy wizard endorsed what Booth was saying, and Wood was duly convinced. Booth's defenders would doubtless assure us that, as so often, at the time Booth made the promise he intended to pay his bill, though heaven knows how.

At this point, Booth dropped a clanger. Before the books were collected from Birmingham, Booth told the Wizard that he was not going to pay him for his financial advice after all, and that it had not been as valuable as he had expected. The Wizard was furious with Booth, and just wanted his money.

Coombes reported this back to Morelli, who immediately saw the possibilities. The Wizard was despatched to Birmingham, with Coombes, where he explained to Wood that he now understood Booth's promises were less than cast-iron, and recommended that Wood take the same view. Wood was now made the same offer, and with immediate payment in full. He accepted, and the books were collected within a few days, Wood becoming a new customer for Morelli for the rest of his life.

Disputes of this sort were no accident. Morelli wanted Booth's kingdom, and didn't mind who knew it. The feud – and it was almost medievally feudal in flavour – between Morelli and Booth lasted for years. But what might have been regarded as a mighty tussle between the King of Hay and the calculating, pasty-faced Midas was instead a pitifully childish display between two men who really should have known better. 'They were like two three-year-olds fighting in a pram,' remembers one Hay bookseller.

As if to show his aspirations, Morelli organised a giant firework display for charity. (This attempt to play the gracious toff was spoiled when he later complained that he was 'disgusted' the crowd of 12,000 people stumped up only £1,050 in charitable donations, the display having cost £10,000 to mount.) He arranged for a Caribbean band to play in mid-winter, charging £11 a ticket. He also distributed posters calling on Booth to complete the repair of the Castle, threatening that if the King failed to oblige, he would hold a public vote to decide if Booth should continue as King or if he, Morelli, should become president. The repairs not having been carried out, on 5 November 1983 April Ashley, strapped for cash as ever, turned traitor – briefly – by accepting a fee of £100 to offer Hay's populace a free glass of sherry each if they would cast their vote by throwing a dart at a picture of Booth. Booth lost the poll.

Some months later, in the 1983 election, Booth stood for Parliament as an independent. He won fewer than three hundred votes. 'My political career was to prove hopelessly vulnerable to Morelli's financial power,' he said. To compound the humiliation, Morelli crawled brazenly into bed with precisely the local Welsh quangos that Booth had most vigorously criticised, applying widely for grants, loans and the like and very often securing them. It was an end to the age of unbridled Boothery.

Where Booth had a certain genial if sometimes artless charm, Morelli's instincts were those of a hard-nosed businessman. He had little of Booth's inherited fondness for the world of books. 'His natural arrogance was incompatible with a trade in which knowledge is more important than wealth,' wrote Booth. He derided Morelli for his failure to join in with Hay's drinking culture, his aggressive book purchasing and his lack of understanding of what Booth had built up.

Morelli, on the other hand, would decide that if books were not selling in Hay he would have them moved to one of his other shops in London, Bournemouth or elsewhere. Booth had underestimated Morelli's determination to make himself a power in Hay. He bought the biggest hotels in Hay and clearly wanted Booth gone. 'My demise must be fundamental to his aims,' wrote Booth in his diary of 11 April 1984.

Another non-recipient of Booth's funds was the Treasury, which sent him a bill for £20,000 after Booth had taken tax from employees' pay packets but failed to pass the money on to the taxman. A winding-up order was issued, the third Booth had faced. Things looked desperate. Somehow sufficient funds were found for Garry Spencer to write fifty cheques to the creditors to whom he owed the smallest amounts of money, to prevent them all turning up in court. But the big bills remained, and Morelli, ever keen to denude the Booth kingdom and hire Booth's most trusted employees, was in no mood to accommodate him. When Booth was declared bankrupt in the spring of 1984, Morelli made sure his accountant was in attendance.

Meanwhile, Michael Bowers, a book publisher, had been put on a retainer to help Booth a few days a week in the writing of a book – long in the pipeline – about his experiences as a bookseller. In the event, Bowers and Booth never discussed the book at all. His earliest days working for Booth were instead spent assessing the value of the books Booth had stored at Brynmelyn. That spring he was appointed managing director of Richard Booth Bookshops Ltd, shortly after bankruptcy was declared. Bowers explains: 'He wasn't allowed to trade through the company that retained the books. He had other companies than enabled him to trade, but the Limited was strictly speaking off limits to him, not that he recognised that.'

Bowers was able to steady the ship to some degree, pointing out at a creditors' meeting with the official receiver that a Customs and Excise claim against Booth for 'an enormous amount of money for unclaimed VAT' was invalid.

Following the creditors' meeting discussions took place about how to address the debts. 'The main danger was that the stock of the Limited could be sequestered – unless Booth offered up some of his private assets,' remembers Bowers. He seems to have been more concerned than at any time previously. He wrote in his diary of 20 May: 'Brynmelyn smothered with flowers: beautiful. I must keep it at all costs.'

The mostly academic reprints at Brynmelyn formed part of the stock belonging to the bankrupted company and Bowers was able to have their value acknowledged among the assets. 'This, I believe, probably lifted the immediate threats to the Limited and Booth's personal property,' says Bowers. The stock at Brynmelyn was put under lock and key in preparation for liquidation. Even then, typically, Booth couldn't resist a degree of finagling. He ordered his staff to break into the site where they were stored and move some of the more valuable books, with a view to selling them elsewhere. 'They knew they shouldn't be doing it, but that is what Richard wanted,' says Garry Spencer.

Michael Bowers says of the plan: 'It would have been very Booth, but I was not aware of it. Then again, I was the last person he would have wanted to know about it.' Even more extraordinarily, some years later the books, or a considerable portion of them, turned up at a recycling depot in South Wales.

Bowers suggested Booth sell the Castle, but that would truly have been a last resort. His recollection does not reflect well on Booth:

During my time at the Limited my main preoccupation was with the weekly wage bill. For much of that time, the turnover was simply not enough to pay staff and buy stock. One side of the problem was that the Limited held quite a lot of slow-moving antiquarian material, the other side was that we were not being offered collections by enough private sellers. Not surprising in the circumstances. The first part we could deal with by making use of the auction rooms (to Booth's disapproval), the second part was more intractable. At first, Booth had shown a willingness not to interfere, but it was clear to me that many of his contacts would be denied to the Limited so long as the business was not in his hands. He was tricky. Never straightforward. His inclinations were neither antiquarian nor literary and his bookselling practice was akin to survival in the jungle, but he had enough cunning to get by. He manipulated his own shortcomings well enough to get people to play along with him, but he wasn't somebody they trusted. Nevertheless, his cynical and unprincipled methods were tolerated to an astonishing degree. Perhaps this is not surprising: book dealers in Hay and elsewhere had no wish to see him go under. Some, from further afield, greatly benefited from his frequent need to offload, rapidly, some of his newly acquired treasures. Also, he was perennially short of ready cash, and he had always seen the Limited as a handy source of cash top-ups. My presence at the Limited clearly frustrated this part of his regular behaviour and there were several devious attempts to get behind my back, one of them involving a company cheque on which my signature had been forged. Naturally, there was no evidence that Booth had a hand in this. The changed situation had turned a chaotic financial situation into a threatening one, and he was making matters worse by continuing to deal 'privately'. He was not prevented from doing this under the terms of the bankruptcy, but it was making life very difficult for the Limited and its staff. Of course, this was a typical Booth scenario: control through chaos. It always produced a messy situation and it always fell to someone else to pick up the pieces. His reputation travelled ahead, and I knew that anyone in my position would be likely to take the blame.

Bowers left in June 1985. By that time, there was a sense that 'old Hay' was more remote than ever. Some of the fast London set had introduced a newer, more liberal ethos and drugs – beyond cannabis – were more readily available. Where crime had previously been low-scale and atomised, by the mid-1980s parts of Hay were getting streetwise. But the low-key policing was having its successes. A young man who in other circumstances might have been facing a stiff fine or even prison was the beneficiary of (by now) Sergeant David Jones's leniency. It turned out to be a good investment on Jones's part. He asked the man to pass on any comings and goings, and to note down the odd number plate, at the house of a neighbour who appeared to be in contact with an unsavoury character from outside Hay. The young man obliged. A few months later, having refined the investigation and passed on the details to his superiors, Jones was summoned to Birmingham and asked how on earth he had made the connection between the pair. 'Old-fashioned policing,' said Jones proudly. He was told by his West Midlands superiors: 'We've been trying to get a connection between these two for three years.' A huge drugs deal had been unearthed. The two men were on a commission of £100,000 each. The full force of the law was brought to bear shortly afterwards.

Not that Booth had much interest in drugs, but two events suggested that the excesses of the high-living era were in decline. One was the death of Blue Boar landlord Chris Fry. The other was the departure from Hay, for America, of April Ashley. She spoke later of how difficult she had found her arrival in Hay, and how much, after a while, she had been made to feel welcome enough to enjoy getting 'rip-roaring drunk' with them.

There was disappointment in how her time in Hay came to an end. Where the *grande dame* persona had provided much entertainment, there was a growing sense that the hammed-up self-importance was more than an act. Richard Booth had appreciated all she had done for Hay. He shared the admiration of her friend Simon Callow – in *The Extraordinary Life of April Ashley*, a 2022 ITV documentary – for her 'astounding bravery and courage'. She was later awarded the MBE and has come to be applauded as a transgender pioneer. But, though Booth remained loyal, he felt she did not appreciate what he had done for her – in terms of providing endless drinks, accommodation, foreign travel and transport. At the same time, she felt he had failed to live up to a number of promises, and they argued spiritedly after he sold some pictures she had asked him to look after. It was a parting that hurt her deeply, but Booth was not alone in his frustration with her. According to Duncan Fallowell, a longtime Hay resident, friend of Booth and the leading Ashley authority – he co-wrote her autobiography while living at Cockroft – she:

> would increasingly smother people and take advantage of them, and it was really a question of personal survival. After I had done the book, I had to have a little distance, and Richard found the same. You helped April with one hand and you suddenly found you had to help her with both

hands, otherwise she got annoyed. She had a very, very free and easy view of life and just thought other people's bank accounts were hers too while she was with them. Richard was *very* generous to her but perhaps not as generous as she would have wanted. April was expecting to be flown in from America, all expenses paid, and it just got out of hand. He himself was close to bankruptcy at the time but that wouldn't carry any weight with April. I suppose to have an aggressive sense of entitlement, which she did have, was necessary to change your sex, but this spilled over into personal relationships too, unfortunately.

The world had moved on, its lustre now somewhat faded. And for Michael Bowers and others, Booth's financial fallibility, so obvious to those on the inside, was now there for all to see. The King's new clothes had been exposed.

Richard Booth Booksellers had gone into liquidation. Among its smaller debts were £8,020 in rates for local amenities. Booth's crown may have been slipping but he remained a local councillor. So when the local finance committee of which he was a member waived the charge (in his absence), there was a predictable rumpus. Booth claimed, with some justification, that he had invested £8 million in Hay, so this was a small price to pay. 'How is it possible to regard the council as having any integrity when a man like Booth can get away with this?' raged one councillor. 'An ordinary small businessman would be dealt with seriously if he fell behind with his rates. It seems there's one law for the rich and one for the poor. He goes around lording it up in restaurants, drinking double whiskies and smoking cigars. There's no shame in bankruptcy – but this guy rubs it in by buying his gardener a better car than I've got . . . and I'm struggling to pay my rates!'

Morelli, too, was to attract unfavourable publicity. *Haywire*, a locally produced gossip sheet, reproduced an article from *Private Eye* suggesting that he had indulged in sharp practice in his deal with the Post Office. The headline on the article was a supposedly punning 'Morelli bankrupt'. Again rising to the bait, he threatened to sue *Private Eye* and have *Haywire* closed down. *Haywire* escaped but *Private Eye* had to fork out substantial damages after it was found Morelli was neither bankrupt nor without morals.

This added fuel to the feud and led to rumours – completely unfounded, though that was beside the antagonising point – that Morelli, already referred to in Booth circles as 'the Sicilian', was related to Frank 'Butsey' Morelli, the first crime boss of Rhode Island and a mentor to aspiring godfathers and other mobsters. Any stick ...

In 1987, to coincide with the general election, a further vote was organised to chart the relative popularity of the two men (about which few really cared, other than themselves). Morelli claimed to have invested £3 million in the town and denied he would ever cut and run, as some had claimed. In a pastiche election statement, Booth, already living on former glories, was said to proclaim of Morelli: 'He may have more mazuma than me, but it was *ME* who brought *HIM* here in the first place! I'm the one who brought all the funny people for you to be amused by ... remember Frank English? Ha ha! What has [Morelli] brought you? Higher priced books, a few sparklers, regimentation and uniformity, unnecessary railings. You all know me, a harmless King Lear, full of Boothoonery. So vote for me, and not the "unknown foreigner".' Morelli won the contest by two votes, twenty-two to twenty, and was now known in some circles as King Leon.

Morelli was certainly not everyone's cup of tea. His proximity to grant givers aroused suspicion, and he gained a reputation for not dealing well with his staff, many of whom were local. There was an element of lofty dismissal among his opponents. This was evident in the words of Boots Bantock who, though he had never met Morelli, wrote the following for *Haywire*:

... So that where there was once spontaneity
There's a dearth, well, you know what I mean
When everything's measured in silver & brass
And most of that fake – so it seems.

But Hay won't renounce her own culture,
and I wonder by Abergavenny,
That on my return, am I right to observe,
Could there be an Italian too many?

But what can we do with the fellow we ask,
with his semi-suburban dreams,
Give him a ticket marked 'Tourist Class'
And send him to Milton Keynes.

But not only was Morelli going nowhere, a new development that was to eclipse Booth entirely was heading his way.

15

Under New Management

'He would listen to Hope ... she was the best thing that happened to Richard.'

Ron Smart

Booth was in love with Hay, supremely egotistical and very determined. The fact that business recovered during the 1980s, despite going back on the old drug, namely buying in bulk from the US, is even more remarkable. He had imported over a hundred twenty-foot containers, each one holding four hundred boxes of books. Now approaching his fiftieth birthday, he was finding the work more tiring than previously, but the drive was as strong as ever. Somehow his luck seemed to have changed. Arno Zohn, to whom he still owed $80,000 plus interest, told him 'forget it', and absolved the debt. Zohn, it turned out, was terminally ill. One version of the story has it that his family were less than pleased to hear of the man's late-life magnanimity.

But most importantly, he had a new, invaluable partner who brought both a discipline and an energy that defied his shambolic leanings. His relationship with Hope had gone from strength to strength in the 1980s. He records how for three years, abetted by Hope's credit card, they travelled through the States, now buying more selectively than before. Though very different in some respects – for one thing he was tall, unkempt and uninhibited, she was small, well-turned-out and more con-trolled – they complemented one another, and nowhere more so than in business. Where Booth was enthusiastic, passionate and inclined to hastiness, she was far more painstaking, businesslike and parsimonious. At one point he wrote in his diary: 'Hope does not like to hear how I made my money . . . it's business!'

They started seeing one another in 1981, and Rob, Hope's husband, imagined that for Booth it would be a passing phase. He was not alone. When Booth's sister Anne met Hope for the first time, she looked her up and down and said, 'Oh, you're his latest', and walked on. But some of Hope's friends felt she was making a wise choice. Though their Hereford Register Office marriage did not take place until 1987, Hope's influence on Booth had long before been clear and growing.

Hope remembers hearing a lot of untrue stories when she began seeing Booth. One was that Booth had had two children who had perished in the fire at the Castle. It was simply untrue, and she has been unsurprised if subsequent stories about him have turned out to be baseless. She was also shocked by the attitude of the staff in the shops. 'When I first started, I would go and buy books and the staff gave me twenty per cent off. I thought, Why all these discounts? I'm not a book dealer. Why are people giving away your stock? It was slack business prac-tice from staff members wanting to make themselves popular.' One Hay bookseller, Doreen Price, stopped buying books from Booth's shops because she felt Booth was being short-changed.

Booth's driver Ron Smart remembers: 'Hope was the one that got the business streamlined. He would listen to her . . . she was the best thing that happened to Richard. She was like a rock to him and he needed that.' 'She looked after him,' says Greg Coombes. 'At first she was mistrusted. I think she fell in love with him and saw he was being belittled, so she was protective towards him and became very spiky towards his opponents and those who were doing him down.'

Booth's recollection on this latter point is remarkable, suggesting Hope had noticed something of which he – though not others – was entirely unaware. He wrote: 'The first problem she identified was that everything, from the family silver to bottles of duty-free whisky, disappeared with regularity from the house.' Stories circulated about copper, radiators, slot machines and so on going missing. Had the trusting Booth really been unaware, or was it that he simply didn't care about a bit of pilfering on the margins? In any event, change was in the air, both domestically and in his business, however much the thieves were contributing in other ways. It was, if you insist, a triumph of Hope over expedience.

In July 1988, the first to go was Charlie Gibbons, a man of 'steadfast loyalty' and a 'wonderful servant', the man who, with his wife Cathy, lit Booth's fires, grew his vegetables, looked after his chickens, pigs and horses, cooked his meals and ran the house. But, Booth acknowledged in his book, '[he] had managed to buy a new car and live in considerable luxury by stealing from me'. He was, it turned out, 'an incurable kleptomaniac'.

Charlie was a kindly, well-known and cheery figure in Hay, and has been compared to the mischievous Private Walker in *Dad's Army*, having an easy charm and an ability to lay his hands on almost anything at short notice. Locals remember his capacity for offering best quality 'spirographs', as he called asparagus, and much else. Booth's friend Ivor Windsor says: 'Charlie had a touch of the taffy rogue about him, but as long as the house was running, Richard didn't care. He was not at all interested.' Another well-established Hay figure reports that 'Charlie thought he was more important to Booth than Hope was – how wrong he was.'

Booth had realised, not before time, that Charlie was being far too carefree with his property, but was unable to prove it. In his autobiography he points a finger unambiguously at Charlie, having caught him stealing a vanload of valuable oak from a Brynmelyn shed. Booth by inclination loathed confrontation, and his shyness often led to incoherent spluttering, but this was unignorable. In time, Charlie's services were dispensed with. Charlie's wife Cathy was furious, and blamed Hope, who had no advance knowledge of the confrontation. 'Who do you think you are?' demanded Cathy, whose services had been done away with a couple of years earlier. 'I'm just the same as you,' replied Hope.

Charlie had had a good run and 'retirement' was in order. In his book, Booth doesn't mention the theft of the oak, but he does say that Charlie was receiving two wage packets every week. According to Booth, his wages clerk Garry Spencer was responsible, also claiming Spencer had given himself an unauthorised wage rise. Both are clear libels if untrue.

The unassuming Spencer denies any impropriety, saying that, as agreed, he was merely following the protocol arranged by his predecessor, which separated Charlie's work at the Castle from his work at Brynmelyn. On his own pay rise, he said it had been agreed in a meeting attended by Booth that this would be awarded if he completed and handed in the tax returns at Brecon before the five-week deadline was up, but the decision had been unminuted and thus forgotten. He did not pursue the matter, having been employed by another disaffected and recently departed Booth employee.

Hope also loyally joined some of Booth's more wayward wheezes. His relationship with Duncan Linklater and his wife

Sally, who had returned to Hay after a spell away and were now living across the road from Booth at the stables in Brynmelyn, had deteriorated. It seems that by this time Booth resented the Linklaters, and in an early version of Booth's book he asserted that Duncan had been involved, with Jim Robson, in the (denied) theft of books.

The story turned into a kind of kindergarten *Jean de Florette*. The friction between the couples was compounded during a dry summer when the Brynmelyn water supply was insufficient to cater for both households. Without warning, Booth cut off the Linklaters' water, requiring them to collect bottled water from Hay, and accused Duncan of all sorts of outlandish antics. Booth said the Linklaters were stealing his water and, in any case, using it wastefully. He believed the Linklaters had designs on taking over Brynmelyn. They said they were simply using what had always been theirs since the purchase of the stables. They tried to reconnect the supply, which had always been assumed to be their right, prompting Booth to chase Linklater out of his garden.

A series of even more childish larks ensued. On a day when Linklater was out, Booth organised the flattening of his neighbour's newly erected fence. (He admitted it, but the police decided to take no action.) The following day, to maximise their irritation and discomfort, he had a ton of stinking pig manure dumped on a strip leading to the Linklater front door.

Having tidied up the manure, Linklater then planted several fast-growing trees on the site. A few hours later, Booth reappeared and pulled them up. 'Richard was always doing things like that, just to annoy his neighbours,' says Lesley Arrowsmith, who, with her husband, worked as housekeepers at Brynmelyn for nearly two years.

These 'garden fence' squabbles took on lives of their own. A second set of Brynmelyn neighbours also had their water disconnected, prompting Arrowsmith and her husband to rig up a secret hosepipe from Brynmelyn for the neighbours' benefit. 'Richard never found out,' she laughs. And the Linklaters managed to keep the pigs from stinking out their end of the strip, though by resorting to means worthy of the dastardly Harrovian stinker Sir Gregory Parsloe-Parsloe from P. G. Wodehouse's Blandings stories. One evening some months later the King of Hay and his lady wife sat down for dinner to enjoy a Booth favourite, home-produced pork, but they had a bit of a shock. 'We found .22 pellets in the pig's skin,' confirms Arrowsmith. Vets and the police were called, and Linklater lost his gun licence.

Booth was as divisive a figure as can be imagined. Some thought him egotistical and childish. Many others, particularly those who didn't know him well, saw him merely as bumbling and decadent – an eccentric force to be tolerated for the cash he brought to the town. If those outside his orbit affected to take his political enthusiasms seriously, it was often with a sense of indulging a child out of touch with the real world. For many, his tendency daily to fire off 'crackpot' ideas invalidated him as a serious thinker, let alone as a visionary to be followed.

Hope, though, was far more than a mere companion. 'She saw a very different side of Richard from what most of us saw,' says one Hay associate. She saw him as he wanted the world to see him. 'Hope worshipped him as a great man, for the real essence of the bloke,' says Greg Coombes. 'She wanted him to have the space to concentrate on the important things, and he was looking for the people who would join him in turning the world on its head. She saw that as a true use of his talents.'

The cementing of this influence was born soon after Booth and Hope began their relationship, when an American visitor, riding with Booth in the Black Mountains above Hay, began talking about the Sioux tribe in South Dakota, where the visitor owned a ranch. She said they were making trouble for the local authorities, claiming Dakota's Black Hills were their spiritual home and discouraging tourists. For Booth, the comparison with the hills – 'my sacred territory' – on which they were riding, which extended even to the epithet 'black', was too obvious to miss, given his complaints about the Tourist Board, the Forestry Commission and the Welsh Water Authority.

'Knowing Hope would be interested, I plucked up courage and asked her to accompany me there,' he wrote. Soon afterwards, the pair jumped on a plane and were heading for Rapid City, South Dakota, sixteen hours from London. They visited the site of Wounded Knee, where in 1890 Big Foot and two hundred indigenous people were killed by US troops. More recently Wounded Knee was being exploited as a tourist site largely for the benefit of outsiders, so nine years earlier Native Americans and their supporters had taken over the town, burned down the tourist museum and held besieging government forces at bay for over nine weeks.

The couple then visited Yellow Thunder Camp, site of a further protest where indigenous people were defying both three thousand troops and attempts to buy off the protesters' sacred lands. Booth wrote sympathetically and movingly about their visit and was clearly inspired by their leader, the charismatic Russell Means.

'We became friends for whom speech was unnecessary,' wrote Booth. 'Henceforth I imagined myself as a Welsh American Indian. We shared the same thoughts on every issue ... The ethics of a leisure society are an insult to the traditional life of a Native American. Tourism was an offensive smokescreen behind which powerful commerce could operate effectively. "We live in an age of brochure culture," I said. Russell laughed and agreed.'

Means visited the UK on a tour of universities and Hope accompanied Booth to hear him speak in Manchester, Bristol and Cambridge, and she was not merely indulging his interest. He wrote: 'Like a mother defending her child, Hope defended the traditional ideals and beliefs of the Native Americans. Our visit to Yellow Thunder Camp brought us together and was the beginning of a relationship that was to last the rest of my life.'

While those seeking an ulterior motive will speculate as to whether Booth's public spiritedness was genuine or merely badly disguised egotism (or, more likely, both), it is undeniable that he did not appreciate incursions on his standing as top dog in Hay. In his mind the council was for small fry, the quangos were dull, interfering nobodies, and Leon Morelli was a pale and crooked imitation of himself, undeserving of the public esteem that both men sought. And, notwithstanding his apparent unselfconsciousness and lack of vanity over his personal appearance, he very much wanted to be well regarded, if only by his own lights. Not unusually, he wanted the respect of those he admired, and, with reason, wanted to be acknowledged as the man who made Hay famous. Which is why he regarded anything 'not invented here' with suspicion. So the chances of a book festival mooted by someone outside his camp finding favour with Booth were thin.

In fact he had talked about doing something similar himself. Nearly a quarter of a century earlier, he had told a BBC Wales interviewer: 'I see it as even more crowded than Stratford. I see people flocking in the streets, I see that we could have a book weekend here and perhaps run busloads of people down from London, call it a book express and they'd come to Hay-on-Wye.' And in 1975 he had talked of a 'book fair' in Hay as a way of bolstering his finances.

The life and times of the Hay Festival would make a

fascinating examination elsewhere. Its chief begetter was Norman Florence, a former actor and theatrical manager who had moved to the area in the mid-1980s, his wife Rhoda Lewis having played Mrs Venables in the BBC TV adaptation of Francis Kilvert's diaries a few years earlier. Florence had originally planned to create a festival in Ipswich, where he had been running the theatre. Charles Dickens, George Crabbe, H. Rider Haggard and others had all left a mark there. Florence had worked on a Shakespeare festival at Bankside for Sam Wanamaker in 1969/70. His mother was a big fan of the National Eisteddfod and Florence's son Peter had performed at the Cheltenham Literature Festival in the early 1980s. A friend recalls Florence senior saying simply: 'Hay is a town of books, what it needs is a book festival.' Others discussed the idea with him and for one reason or another drifted away, so it was the Florence family that came to be identified with the festival.

The Florences spoke to as many people in Hay as they could. There was a degree of enthusiasm, but uncertainty as to how involved Booth would be. They tried to make contact with him, but he was hard to get hold of. 'There was a wary scepticism among the locals who had known Richard for a long time and had dealings with him about working with him on a new project that was independent,' recalls Peter Florence, who succeeded his father as the festival's director. Eventually John Grant, owner of Hay's long-established newsagent and a highly respected local figure, and Norman and Peter Florence managed to meet Booth at the Castle.

'Richard was quite animated and entertaining, but a little hard to understand,' remembers Florence. 'He wanted it to be called the Richard Booth Festival of the Second-Hand Book, to hold it only on 1 April every year to commemorate independence day, and for it not to include any living authors. We agreed that we were probably on different tracks and parted quite amicably.'

Those who know Booth well insist his demand would have been delivered with a whimsical giggle and little expectation of success. He wanted his due – to be recognised for what he had created – and for the festival to play to the strengths that had brought prosperity to Hay, rather than those of the new book trade. 'Why should the town promote new books that it does not stock?' he asked later, though Hay did have a shop selling new books at the time. More to the point, he said, was that new books in themselves would not bring in book buyers all year round when they could be bought on any high street in the country, whereas Hay's second-hand books were a proven attraction.

Talking of the 'natural integrity of the second-hand book trade', he said inexpensive, high-quality literature will always sell, and the festival was in itself nothing to do with literature. 'Shakespeare, Molière and Tolstoy are immortal compared to low-quality literature which may achieve a quarter of a million sales.' 'He was incandescent,' remembers Ivor Windsor. 'This is where the ego came in ... why should this interloper be pissing on his patch?'

In December 1987 it was announced that the first festival would be held in April the following year. Norman Florence was to be the artistic director and Brian Battin, mayor of Hay, its chairman. Simon Callow, Prunella Scales and Julian Glover were to perform (with others yet to be named), and a request for 'Friends of the Festival' was made.

The festival went well, boosted by a small army of local volunteers anxious to do their bit for the new venture, but Booth – his ego consciously unstroked by the Florences – was having none of it. He wrote an A4 leaflet ridiculing the organisers, sponsors and performers and making unfounded allegations of sharp practice by the organisers. Margaret Drabble, a former guest of Booth, was dismissed as 'Margaret Dribble', and he mocked a number of local notables. Two festival ticket sellers told *Haywire*, in admirably temperate language, that it was 'wicked of Mr Booth to say the things he did. If he knew the hard work that went on behind the scenes by volunteers he would blush with shame!'

Hugh Muirhead, husband of one of the co-organisers, wrote an even more furious denunciation of Booth, launching a personal attack on his motives. 'Booth,' he wrote, 'previously thought by me to be an extremely amiable, eccentric poseur, with a taste for buffoonery, has proved to be a mischief-making, malicious character and no friend of those who are community conscious in a practical way: a way, I fear, he will never be able to emulate, unless he learns how to stop carping, complaining, knocking and protesting. The whining of a "barber's cat" in alleyways, doorways and dark corners of bars has never been an attractive sound.'

The Florence family responded initially with silence, seeing Booth's behaviour as demeaning and speaking for itself. Ever keen for a reaction, Booth seems to have been enraged even more. The festival, he said, was exploiting Hay's workforce while leaving its people uninvolved in its events. 'Who is this Norman Florence?' he said. 'He has bedazzled many old dears into thousands of hours' voluntary service for his own benefit. Through his mysterious machinations he has created a self-perpetuating clique of "director" who, having used Hay as their launching pad, give no account of their spoils. Are these spoils being transferred to a Swiss bank? WHAT IS GOING ON? WHY DO THE PEOPLE OF HAY FEEL THEY ARE NO PART OF THIS FESTIVAL?'

The mayor Brian Battin replied: 'Booth has upset so many bodies and councils that they will not have anything to do with him. They have given him grants and he has done nothing with them. He criticised the festival before it even started. Now he is going about slandering Mr Florence, suggesting that he has run off with the whole £24,000, which includes grants. It is preposterous!'

Any hope that this pitiful squabbling might die away vanished when the *Sunday Times*, owned by Rupert Murdoch ('I simply distrust everything he does,' said Booth), announced it was to give £10,000 in sponsorship to the festival the following year. The speakers included P. D. James, Ruth Rendell, Ian McEwan, Mary Wesley, Julian Barnes, Michael Holroyd, David Hare, Beryl Bainbridge and Heathcote Williams, all at the time at, or near, the height of their powers and sellers of large numbers of books. It was an undeniably remarkable step forward in just the second year in operation, but the looming spectre of Rupert Murdoch fed the sense that big money was taking over.

Booth continued to protest that the festival was not popular with local people. This was true, in that the number of Hay inhabitants who attended was not great. But when asked, local shopkeepers, pub landlords and hoteliers expressed delight. The sense remained that the festival schedule did not contain enough 'for local people', a cry that has long persisted. 'I am open to suggestions,' said Norman Florence.

When the Florences did come out of their tent, or perhaps their sponsored marquee, they wondered why he regarded doing something for the town as the prerogative of Booth alone. Their early contact with him had been unfortunate. Booth agreed to sell twenty tickets for the festival at £2.50 at the front desk of the Limited. They sold quickly, but the £50 they raised disappeared. 'What is the matter with the man?' asked

Norman Florence. 'Why does he want to destroy this beautiful "happening"?'

Booth grumbled that the Florences were not revealing how much their performers were being paid, complaining – in the face of the evidence – that other festivals did (and do) so. Booth even informed the police, who took away the accounts book, returning it soon afterwards and taking no action. Booth also got up an anti-festival petition among the town's booksellers.

Some admitted they had signed it just to shut Booth up but his nose for a popular grievance was not baseless. He touched on a feeling that retains a resonance today for literary festivals both in Hay and elsewhere. Alan Halsey, who ran the poetry bookshop, was miffed that the Florences had shown little regard for those who had made Hay popular. 'There was little or no consultation with the booksellers,' Halsey told the *Independent*. 'I think in all sincerity they thought the festival would benefit everyone. I don't think it occurred to them we'd see it in a different way. That's what really annoyed people, that they used Hay, the Town of Books.' Peter Florence's reply was not conclusive: 'This is not a festival for boosting the book trade. It's a celebration for the way people use words. Selling books is not important to the general populace.'

Booth put it about among his supporters that he was excluded from the festival, which is a very Boothian way of saying he excluded himself, because its organisers had a different vision from his. If he was trying to get a reaction, it didn't work. After the festival had been going for a couple of years, Peter Florence said he had never spoken to Booth, and by that time, and long before, Booth had made plain his dislike of what the Florences were doing. (He called Peter Florence 'Little Napoleon'.) Looking back, Florence now says: 'We put the low-level hostility of the first few years down to what people in Hay affectionately call "Richard being Richard". We all took it in a knockabout spirit. Richard always had a knack for what would make him a media story.'

Nonetheless, the anti-festival campaigners continued with Neapolitan-style laments for the heartless rejection of their leader, the man who had done so much for the town. By the third year, though, the festival was indeed boosting the book trade, and, like it or not, was pulling in people of the standing of John Pilger, Arthur Miller (who famously asked: 'Hay-on-Wye – is that some kind of sandwich?'), Jonathan Miller, Melvyn Bragg, Germaine Greer, Jan Morris and Enoch Powell.

But Booth's resistance was as firm as ever. 'There's a nasty atmosphere developing in Hay,' wrote two book dealers in *Haywire*. 'Booth knows this festival thing is big. It's bigger than he thought it would be and he can't control it, it's all beyond his control . . . Booth is trying to make the whole town adopt a pro-Booth, anti-festival attitude.' To that end, he tried to organise a topless chainsaw competition, but ditched the idea for lack of contestants. But he did organise a team of people with chainsaws to rev them up in order to make a poetry recital inaudible, and would drive round tooting his horn near the performers' tents. 'Honestly, he's just like a baby who can't have his own way – with his nappy round his knees.'

For all the hostility, it was unavoidable that there should be some collaboration. (One friend of Booth told him that if he really wanted no overlap, he should close his shops during festival time.) At that time the Castle was playing host to a Booth antiquarian bookshop on the ground floor, specialising in Native American books – reflecting one of Hope's enthusiasms – as well as a variety of markets, where local producers and Hay's more alternative crowd could sell their wares. The Castle garden was made available for various events, and for many years Giffords Circus would perform there.

In 1991 the festival sold over twenty thousand tickets and was clearly not going to go away. The presence of the festival allowed Booth a soapbox from which to complain about supermarkets, Leon Morelli, the Welsh Development Board and Tourist Authority, the state of Cusop Dingle and much else. His friends thought he was out on a limb. 'I shouldn't bother too much about the festival,' said Frank English, speaking for many of those with Booth's interests at heart, in 1992 shortly before he died of throat cancer. It was remarkable English had lasted as long as he did, such was the damage he had inflicted on his liver. Some saw English – master carpenter, polymath, wit, drunk – as the real genius behind the Booth business, and certainly Booth valued his opinion very highly. In London he moved in sophisticated circles, but his leanings were irresistibly low life.

Booth has been described as homophilic, and he was admirably understanding of the stigma that was attached to homosexuality. Frank English was gay, and for his entire life engaging in homosexual acts with those under twenty-one was illegal. In his eyes, though, impressionable and vulnerable young men in pubs were fair game. He was rather more menacing than a forgiving and light-hearted 'older man' caricature of the time allowed. Those who knew to steer clear of him were free to guardedly enjoy his caustic humour from afar, treating him as 'just Frank'. To some he was helping young men discover their true sexuality; to others he was merely predatory and disgusting. One or two of his targets just punched him on the jaw. Others succumbed, sometimes to the distress and anger of their relations. Booth's instinct in almost all matters was, in modern parlance, to be 'non-judgemental'.

Among mainstream bookshop opinion, English is regarded merely as 'a character', a singular adornment to the Booth circus. He was almost always paid in cash, prompting a constant sense of frustration from the authorities. On one occasion, he got wind that the Inland Revenue were in town looking for him, having been told he liked a drink. At lunchtime, when the Wheatsheaf pub was moderately busy, they saw a man matching English's description drinking at the bar. English denied all knowledge, but assured them he would give them a hand. English accompanied the taxman round the Booth bookshops asking: 'This gentleman is here from the Revenue. Has anyone seen Frank English?' His colleagues didn't let him down.

His drinking habit was to bedevil his later days, and a friend reports that he used to see pink elephants coming up through the floorboards: 'He was up all night nailing up the holes.' Booth claimed that Marianne Faithfull's haunting song 'Broken English' was written with him in mind, though there is scant evidence.

Meanwhile, the haphazard expansionism continued. Despite the financial pressures, Booth continued to offer a protective arm around those he liked. Rosie Hayles and her daughter occupied a large house in the middle of Hay. Her story is typical of the human, kind Booth, who admired Rosie's straight-dealing and judgement, but it also manifested the flawed paternalism he showed some of those he encouraged.

He liked Rosie very much and in 1990 suggested she use some of the spare space in the house for a shop, where she could sell some cookery books he had bought in the US. In fact there weren't that many, and they were largely unsellable, the recipes American-aligned and measured in cups and so on. They agreed to use the rest of the shop for selling children's books, and to the fury of his existing employees in that department, Booth, having found a new best friend, cleaned out his own shop to stock Rosie's.

Stung by criticism from his established employees, Booth's attention then reverted to his original children's department, which was assiduously restocked while Rosie's new venture was ignored. She had no choice but to do the restocking herself, punctiliously keeping records and running a tight ship. His neglect gave her the opportunity to make a necessary move and learn the trade. After a year, most of the stock was hers.

She was grateful for the start he had given her, but when she told him he should stop paying her wages, he was extremely hurt. 'I think he saw it as a lack of loyalty,' says Rosie. 'He may also have thought I had been stealing his stock, which in fact I was completely scrupulous about, or perhaps I was the latest example of people who found him impossible to work with so they set up on their own. I would have worked for him for ever. I had never been self-employed but I had little choice. It had become impossible working for him.'

16

An Exportable Model?

'Hay as a book town has had an astonishing economic effect on its region.'

Professor Tony Seaton

The Booth bookshops continued to be a subject of international interest, and a feeling had been growing that Hay's experience might be a blueprint for the development of 'book towns' elsewhere. The first by some distance – in the early 1980s – to seize the idea was Redu in the Ardennes, where Noël Anselot, a former oil executive, had set up the first of thirty bookshops. Anselot acknowledged that Booth had taught him everything, referring to him as his 'father'. One day in the late 1980s, Booth reports in his autobiography, he received a call from Michel Brabant, a French businessman who owned several printing presses in Montolieu, a small town near Carcassonne in the south of France. Brabant, alarmed at the town's dwindling population and the probable closure of the local school, wanted Booth's advice as to how to create a book town. Booth contacted the French-speaking Anselot and they agreed to make the trip.

Hope accompanied them on the sleeper train from Brussels,

but she woke up in agony, with kidney trouble. The emergency cord was pulled and Hope was rushed from the train on a stretcher to Montauban hospital outside Toulouse. The hospital was not equipped to deal with her problem, so she was moved – by now with a life-threatening condition – to Toulouse hospital, said to have the largest kidney unit in Europe. 'I remember speaking to Richard on the phone at the time,' remembers Vera Taylor, one of the witnesses at the couple's wedding. 'He was *so* worried.'

Hope recovered and Booth was able to resume his trip. Montolieu did indeed metamorphose into a book town, and Booth even opened his own bookshop, Librairie Booth, there in 1989. He and Hope funded the venture entirely, paying for a shop assistant (whose early months there were quiet, allowing her to weave the wool from her goats on a loom).

Anselot followed suit and opened his own shop, but all the time, Booth recalls, there were differing views as to how the town should develop. Anselot and others wanted to 'let people in different parts of the world do it in their own way', whereas Booth wanted his shop to provide a lead, and for the town itself – with Italy and Spain so close at hand – to be the home of the world's first truly international book town. Anselot, a man no less confident of his opinions than Booth, placed books themselves on a pedestal, ideally with local subsidies helping to keep them there. For Booth, what was important was the sustainability of the rural community and the maintenance of traditions. In 1992 Hope's daughter Lucia opened the Café du Livre, and soon the restaurant and book-shop expanded to become a writer's hotel, the International Inkwell, later written about in the *New York Times*. Here again was the Boothian 'if you build it, people will come' determination. The financial and emotional input provided the crucial foundation of Montolieu – *village du livre* – which continues to flourish.

Miep Van Duin from the Netherlands has been a bookseller in Redu since the early 1990s. She remembers Booth fondly, for his humour, his reading and remarkable memory. Her first visit to Hay was in 1992, when, she recalls, the town crier led a formal procession through Hay to mark the visit of six distinguished guests from Hay's Belgian counterpart. Booth didn't want to take part in any formal march and stood on the sidelines, but then, she remembers with a chuckle, 'Hope ordered him to join in.' Later that evening, at dinner at Brynmelyn, Booth found himself less than entertained by his guests and fell asleep at his own table. Gamely, Hope decided the show must go on, asking Miep's husband Jan to carve.

Countless entries in his diaries begin 'up at 5.00 a.m.', 'drove to Sheffield before breakfast' or 'up early to drive to Bradford then Bristol'. This may explain an intolerance of long dinner parties and a tendency to nod off, which particularly annoyed fellow town council members. The drive to 'do things' remained strong, and over the next few years Booth enjoyed invitations to towns on both sides of the Atlantic to explain how they might emulate Hay. He was never paid, but was always received rapturously. Sometimes his opinions were accepted. At others a differing, local view prevailed.

Bécherel in Brittany and Bredevoort in the Netherlands were on the agenda, the difference between his and Anselot's views becoming ever more apparent. It emerged that Anselot was rather more obviously financially self-interested than Booth, possibly with a view to investing in property. 'If a book doesn't sell, it's not economic,' said Anselot. Booth's view was that book towns do not have to be commercially based in order to succeed. 'Non-commercial activity has its own virtues.' He continued:

'Making myself a king has definitely been a loss-making activity. Nevertheless, looking back on the time when I was not a king, I feel it is justified.'

Booth wanted specialist shops, and suggested, for example, every book town should have a special collection. So one might be a major centre for, say, flower arranging, with another majoring on lighthouses or cricket.

Saint-Pierre-de-Clages in the Swiss canton of Valais was added to the list of book towns, but again Booth and Anselot disagreed. The Belgian wanted small shops and a book fair; Booth said the town needed the stimulus of a mega-shop. Fontenoy-la-Joûte, in Lorraine, was another, but once again the influence of Anselot was clear. Booth regarded his inability to speak French as the chief impediment to the acceptance of his ideas. His faith ever in folk wisdom, he mentions how men in a local bar contemplated him solitarily pouring a Ricard. 'I think they saw me as a victim of the French Establishment,' he wrote.

Stillwater, Minnesota, also had book town aspirations, but any comparison with Hay was misleading. It was already a large town containing thousands of books, many of them bought or sold by Booth to his friend Tom Loome, by now back home. Nevada City and Grass Valley in California were the subject of a successful visit, though it is hard not to conclude, reading Booth's autobiography, that every trip where Anselot was absent was more successful in Booth's eyes.

Norway's Fjærland joined the roster in 1995, followed by Wünsdorf-Waldstadt, a town in formerly communist East Germany, though the latter failed to be given the stamp of officialdom as a German book town, which to the seditious Booth was a badge of honour. As had happened throughout his career, he had countless positive and well-intentioned ideas for how the town might develop a specialism or unique selling point, though once again – as he put it – 'my convictions were not shared'.

Book towns seemed to be booming. As Tony Seaton, a lecturer in tourism at the University of Strathclyde, put it, 'far from being a lightweight venture, Hay as a book town has had an astonishing economic effect on its region and, to some extent, Wales'.

The late 1990s brought a number of changes to Booth's life. In 1995, he gave up drinking for several months in the hope of improving a waning sense of balance. He was unable to stand on one leg and was deaf in one ear. A chance meeting with one of Hope's relations led to diagnosis of a huge acoustic neuroma (brain tumour) behind his left ear. Though the tumour was benign, it was so large and inaccessible that the chances of him surviving two seven-hour operations – one to open up and calm the brain, the second to remove the tumour – were 50/50.

He did survive, evidently due to the skill of Professor Bell of the Atkinson Morley Hospital in Wimbledon, who he praises to the skies in his book. He needed several weeks of recuperation, and the operation left a mark on his physical appearance, his face now lopsided and suggesting that he had had a stroke. He had also had a major prostate problem which required an extended stay in hospital. He was eventually discharged, though needed a walking stick thereafter.

This brush with mortality would have slowed up most people. As 1998 and his sixtieth birthday approached, he might have considered his work done. When he opened the first bookshop, there were two places to stay in Hay. Now there were more than a hundred berths and thirty-nine bookshops, but the fire in his belly burned as strong as ever. In 1997 he had voted Labour for the first time in his life. The change in national politics offered a new opportunity for him to bend politicians' ears about the corruption of local government. But diplomacy, magnanimity and sharing the credit were never his strong suits. He was displeased when in the same year his former alumnus Noël Anselot was awarded the *Légion d'honneur* by the French government. Jess Gill, whose grandmother was Booth's aunt, wrote to President Mitterrand, pointing out that as the begetter of the first book town, her Uncle Richard should have been given the award instead. It was conceded that he was indeed the 'grandfather' of book towns, but the award would nonetheless go to Anselot. Invited on French TV to expand on this, he asked Gill, a fluent French speaker, to convey the strength of his anger. He knew enough French to realise that she, seeking to protect him, was not giving full vent to his feelings. So in order to make a mark he recited what he knew of the sex life of Marilyn Monroe, in his poor French.

He lobbied with his distinctive vim and passion for Dalmellington, in East Ayrshire, Scotland, to be given the status of book town. He said it was more deserving and in greater need than Wigtown, which overlooks the Solway Firth, where bookshops were already well established, and which eventually triumphed. Typically, he could not help criticising the decision, which he regarded as a stitch-up and which ended his friendship with Noël Anselot. The judges' choice, he said, was based on conventional tourist-trade thinking. 'Together they disregarded my thirty-five years of practical experience,' he wrote. He retained an association with Dalmellington and accepted the use of three factories rent-free from the local authority.

The twenty-first anniversary of the declaration of independence in 1998 was an opportunity for his supporters to pay yet further homage, declaring they wanted him crowned 'Emperor

of all the World's Book Towns'. A banquet for fifty was held at
the Castle. At the end of the meal, Booth, dressed all in white,
rose to make a speech not of basking self-congratulation but of
fury at the bulldozing of half a mile of ancient hedgerow and
the use of council land for a million-pound property development, agreed without proper democratic oversight, he said.
This was not a man to go gentle. 'Democracy is best protected
by royalty,' he announced. A rain-sodden coronation followed,
with the town crier praising 'a thriving, vibrant town, and
undoubtedly the world centre of the second-hand book trade,
all due to his foresight and industry'. With the town at that
point boasting three dozen second-hand bookshops, there was
not much disagreement.

He banged the drum for rural revival as loudly as ever.
Socialism was something he had long denigrated. In 1998 he
opposed the introduction of the minimum wage but that did
not prevent him standing as a candidate for the Socialist Labour
Party in the 1999 Welsh Assembly elections. In language not
often heard on left-wing platforms, he announced: 'The only
way to revive the rural economy is to bring back animals
and peasants, not make phoney publicity stories about job
opportunities.'

But perhaps his most spectacular change of heart was towards
the Hay Festival. His publicity gene had previously worked
overtime, leading to denunciation of the 'Rent-a-Literati' and
production of 'Arts, Farts and Tarts' T-shirts. The volte-face
was all the more remarkable given how wounded he felt at the
time of its inauguration. Not only had it not been his idea – or
at least not in its eventual form – but despite his extraordinary
contribution to the town's prosperity, it was almost as if the festival organisers were embarrassed by him. Many of his friends
remain angry about this.

While purportedly acknowledging his importance, Kate Hadley feels, the organisers took advantage of him. 'He let himself be ripped off by Hay Festival people swanking around being condescending and that hurt him quite badly. He allowed himself to be mocked, in that he would be invited to cocktail parties when they had celebrities there, because he was Richard Booth, and his presence would underwrite the festival, but they would be mocking him at the same time. It was really horrible.' This would doubtless be denied by the festival organisers and allowance should be made for the sensitivity of a close friend, but it was not the show of regard and gratitude to which Booth's supporters felt he was entitled.

In 2001, in the biggest coup of Peter Florence's time in charge, former US president Bill Clinton spoke at the festival. In a phrase that became famous, Clinton referred to it as a Woodstock of the mind, adding 'a town with one bookstore for every thirty-two people is all right by me'. Booth was invited to meet the former president, and told him of a curious coincidence. One Hay visitor, film director Stephen Weeks, had been browsing in one of his shops recently and picked up an ex-library copy of *Life on the English Manor: A Study of Peasant Conditions 1150–1400*. Weeks paid a pound for it. Previously it had been had taken out from the Arkansas Seminary library, from which the book had been purchased. There was only one previous reader. His name was Bill Clinton. The former president's reaction is not recorded, but Booth is said to have been moved on by a security person. Booth cannot have been best pleased, either, by Clinton referring to Hay as having been 'created by its festival and thirty-four booksellers'.

Not only did he feel a sense of personal affront at the festival's independence from him and its reluctance to embrace his beliefs, he also felt strongly about its dependence on big-business sponsorship, which represented the sort of commercialism inimical to his vision of a second-hand economy that might one day lead to a green economy and 'trickle tourism'. And many of Hay's shopkeepers, whom Booth had sought to represent, felt that since 2006, when the festival rented a greenfield site down Brecon Road, it was of even less benefit to the town itself.

It seems it was Ivor Windsor who eventually persuaded him to bury the hatchet. 'I told him, entirely between him and me, that if you can't beat them, join them. The Castle was in a dilapidated state but it could be a very imposing backdrop for festival events and this thing was here to stay. It was going to be in his interests to have an accord with whatever was going on, and all it was doing was making Richard look small-minded.'

It helped, of course, that Booth had his own book, an autobiography published in 1999, to promote. It had been many years in the preparation, and he was able to call upon the help of Hope's daughter Lucia to impose some sort of order on it and complete it.

In *My Kingdom of Books*, he puts his about-turn in part down to accepting festival organiser Peter Florence as being an honest man. There was a sting in the tail, of course, though of the pots and kettles variety. 'Only an honest man would have driven ahead in his desire to promote it with so little tact,' he wrote. His hope was of linking the festival's success with that of the book towns. He was not to know that while one was growing, the other, as we have seen, was heading in the opposite direction.

Anybody who thought Booth, having reached his seventh decade, might lose his vim was mistaken. The hostility to Morelli was unrelenting. Morelli, never less than a controversial figure, said in 1998 ... 'I can't think why Richard has to personalise things so. I have nothing but respect for Richard. From the time I arrived here, he is the man who made Hay what it is. But he is eccentric.'

He continued to preside over the Limited, a site of sentimental importance to Hay, having been the venue for countless agricultural sales and only recently the home of Robert Williams Ltd, for long an indispensable hardware store. The Limited retained a Boothish sense of clutter, notwithstanding Hope's dogged if not always popular attempts to bring order.

But cash flow remained a problem, and rumours of thieving persisted. On one occasion in the late 1990s, a number of science fiction books went missing from the Limited. They disappeared while Violet Jenkins – previously co-owner of the Mason's Arms and now with responsibility for that section – was on duty. The finger of suspicion was pointed at her. It seemed unlikely she was the culprit, given her family's long and loyal service and friendship with Booth, but that had been said of others and turned out to be true. Given that there seemed no other credible candidate, one day, when Booth was away, she was dismissed.

'Mum was devastated,' remembers her daughter Sue, who now works at the Limited under its current ownership and is, like her parents, a standard-bearer of what longstanding locals refer to as 'old Hay' – quiet, unshowy, unassuming decency. Vi's son Kelvyn remonstrated with Booth when he returned: 'She's the most loyal person you've got working for you, and you know it.' Booth agreed that was true. She was as straight as they come. 'Get Violet back here,' said Booth. 'She works here as long as she likes.'

It was an unfortunate episode from which everybody learned. The person who had ordered the dismissal was Julie Peacock, who had been hired, like so many before her, to introduce more rigour to the business, though in her case the mandate was much stronger than for previous incumbents.

Understandably, like a potentate who seeks foreign successes when domestic ones are becoming scarcer, Booth continued spreading the word abroad about the glories of Hay and its successful formula. But he saw no mileage in sharing the limelight with his colleagues in Hay. One day in 1997, Chris Arden, who owned a shop and was chairman of the Hay Association of Booksellers, happened to be in Bredevoort. He was about to return home. As he was saying goodbye Miep Van Duin said, 'See you next week.' Arden was thrown by this. Why would that be, he asked?

The notion of book towns had become widely known – both Redu and Bredevoort were claiming over three hundred thousand visitors a year – and the Western Norway Research Institute had been given nearly half a million pounds of European Union funds to foster international collaboration between them. Arden and another bookseller, Mark Westwood (also chairman of Hay's Chamber of Commerce), had no idea it was holding its inaugural meeting at the Castle in Hay. The organisers had intended for the 'European Book Town Network – a Telematics Application based on a Model for Sustainable Rural Development based on Cultural Heritage' (in other words, an intranet for second-hand booksellers) to include a variety of shops from each book town, but Booth had omitted to tell any of his approximately three dozen fellow booksellers in Hay.

There was £80,000 in funding at stake, which Booth had no intention of dividing up. The scheme's project manager, Norwegian Ingjerd Skogseid, does not remember the details, but insists all his expenses had to be accounted for, and he was required to provide matching funding. It was the sort of bureaucracy he found unbearable, but evidently the rewards made it worthwhile.

Specifically, according to the International Organisation of Book Towns (IOB), the plan 'proved to be very useful for the partners from the book towns to get acquainted with the then new telematics, and with each other. In the beginning hardly anybody ... used other means of communication than letter, telephone or sometimes fax. However, in the space of two years, the booksellers became familiar with the use of the internet for personal contact, publicity and book selling.'

The shorthand belief in Hay was that the money should have been spent on computers – and wasn't. There seems to have been no benefit from the EU money, and certainly none outside the Booth bookshops. An irate Mark Westwood challenged Booth as to why, when the very intention was to improve communication between shops, the other Hay shops had been excluded. Booth even tried to pretend that some of the money had been shared between Hay's other booksellers, asking Anne Brichto and Derek Addyman if, in case someone came in and asked, they would lie, by confirming that the computers they were working on had been provided by EEC funding.

It was true that Booth had spent many multiples of that figure on Hay. It was also true, though, that it occurred to no one else that the money should not be shared. Hope Booth remembers the frustrating amount of red tape involved in their dealings with the Norwegian outfit, but agreed that her husband was 'not very good at sharing'.

It was not the last time the organisers would have to spell out the rules for Booth. As in Hay, where he would buttonhole people to proselytise about the possibilities for international book towns, he would constantly speak about items not on the agenda, and in the end had to have a time limit imposed on his interventions.

Such formal, legalistic stipulations went against the grain, but he did accept the time limit. One of his problems was an admirable one: over-enthusiasm. For example, he would constantly badger the Norwegians, pointing out there were more of their compatriots in Minnesota, Wisconsin, Iowa and the Dakotas than in Norway, so they should export more to the States.

Booth's book town counterparts found him frustrating, but they acknowledged his importance to the book town movement, his good intentions and his humanity. In July 2000 at the final project meeting of the Norway-based project, held during the Second International Book Town Festival in Mühlbeck–Friedersdorf (Germany), Booth was made honorary president of the newly formed International Organisation of Book Towns, registered in April 2001. The IOB was to have an executive committee to handle policy, with Booth presiding (rather than executing) from 'upstairs'.

The friction between Booth and Westwood was to get worse. In March 2002, a meeting of a different organisation, European Booktowns, was held at Montmorillon, near Poitiers. Booth was not invited but the Chamber of Commerce, of which Booth was not a member, was asked to send a representative. This pushed Booth over the edge, prompting him to ban Westwood from his shops. Westwood wrote to him a few months later, pointing out that they had been friends for twenty-five years and 'it is clear your betrayal of this friendship derives from my attendance [at Montmorillon]'. He accused Booth of slander and libel, of concealing information from other Hay booksellers to prevent them having involvement in the book town movement and of behaviour at odds with the aims and spirit of the movement and with his position as honorary president of the IOB.

None of these claims appear to have been denied. The

following year, he put up notices around Hay announcing a tea party at which the public execution of 'three scoundrels' was to be discussed. He proposed that over 'delicious morello cherry sandwiches' (charge: £2.00) the people of Hay should decide which method of execution should be applied to Westwood and two other men, with whom he was in dispute over the questionable award of a grant.

The wife of one of the other two men did not think this a laughing matter. As a result, Westwood half seriously alerted the police, suggesting this was an incitement to murder and an offence under the 1861 Offences Against the Person Act. In the event he was cautioned under the Harassment Act. Booth agreed to lift the ban on Westwood entering his shops, but the next time he appeared he showered his opponent with abuse in front of staff and customers.

The internet took an almighty toll on second-hand book-shops in two broad respects. Now everything was available online, and the chances of picking up a bargain plummeted. The uncertainty and latitude that went with the pricing of books also went out of the window. In the new age, both sellers and buyers knew too much – they could consult a personal computer, latterly a smartphone, as to the value of a given title. The edge had come off specialisation, affecting book towns and second-hand shops more generally.

But the other effect was a threat to books themselves. The ability to download a book electronically onto a lightweight device like a Kindle was seen at one time as a threat even to new books. Was this the end of the printed page? This new develop-ment might save many trees but kill any number of bookshops.

In any event, it was not good news for book towns. 'In Belgium and France the impact of the internet took a while longer to be felt,' says Miep Van Duin, 'but you felt the German and English speakers were spending less and less. Then you had the 2008 financial crisis, and since then trade has gone backwards ... The lesson is that it is not what Richard gave us in particular but what that time gave us. We have to move along with the changing of the time.'

Reg Clark, one of Booth's most loyal supporters, says his boss's commitment to book towns was, paradoxically, not entirely beneficial to his own kingdom: 'My own view is that Richard's efforts to promote his vision of the book town worldwide, whilst undoubtedly benefiting declining economies in other countries, ended up rather diluting the uniqueness of Hay.'

17

The Open Road

'Richard was always a welcome guest. Sometimes very tiring, but we also laughed a lot.'

Werner Borchert, Wünsdorf bookseller

For Booth himself, though, his travels gave his ambitions a sense of universal relevance. 'The book town thing gave him a sense of being needed and wanted again ... he'd been rather sidelined, by the coming of the Hay Festival and the arrival of Morelli's money,' says Clark. 'Now, as president of the International Organisation of Book Towns, Richard was lauded once again internationally.' In Paju Book City in Korea, he was welcomed like a pop star and in Malaysia he was interviewed in full regalia on national TV.

Despite deteriorating health which now required him to use a walking stick at all times, in the early 2000s Booth continued to fly the flag. His judgement was not flawless, though.

A discharged prisoner came to him and Booth was pleased to be able to offer him a chance to cultivate an interest in criminology, doing deals with a college in New York. Booth later caught the man reverting to type by stealing books to sell on the side, which quite amused him.

Less easy to laugh off was the denouement of the attempt to create a book town in Blaenavon, a run-down mining town thirty miles south of Hay. The town could not sustain the interest and optimism first generated by local subsidies, which had enabled ten bookshops – stocked largely with the overflow from Booth's Hay bookshops – to open simultaneously in properties provided with council help. Booth's main partner in the venture was a charming businessman, with enthusiasm comparable to Booth's own, called James Hanna. He had sold what might then have been called 'soft porn' in Hay, complemented by vivid descriptions written by Hanna himself. This should have sounded alarm bells, but the essentially liberal, or libertarian ethos – where 'smut' used to be sold alongside serious feminist tracts – meant that any signals went ignored. Hanna turned out to be a much worse man than he had seemed, not staying long in Blaenavon and returning to his native USA where he committed rape and child pornography offences. In 2013 he was sentenced to two sixty-year prison sentences.

Come rain or shine, though, Booth's belief in the power of books was undimmed. Though Margaret Drabble had found him uninterested in literature, and antiquarian booksellers questioned the depth of his knowledge in their field, he remained a keen reader. He would have a pile of books by his bed, and would have three or four on the go at once, always on top of the contents of each of them. 'He read books on the life of plants, or aquatic resources,' says Hope. 'Anything might take his fancy. He could talk to you about the history of Kellogg's if you wanted.' He disapproved of two books in particular. One was the memoir of Conservative politician Peter Walker, later Baron Walker of Worcester, which enraged Booth for its glossing over of the author's early 'corporate raider' (often asset-stripping) dealings with the controversial Jim Slater. The other was one he singled out from a genre with which Booth had reluctantly become familiar on his travels. He loathed business books which celebrate entrepreneurial brilliance. 'I have seen them in airport bookshops all over the world and no lower form of literature exists,' he wrote in his autobiography. 'If you wanted to condemn me to hell, you could do so with twenty copies of Donald Trump's *The Art of the Deal*.' He enjoyed crime fiction, particularly Ed McBain, but his favourite genre was non-fiction about serial killers.

He travelled as much as he was able, accompanied by a driver and minder. One of them, Colin Stark, would be given a list of dos and don'ts (no drinking, no smoking, a shower every day, etc.) by the ever-vigilant Hope. They travelled to many book towns in Europe. (One airport security officer, having seen Booth's orb and sceptre on the X-ray machine, referred to Booth, apparently in all seriousness, as 'Your Majesty'.) Even at pensionable age, the naughty adolescent was not dormant. When in Mundal in Norway, for the opening of their book town, he ran a German flag up the pole. 'We didn't half cop it, particularly from the older people,' remembers Stark. And, also in Mundal, Stark left Booth alone for a few minutes, warning him 'if anything happens I'll get a bollocking from Hope'. Booth allowed himself to be led astray by his hosts for a quick drink. 'I said, "You stupid mad bastard, don't you ever do that again."' Like a cowering cur, he'd say, "Sorry, Starky".'

In latter years, others who also took the role of 'tour manager' (driver, carer, companion, book packer), both in the UK and abroad, were Mike Price, a carpenter by trade who worked for Booth for sixteen years, from Hay, and Booth's great-niece Jess Gill. Price remembers turning up at Brynmelyn at five o'clock one morning and having to roll the car down the hill, to avoid the ignition waking Hope. He also recalls the strictures as to what Booth was permitted to do, given his frailty and need for medication. He had a favourite cigar shop in Saratoga, New York state, but sometimes Hope would confiscate any purchases on his return. (One box ended up as a Christmas present for their gardener.) Price tried to prevent him drinking, but occasionally he would sneak out to a liquor store for a bottle of whisky, which never ended well.

Jess Gill, a veteran of trips to South Korea, Malaysia, East Germany and the US (six times), decided there was no point in a blanket ban on fun, and agreed to institute a quota. He would be allowed two cigars, two whiskies and a glass of red wine a day, but even this was not guaranteed to prevent mayhem. When enthusiasm overtook him, he would be inclined to jump out of the car before it had stopped moving. On another, while supposedly advising on the best route through Nebraska, he allowed his cigar ash to drop onto the maps at his feet. After the car filled with smoke, Jess brought in a ban on smoking in the car.

His co-travellers remember him with nothing but fondness, his days on the road possibly being those of maximum fulfilment, affability and escapism, even in his late years. 'He was good as gold with me,' says Mike Price, who on one US trip drove him six thousand miles in sixteen days. 'He was such a nice man when we were out on the road.' There was constant laughter and incident in the search for more books. It was his liberation.

Being his minder was not a job everyone would have wanted. 'He was very imposing, an important figure,' says Stark. 'Once I travelled with him, I didn't want to stop. He knew how far he could push me, and I knew how far he'd go, and we never had a row. I knew that if we had fallen out, who was going to look after him? His wife had given me the responsibility of looking after him and I had to fulfil that.'

In Wünsdorf, the couple struggled to make themselves understood. Their German was limited to Stark's 'tiefer, tiefer, tiefer' and 'wir haben einen Wassereinbruch' ('deeper, deeper, deeper' and 'we have a leak') acquired from a rich familiarity with *Das Boot*, the film about life on a wartime U-boat. Typically, Booth's personality was sufficient to overcome this unfortunate evocation of the Nazi era. His interest in military history, and the fact that the Kaiser, Hitler and the Russians had all been militarily active in Wünsdorf, gave him common cause with Werner Borchert, who headed Wünsdorf's book town aspirations. Borchert says Booth was always keen to visit German gardens including Sanssouci (Frederick the Great's summer palace) and Bad Muskau.

'He used to say, "You East Germans are the best Germans,"' remembers Borchert. 'He was a volcano, full of character and ideas, but he also had idealistic hopes about the cooperation of book cities with different languages. He wanted to send us thousands of books in English. It took a while for him to understand that there was no market for it here. Richard's trademark, in addition to his wonderful laugh, is of course the stick. He once walked through one of our used bookstores with this stick and used it to sweep books off the shelves that he thought had no chance of being sold. Richard was always a welcome guest. Sometimes very tiring, but we also laughed a lot.'

Borchert agrees that the internet has brought havoc to the book town movement. In the last twenty-five years, Wünsdorf has lost half its booksellers. 'In the internet generation it is really very difficult to make money with old books. We are fighting it, but for how long?'

The book town flame still burns bright in some parts of the world. Jess Gill travelled extensively with Booth, and he was treated almost like the royalty he aspired to be. Her conclusion as to their uneven record is that book towns need an individual with a certain drive to sustain a town's focus on the importance of second-hand books – in short, they needed their own Richard Booth. 'Very often, they couldn't replicate Hay because they couldn't replicate Richard.'

Booth's commitment to bookselling remained strong. A local book dealer, Andrew Morton, whom Booth would cheerfully refer to as 'cuntface', noticed that Booth had put a warehouse on Forest Road, just outside Hay, on the market. Nominally the price was £125,000. 'I knew that Richard had recently bought the BBC library, and that it was at least four times bigger than he realised, so he needed the space to store the books,' says Morton. But he also knew that Booth always liked a quick deal. He pressed all the right buttons, offering Booth a good deal less than the asking price, and that Booth could keep his books there for a year. It did the trick. Booth accepted. What's more, contrary to the expectation of some, he moved his books out on the dot one year later.

There had been changes of venue in the previous four decades, and Hope was striving mightily and protectively to put things in order, but the prevailing ethos remained undisciplined. His bookselling base camp remained the Limited, which retained the promise of offering an unexpected treat. Bruce Robinson had a particular fondness for the Limited. In the early 2000s he began the research for his acclaimed book about Jack the Ripper, and Booth would encourage him to rootle among the Victorian periodicals on the top floors. 'He'd say go and fuck off up there, there's nothing but a dead rat,' says Robinson. 'It was amazing, like a great library. It was like mining gold.' He admits that on occasion if he thought something was over-priced he would rub out the price and take it to the desk.

He remembers one employee 'like the fat boy, from *Pickwick Papers*', who used to love burning books. 'He'd say, "Argh, that'll burn real good, them, they'll burn good!"' He remembers spotting a first edition of *Dracula*, in the original cloth. 'Even then it would have been worth £150 or £200, and he was going to burn it. I said, "You can't burn that, it's a really rare book." He said, "Oh, is it?" And he shoved it under his coat and that was the end of *Dracula*. God knows what happened to that when the book changed hands.'

Booth's enthusiasm remained for a sale, almost regardless. 'The price didn't matter to him. It was a bit like Thomas Edison's indifference to money. He was very weird. I remember I wanted to buy four volumes of *Who Was Who*, which had been published in the 1950s, and went right back into the Victorian era. I asked Richard what he wanted for them. "I don't fucking know," he said. "Give us a fucking fiver." The woman who worked for him nearly fainted. They could have got a hundred quid.'

Hope, who when it came to money was as economical as her husband was incautious, knew that if the sums were not adding up it needed to be remedied. This did not mean she saw bad faith at every turn, more that she was inclined to challenge Booth's laissez-faire attitude and willingness to let favouritism impede the haphazard pursuit of professionalism at the Limited. Even the trimmed-back Booth enterprise was struggling and costs needed to be cut yet further. The business was not sustainable.

The most notable casualty of this approach was Cotters. A

true aesthete, he had worked for Booth for getting on for four decades and had not only added an extraordinary degree of expertise to the Booth operation but his eccentricity, enthusiasm and engaging manner lent a distinctive air to a visit to the shops.

Cotters and Hope had never got on. When she arrived in Hay, he – already by then one of the longest serving members of staff – felt understandably proprietorial about how best to mitigate and manage Booth's excesses. She, on the other hand, could see the chaotic way things were proceeding and knew change was needed. The question was, who was to make the change? Many managers, accountants, lawyers and directors had tried without success to steer Booth towards discipline and moderation. The arrival of Hope at Booth's side, emphatically not someone to trifle with, was never going to go unnoticed. One Booth-watcher later described the implicit tussle between Cotters and Hope as 'the battle for Richard's soul'.

With the writing on the wall about the direction the business was taking, Cotters's services were dispensed with. It was a 'ravens leaving the Tower' moment. Cotters's employment with Booth extended back to the pioneering, expansionist days; he was the only bookselling employee left from that era.

His departure remains an area of some sensitivity and opacity, which Booth sought to mitigate by writing him several warm, kind and heartfelt letters citing his financial straits. Cotters, with his warmth and humour, was an engaging and knowledgeable point of contact within the old Booth empire and Booth, after taking advice, undoubtedly felt conflicted about losing his best-read staffer.

Also surplus to requirements was Mike Price, who had worked for Booth as a driver and odd-job man for sixteen years. Booth refused to pay him any redundancy money. Price sought help from an employment expert who turned up at a meeting with Booth. If he didn't pay up, she said, he would be taken to court, which would cost him twice as much. Booth admitted defeat, and told her darkly: 'You have just broken off a good relationship.' In fact, the relationship survived, after the redundancy was paid, Price expressing willingness to take his former boss on another US trip (which never materialised). He continues to speak warmly of him.

It is tempting to wonder what might have happened had Hope appeared on the scene ten years earlier. Though not universally loved by those who knew Booth before she arrived, her resolution, discipline and sense of order were among the qualities her husband's business needed, yet in the end even she was unable to prevent its demise.

Personally, by general agreement, Hope was good for Booth who, an old Hay friend says, was essentially a little lonely and in need of such love. His relationship with his surviving sisters improved considerably as a result of Hope's influence. 'She was very good at nurturing him in the ever-changing world,' says Ivor Windsor. A former Booth employee, and not a great admirer of Hope, says: 'Booth did love Hope. It is also true that when he was ninety-nine per cent bust she used her credit cards to rescue him. His relationship with Hope was easily the best ... And Hope definitely loved Booth, which made him happy.'

Certainly neither of Booth's previous wives would have been equipped to harness and redirect his quixotic management style. Elizabeth was always inclined more towards family life and Vicky, as can be seen in her life after Booth, was to develop in directions unimaginable of his first and third wife. At one point while she and Booth were arguing about whether to get divorced – his mind was already fixed – Vicky said dramatically that she wanted them 'to die together', i.e. for them to never to separate. How either ever thought they might last more than a few months together remains a mystery. Had Vicky's entrapment by drugs not been so sad, it would have been comical. Both married believing the other would make them rich. Both were wrong.

The very existence of Vicky (aka Tola) as Richard's second wife is known about by a diminishing number of people. The marriage was brief and tempestuous. Knowledge of what happened to her subsequently is known by fewer still. It is an extraordinary story.

After she and Booth were legally divorced in February 1977, she moved out of Hay, living latterly on the edge of the Black Mountains. Drugs continued to be a central feature of her bohemian life, and she was moving among musicians who shared her habits. Among them was Jim Capaldi, of Traffic, whose links to Birmingham and his native Evesham remained strong. Another Eveshamite musician was Gordon Jackson, a songwriter who owned a leather shop with another Traffic acolyte, Mick Baulch, in the town to supplement his income

Don Carless, the Birmingham businessman who had helped put Traffic together, used to drop in, as did Dickie Moule, editor of *Haywire*, who, fatefully, eventually introduced Carless to Vicky.

They began a relationship, her friends relieved that after the trauma of her time with Booth she had seemingly fallen for someone better attuned to her needs. Carless had also owned coffee shops, an antique shop and other small businesses, but, as we have seen, his entrepreneurial skills did not end there. If Vicky had ever contemplated getting off drugs, Carless, himself in their grip, was unlikely to help.

He was also attracting the attention of the police. On one occasion, after Vicky had asked Don to supply five hundred tabs of LSD, he left them on a prominent table in his antique shop, where they were spotted by an undercover policeman. It led to the first of several convictions.

At that point Vicky showed little sign of wanting to change, continuing to take drugs as copiously as her birdlike frame would allow. And her left-wing leanings were still well to the fore. She launched a plan with some anarchist Catalan friends to contaminate the Barcelona city water supply with LSD, though it never came to fruition. She used cocaine extensively, as did others in that circle. One of them, Traffic's flautist Chris Wood, fell into a serious state of addiction.

In the winter of 1978, Vicky, just turned forty, learned she was pregnant. What might have been a culminating moment of domestic happiness was shockingly undermined when, days before the baby's birth, the father, Carless, was again arrested and charged with supplying cocaine. Quite apart from the child's birth, this was to be the start of an even more chaotic few years.

It was clear to Vicky that motherhood and hard drugs – mostly cocaine and LSD – would be an unhappy mix. The baby, a boy named Guy, was born in May 1979 with an amphetamine/cocaine withdrawal problem, for which he needed urgent treatment, and which brought Vicky to the attention of social services. Why was this baby born with an addiction, they demanded.

Carless was sent to prison. He was given compassionate day release to visit Vicky and young Guy, then just eight months old. He had not the slightest intention of returning to prison after his day release. Instead, having arranged to have a fake passport created in the name of Hugh Lynch, during his 'day out' he told Vicky to go with their young son and meet him in Barcelona. With his forged passport he then drove through France to be reunited with Vicky and his son. They were on the run in Spain for six months, Carless shunning photographs and staying away from any form of officialdom. His in-laws in the Canaries wanted nothing to do with them, and eventually, when drunk in Cadiz in southern Spain, he revealed his real name and was arrested. He spent time in prison in Cadiz before being returned to the UK.

Carless's involvement in drugs had extended well beyond providing the occasional bit of weekend recreation for Birmingham's young music fans. He had visited Afghanistan with a gang and was on a percentage of the profit from smuggling heroin to the UK. He used a house owned by his mother Connie as the stash house, where several tons were stored. The police had caught up with his involvement and in September 1982 he was sentenced to six years in prison.

On his release, he returned to live either with or next door to Vicky. He had been addicted to heroin since a 1974 trip to India, and one day he passed out when he was at home, alone upstairs, only to come round as a fire was blazing in the sitting room below. He escaped but went back into the house to rescue a box of jewellery and was trapped. Two passers-by managed to drag him out, but he had received 90 per cent burns and was paralysed as a result. He lived on, mostly in a wheelchair, for another eighteen years, occupying himself with his art and enjoying Jim Capaldi's occasional returns to his native UK, always an opportunity to enjoy some high jinks with an old friend. His musician friends – Capaldi and Steve Winwood and others – rallied round, playing the odd charity gig for him, but it was an unhappy final few years. Carless died aged seventy-eight in 2002.

Vicky, from whom Carless had separated in the 1980s but with whom close contact was maintained, found more steadiness in motherhood than might have been suggested by her turbulent first four decades. She continued to practise yoga and lived a more measured, spiritual life than before. She was, says her son Guy, now in his mid-forties, 'a wonderful mother, a very spiritual person . . . she and I looked after one another. To me she was absolutely not a rebel on a disaster road.' She taught autistic children for some years, never seeking to make money out of it. 'She was never a victim in that she was always cool, following her own path.'

He says he never had any sense that Vicky harboured bad feelings towards Booth. 'She might have felt a bit in the lurch initially, but I don't think she was hanging around waiting to get back together. I don't think she was really hurt by it . . . she just went off and did her own things. She held him in high regard right up to the end of her life, and they were always super friendly with one another and happy whenever they happened to be in contact.'

In her previous, Hay years, he acknowledges, she had been more than a handful.

I feel sorry for Richard, to tell you the truth, having to deal with that, this crazy Canaries woman. She had chosen the crazy hippy path. She smoked a lot of marijuana, for the escapism. It was a wacky time and those two were two massive people, doing their own thing and really going for it. I think they found in each other things they admired and liked in themselves. She was very beautiful, very stylish, very much ahead of her time in terms of women's liberation. Women are very much independent these days, they are not held back like they used to be, and I feel she was very much on the early curve of that, for single-minded women not being pigeonholed by men, or a career or anything ... she was wild and wacky but very strong-minded in insisting on doing her own thing.

You have to understand the risks she took ... I could never understand how she could leave a level of luxury and comfort and go off and do her own thing ... because in Birmingham we did not live in luxury, we went through a lot of hard times ... but she valued the freedom of being able to do her own thing more than anything ... When I heard Vicky had chucked Marianne Faithfull's suitcases out of the Castle because she thought Richard was having an affair, I thought, Fair play, Mum, because Marianne Faithfull ain't no one to mess about with. My mum would have felt, What the hell? Good on her. That said, it was all a bit too much for Richard. At that time in her life, he wasn't really exciting enough for her.

Asked if it might have been his mother who put LSD in the elderflower wine at one of Richard Booth's parties, he said: 'That sounds like my mum.'

Booth always spoke fondly and regretfully of Vicky later in life. They remained in infrequent contact. After she died, in 2018, Booth was in touch with Guy, by then a DJ, speaking very warmly and offering to try and fix up gigs for him at universities where he had contacts.

Would Booth have liked to have had children? As on so many Booth-related questions, the world is divided. 'We should all be grateful he didn't have children,' says one close friend and admirer. 'He would have been a maniac of a father. A friend says, "Either have a baby or be a baby", and he needed to be a baby.' If he had a vasectomy, as some claim on the basis of no discernible evidence, 'it was one of the most appropriate things he ever did,' said one former colleague. More credible is that he was infertile. 'He just wanted to have lots of sex,' says the same friend. 'He wanted to be the only child in the relationship with his wife. He wanted to have all that attention.'

Around the age of forty, though, he showed signs of wanting children, but it never happened. By general agreement, he was an exceptionally supportive stepfather to Hope's children Lucia and Orlando, and showed great fondness for his blood relatives. His relationship with younger children was very different from those he displayed in the 1960s and 1970s. Generally, children were not his thing, but when it came to the offspring of those close to him, he was as sweet and gentle as could be.

Kate Hadley remembers him showing far more tenderness than many would have believed. 'When I took Thomas [her son] down some years later, Richard and [a colleague] spent hours on consecutive days teaching him to walk, across the hall at Brynmelyn between them, both with arms outstretched as he toddled across and fell into them. 'Come on, boy, you can do it. Oh, good boy.' Richard's face was illuminated by such a vast, tender smile. And when Tom was unwell in the night he came and sat up with me and helped nurse him, getting bottles, nappies and such, and me tea.' Others speak of his kindness in hamming up the role of King with young children – bestowing knighthoods on them and so on – not that he didn't normally enjoy the part.

Though he would not have wanted to admit it, some of his attitudes did soften – including his attitude to the Church – the most striking example being his acceptance in 2004 of an MBE. 'This is a tremendous honour,' he said, 'especially because

I have taken a radical position in the past. I was surprised and delighted because they don't normally give things like this to people like me.' By way of levelling the score, Buckingham Palace saw fit to award an MBE to Peter Florence the following year.

Epilogue

The further injection of cash into the town by Leon Morelli and the success of the Hay Festival should have added to the prestige with which Richard Booth was regarded. Yet he was unable to enjoy the blooming of these other flowers, and if anything he is less well known as a result of them. They enhanced Hay's fame and prosperity in one way or another, but they were not much to his liking, and going with the flow was not in his nature.

Probably the most painful loss in the stripping away of Booth's assets was the sale of the Limited in 2007. For nearly a quarter of a century, since he sold the Cinema bookshop, he had presided over the large, cavernous three-storey building in the heart of Hay, sustaining the type of ramshackle but promise-laden shop that had made his reputation in the late 1960s.

But the Limited was losing money, too. Booth's enthusiasm was still there, but the flesh was weak. He was tired, the internet was asking new questions of every second-hand shop in the world and, even without proper heating or sanitation, the overheads were considerable.

The forefathers of Oregon-born businesswoman Elizabeth Haycox had migrated to the US from Ludlow, an hour north of Hay, and she and her investment manager husband Paul Greatpatch came close to buying a second home there. Then the couple become regular visitors to Hay in 2002, infected like so many by the festival bug and the hope of picking up the odd book bargain. Three or four years later, they noticed that the Limited bookshop was for sale. Undeterred by the cold and damp, the mustiness, the poor quality of the stock and the continuing unprofitability of the shop, they saw possibilities, but it meant effectively starting from scratch.

Given Booth's resistance to new books – he used to say 'new books are for the ego, second-hand books are for the intellect' – there was an irony in the fact that the couple used Powell's bookshop in Portland, Oregon, as their blueprint. It had managed to make a success of selling both new and, in US parlance, used books under one vast roof, and she and her husband hoped this might work elsewhere. In 2007 they paid a million pounds for the Limited and, on advice from a Powell's expert, £100,000 for the second-hand stock (half what Booth had been asking). A condition – theirs – of the sale was that the building should bear his name, and that no other shop in the town should do so.

The million pounds was intended to be used to secure the future of the Castle, still the Booth flagship, but still in a state of disrepair and in danger of becoming a white elephant – privately owned, soaring above the centre of Hay but in need of serious investment.

The Haycox/Greatpatch team managed to turn the Limited around. Their time in charge didn't begin well. On arriving in the shop, they were told by a member of staff that there was 'a rat in the basement, and it's *not quite dead*'. Things could only improve after that. The place was blitzed, and in time a café and a small cinema were opened, the shop's interior spruced up – and better lit – but the intended essence of the shop, as a cornucopia of almost any book you could ever want, was retained.

The relief to the Booth coffers was to prove short-lived. He continued to owe money to the banks, and the Castle remained an enormous drain. For decades he had borne the costs it provoked. Where some criticised him for allowing it to become run-down and by now in need of a huge refurbishment, he prided himself on shouldering the job of patching it up. He was the one who nearly fifty years earlier had taken the responsibility, on behalf of the town, for its upkeep, haphazard though that was. Who else, after all, would be willing to do so? Selling it had always been unthinkable. Hope was more aware than anyone of what it meant to her husband. It had been the great enabler, allowing Booth to play the King in the centre of town. Symbolically its sale would be the end. Plus, he was still enjoying it. 'People thought he was incredibly rich because he owned the Castle,' says Hope, 'and he used to be a bit naughty, saying, "I've got a rotting castle in Hay, do come and stay", and my heart would sink.' But the Castle heating was no good and the whole thing was a hassle. 'Then one night the estate agent came and he said to Richard: "You can't keep both. You have to sell either Brynmelyn or the Castle. Which is it to be?" Richard thought about it for a bit and said, "The Castle."'

The Haycox/Greatpatch revamping of the Limited led to yet more ambitious thoughts. Maybe, with the help of public money, they could turn the Castle into rather more of an agreeable tourist hub than it had been hitherto? They had considered making an offer for the Castle before, to use as a place to live, but it was too public and didn't feel right as a home. Nonetheless, they saw its potential both as a historic site and as a meeting place. Plans were hatched, feasibility studies launched, banks consulted, and a huge new look for the Castle emerged.

'Bloody hell!' said Booth, as he encountered Paul Golding, a shop owner acquaintance in Hay. 'Some stupid arse has just given me two million for the Castle.' A little graceless, perhaps, but his delight was understandable. Whereas thirty years earlier the sale of the Castle would to him have been ludicrous – though Penelope Betjeman was one of several people who encouraged it – things had changed enormously. He was over seventy, his mark on Hay was clear and, as ever, he needed the money. His beloved Brynmelyn was in urgent need of repairs which the Castle was making impossible. The fact that two businesspeople and a large state-run quango were teaming up to move him out of the Castle was of not the least concern. Indeed, it was a very amicable handing over.

With the help of around £7 million from the National Heritage Lottery Fund and the initial £2 million of their own, the couple were able to secure the future of the Castle. Though some architectural purists are not entirely happy, the result is generally seen as a success, and the Castle is now a true focal point for visitors to Hay. It has a café, a bookshop and it runs cultural events, and most of it is now used by the public to a degree it has never been.

The Castle turned out to be Booth's pension. As with so many businesses, the core assets were the properties, and his efforts in putting Hay on the map had the happy ultimate corollary of fattening his own bank balance. Now Hay's new benefactors were providing the feather-bedding for his retirement. He and Hope bought a house in Marbella to which, for about a decade, they escaped for a month or so to avoid the cold British winters. Although growing frailer and now with the assistance of a carer following a stroke, he retained a sparky sense of humour. Often he and Hope would invite friends to stay at Brynmelyn, or he would venture out, with the help of a wheelchair, sometimes visiting his beloved Llanthony, of whose priory L. T. C. Rolt said 'no building in Britain has so majestical a setting'. He died very peacefully on 20 August 2019 at home in Brynmelyn, aged eighty, with people who loved and cared for him.

The last decades of a life can be melancholic and suffused with disappointment. The high-water mark of Booth's influence had long passed, and the man who made Hay famous was indeed a diminished force. He continued to dream and to look forward, his presence a reminder of an age of expansiveness, humour and fun, his friends protective of his name and his reputation, but the world had moved on. Relations with April Ashley seemed repairable, and when a friend suggested they meet up again, he was not against the idea. It is probably fair to assume both regretted never rebuilding their bridges.

Was that sense of having been eclipsed true of Booth? He had had to sell the Cinema, the Castle, the Limited and Cockcroft House, the cornerstones of his bookselling business. He no longer had a shop in Hay, his latest venture (entitled The King of Hay to avoid breaching the terms of the Limited's sale) having come and gone in no time. The book towns, his blue-print for rural sustainability, were having an indifferent time, and many of his concerns about the viability of country towns remained unanswered. Property prices around Hay reflected the wishes more of visiting outsiders and blow-ins than of locals, and the local environment was denuded by supermarket-driven industrial farming techniques. Hopes for a revival of the horse economy now looked positively flat-earthist. Perhaps most woundingly, rather than being taken seriously as someone with a deep love and commitment to the town, he was patronised by many, who saw him as an egotistical self-publicist, a bit of a joke. They hadn't minded him buying them drinks, though.

Hay has long (possibly pre-Booth) had a tradition of

individuality among its shopkeepers, and now has, for example, a flourishing stationery shop, a hardware store, a delicatessen, a decorative lighting shop and guitar shop. But its fame alone would not in itself have been welcomed by Booth, because Hay is now at risk of being famous for being famous. Many modern-life developments are not unique to Hay, but it has its own variants. The town brings in day-trippers to buy ice creams and knick-knacks as much as books, even if more than twenty bookshops remain. Many 'old Hay' people will tell you they never go into town these days. They are less likely to bump into old friends than they would in the supermarket at the edge of town. The sense of community, still there out of season and out of sight to the casual visitor, is strikingly strong. Hay has a number of mutual help groups and an ethos of good neighbourliness is potent. But it has adapted to accommodate the tourism of the holiday let and the B&B. The sheep and cattle market has closed. There used to be a slaughterhouse on the high street and a handful more nearby. Now there is just one within a twenty-five-mile radius. The landscape – its contours still unwreckably beautiful – has for years been 'kept tidy' and frequently denuded by the nitrogen and pesticides required by supermarkets, cheap imports and an ever-tightening subsidy regime that might have been designed to put environmentalists and farmers – feeling beleaguered and struggling more than ever to turn capital into income – on opposite sides. The mania for cheap food hides poultry concentration camps behind ever-threatened hedgerows, while the overstocking of sheep prevents anything growing on the hillsides, buzz-cutting what should be a biodiverse haven out of existence. Treeless hills can do nothing to save soil and rainwater from crashing downhill towards a River Wye already overwhelmed by being used as an agricultural drain. Less than 2 per cent of the food eaten in

Wales is produced in Wales. The principality has at most half as many birds and butterfly species as it had in the 1970s. Only 0.1 per cent of farmed land in Wales is used for growing fruit and vegetables. Booth would have found all that a profound disappointment.

Nonetheless, melancholia was not part of who he was. His mantra, one ally recalls, was that whatever happens is always for the best. Hope says he was always looking forward, fired by some new-found enthusiasm, often starting the day breezily going downstairs from his bedroom, lustily singing a Rugby school song. His office looked as if the fax machines had exploded, so many plans did he have on the go. In 2012, three decades on, he even put out feelers to see if the then ailing Leon Morelli might agree to sell him back the Cinema, though he didn't have the money to buy it. He would meet friends for lunch and let off steam about the wickedness of Rupert Murdoch.

If he needed consolations, there were plenty. He was supported, and looked after, with remarkable devotion by Hope, who also helped improve his imperfect relationship with his sister Joanna. He had taken a great many people on an amazing adventure. In researching this book, so many people spoke of the debt they owe Booth. Many laughed with him. Many more also laughed *at* his unaffected eccentricities. This, though, is at no cost to their fondness for him or their gratitude to him for the opportunities he gave them and the faith he showed in them, whether it was giving them a start, sending them off for a day's book buying, travelling abroad or simply filling in for his domestic shortcomings.

He hadn't set out to do anything very specific. The bright, unfocused son of privilege got lucky by being inspired, and he changed a small market town into a global brand. It was credited with being the world's largest second-hand bookshop, very much of its time, and as such was an extraordinary thing. He gave the town a specialism that in 1960 no one would have imagined.

It was down to exceptional force of personality, a belief, based in part in a sentimental attachment to Hay and in part to an ego-driven vision of the possibilities of something he had stumbled upon. He was not a genius, and there are aspects of his record that suggest personality disorders that he never learned – or apparently wanted – to hide, for whatever reason. Much of his character appears unformed. A number of people spoke of him as if he was still a young boy, playing at being a king, forever trying on garb from the family dressing-up box. In that world, he is at the centre of his own self-designed fairy tale, where he is the wise and beneficent one, complete with castle, and those who cannot discern his qualities and wish to do him down are thieves, brigands and scurvy knaves.

In his diaries he sometimes imputes motives to people quite unnoticed by his colleagues. And his single-mindedness at times caused needless upset. 'He wasn't a deliberately cruel man,' says Ivor Windsor, 'he was just childishly egocentric. He didn't have normal, ordinary reactions and emotions. He wouldn't have realised how he had upset someone.' Kamma Andersen admires his brilliance, but saw something was missing: 'I don't know if he had the ability to self-reflect on things. Maybe he just func-tioned on a different plane. There was an effective lack of filter.'

His relationship with his father, who built a library at Brynmelyn, is telling. He was a disappointment, in failing to be fit enough or keen enough to join the army, and was so impelled to be his own man that he spurned *any* conventional career. Yet it was books, the interest he shared with his father, that guided his life. Few men escape the conscious or unconscious influence of their fathers, and Booth certainly did not escape his. 'There was not a lot of displaying of love in that family,' says one shrewd Booth-watcher. Critics of old-school parenting say that such fathers put little into their sons and expect a lot back. In short, emotional neglect and high expectation are unlikely to produce happy, balanced sons.

He is open to the charge of being manipulative, and some of those who worked for him were extraordinarily loyal and hardworking, going way beyond what might laughingly be called their job descriptions. The words 'You'll do that, won't you, Pat?' (or Sue, or Andy, or whoever) were often to be heard, his remarkable forgivability always winning the day. Those of whom he was fondest are among the most transparently decent, straightforward and honest people one could encounter. Would he like them just for their malleability? Hardly. He would invite them to the Castle, however socially uncomfortable they might feel, and make a special fuss of them, seating them next to him at dinner, for example, to put them at their ease. In defiance of the blinkered selfishness imputed to him, there could also be a thoughtfulness that his critics probably never saw, whose existence they would doubt.

That was an era of labour relations unrecognisable today, and, as his friends agree, Booth would not have survived long in what he might have called 'wokeworld', but the personal loyalty he inspired in those who lasted the course is exceptional. 'They excused him, they covered for him, they stayed for years with him, they saw what he wanted to do for Hay – it's extraordinary,' says someone with no interest in praising Booth. Look no further than Mike Price – who worked happily for Booth for sixteen years and still adores him despite Booth having to be threatened with court before he would pay his due redundancy.

But where he did try to manipulate, he was not always very good at it. Often, he committed acts seemingly blind to their consequences, again a mark of a childish mind, in the body of a highly intelligent man. The writing of cheques knowing they would bounce is one example. Those who see sociopathy in him would say this is typical: all that mattered to him was getting the deal done. The awkward bit of paying for it was remote, so far down the list of priorities as to not even register. His defenders would say that if he was asked he would have said he had every intention of paying. It just might take a while.

Similarly, the 'Caerleon car story' is more curious than defensible. Val Haynes, one of the few who refused Booth's offers of pub drinks because she knew how much others took advantage of him, remembers a visit to South Wales when he shunted the cars in front and behind to get out of a tight parking space. 'He left a note for the owners saying, in effect, "Sorry for the damage, my fault, Richard, King of Hay", but when one of the drivers arrived at Cockcroft House bearing his note, Richard hid in the office.' It wasn't wise or easily explained. It was 'just Richard'.

Similarly, he would hire people in a burst of enthusiasm, blind to the certainty of a new favourite coming into imminent view. On one occasion he employed someone to run an ecology bookshop. 'The guy in question turned up on the agreed date, having moved to Hay and arranged for his family to follow, and Richard had completely forgotten about it,' remembers a colleague. 'You just hope the guy hadn't burned his bridges elsewhere.'

But when inspiration struck, he ran with it. 'What Richard did was facilitate everybody's hopes of a big dream,' says Kate Hadley, 'He had physical daring and strength and energy to do such out-of-this-world things while holding to a deeply intellectually moral code of thought and curiosity. It was a kind of Whigite bohemian cocktail, a privileged stance laced with both indulgence and abstemiousness.'

His problem was that he was more impresario than business-man, more showman than bean counter. The cavalier had no time for regulation and puritanism. (He loathed Leon Morelli, but refused to join widespread disapproval of Morelli's sexual promiscuity.) The tax authorities were as certain to be inquisitive about his cash-heavy business dealings as a monkey would be by a handbag.

Booth never saw the degree of gratitude to which he felt entitled. Ivor Windsor says: 'He was a great patrician. He really did feel that Hay was his fiefdom and that people should feel that and feel blessed for all the help he has given them.'

Rosie Hayles agrees: 'He was desperate to be well thought of but on his own terms ... he wanted to be popular, he wanted to be King of Hay, in a jokey, fun kind of way. He wanted to be seen as a local, as long as he could be seen as the leader of the locals.' Alex Williams remembers returning after a day's book buying. 'The business was his family, it really was. It was all he thought about. One day when we were driving back, he would say, "We're just approaching the kingdom". He really thought of himself as the leader of the family in Hay.' Delusional or not, he felt it strongly.

He loved Hay and the idea of it being distinct from both England and Wales, a Marcher-lord town where people think the law doesn't apply to them. And with that attitude came the louche behaviour of him and his friends. 'I believe Booth brought a strain of thinking that was positively immoral,' says one senior local. 'That sort of behaviour may be thought sophisticated in London, but not round here.' He brought money to Hay's businesses but for those of a more puritan frame of mind it was accepted guiltily, Hay's successes sometimes being ascribed as much to the character of its people as to Booth's drive.

On the other hand, the presence of the festival compounded the ambivalence in the town towards Booth. As one of Booth's earliest customers, Haydn Pugh, now a successful record-shop owner, puts it: 'The thing that annoys people in the town is when people say, "Where would Hay be without the festival?", as if that is all Hay is, its festival. What they forget is that without Richard Booth there would be no festival, which in the late 1980s arose from Richard having created a new concept, a town of books. Nobody would have heard of Hay otherwise. But now I worry that the festival, with its out-of-town site, seems to be disassociating itself. The journalists and photographers all used to spend time in the town, but the festival seems to be moving further away from what used to be its roots. A lot of people and new businesses do not realise Hay is still successful as a result of Richard Booth's legacy.'

There are too many examples of his extraordinary behaviour to dismiss this cheaply as 'just Richard'. Which psychological category it falls into is beyond the expertise or capacities of this author. It is hard to know how we would react had we been responsible for the death of a passenger. It would presumably be life-changing, and a friend says Booth was deeply affected, yet he showed almost no outward sign to the wider world. Whatever the reason for his failure to make personal contact with the grieving family – shame, a sense that nothing could bring the boy back and that nothing could be gained for him or the family by it, a squeamishness about confrontation, a loyalty to a man he felt was also culpable, who knows? – it surely places him in an exceptional category. Most of us, even if driven only by a fear of 'what people might think', would take some steps to, in modern parlance, 'reach out'. His choice not to do so says a little of his stiff-lipped heritage, but not everything. At one end of the scale, ostentatious empathy is to be avoided, but his willingness to appear impervious to the family's grief is hard to explain. It is taking 'what cannot be cured must be endured' to extremes.

It is all the more remarkable in a man with chameleon-like qualities. He could adapt his version of events according to who was hearing it. He could be what he wanted to be in any circumstance, suggesting an acute and reflexive degree of sensitivity and a capacity to respond as a situation required. Yet so often precisely that sensitivity seems to have been missing – lecturing Miami prostitutes about the Welsh Development Agency, or trying to pass off late payment of an employee's wages as a wedding present. He would cause upset or offence, apparently unaware of having done so, of how he came across. So what happened to the all-seeing, adaptable chameleon? Maybe it only applies in high-focus situations, and Booth was nothing if not single-minded.

One person described him as 'the kindest, gentlest, most sensitive person I have ever met', but to his critics, for all the innocence, he was not a nice man. To them he was selfish and uncaring and, as one shopkeeper who had a lot of contact with him put it, 'a bit of a dick'. Maybe people who achieve things are very often not conventionally 'nice'. Yet there is too much fondness for him – even among those he did not treat well – and too much understanding for what he was trying to do for that to be the end of the story.

There remains no consensus about his personality, but what is beyond question is that Hay would not be what it is today without his determination. His critics say that success was achieved by accident, that he had no altruistic vision to create the world's largest second-hand bookshop – it just happened, the unexpected consequence of an egomaniacal drive. Perhaps, but his impact cannot be denied.

Michael Bowers has no time for Boothist exceptionalism:

Richard Booth always believed that Hay depended upon him whatever he did, and however he did it. To him, the whole thing was a game in which he could write the rules as he went along. He believed he would get away with it; he is still getting away with it. The process of mythologising Richard Booth had begun before I met him. What surprised me was that it continued unabated, initially in the hands of people who should have known better (actually, they did know better), but now through people who know little or nothing about him. I know that it is human to prefer a good story to the truth but, in the case of Richard Booth, the unvarnished truth should be a more compelling story.

Accident or not, with what might be called his 'Fitzcarraldo for farming country', he made a difference. Peter Florence, who was responsible for the festival's greatest years of expansion, offers credit to Booth's role. 'I think it's absolutely true to say that Hay's book town identity owes a core and fond salute to Richard – his vision, his genius for publicity, and his anarchic spirit. His golden years in the seventies and early eighties just sound like fun and adventure, and a really innovative business idea. And every successive generation here moves the story on, sometimes in harmony, sometimes in discord, but always productively.'

Those golden years have indeed gone, but they are worth remembering. Collector Ian Sanger looks back fondly, as many thoughtful book buyers must do:

For a reader or a collector it was a unique, immersive experience to visit Hay. When you arrived after a long day you would think: tomorrow, maybe this evening still, go and take a look. You never know what you may find. The B&Bs, the pubs, the surrounding farmhouses were filled with questers, pilgrims, fanatics. Breakfast conversations, more often monologues while the tea grew cold, might elucidate the bibliography of any field, from anchorites and archery to *Zadig* and Zen.

That so many people with such a variety of interests should make a point of coming to Hay, where there was originally nothing of note to draw them there in hundreds, was an extraordinary phenomenon and achievement.

But the key point is that while the memories are of something different from what we see today, there is a legacy of more than memories. Derek Addyman welcomes the festival, but calls it a once-a-year 'bonus' to an essentially steady business. Certainly there has been rationalising since the days of there being forty bookshops in Hay. Two of its outlets are effectively conglomerates in which a single shop window might display the books of ten or twenty booksellers, who share rates and rent, but apart from those there are still around twenty free-standing bookshops in the town. 'It isn't that after Booth died everything closed down,' says Addyman. 'Not at all. London and the country more widely has lost a lot of its second-hand bookshops, but Booth left a real legacy here. It remains a town of books and a mecca for book buyers. Hay remains sustainable, which was part of the Booth ambition, and the viability can be seen in the fact that new shops keep opening.'

Simon Finch studied at Bristol University in the 1970s and spent a lot of time with book dealer Tony Heath, travelling the West Country and beyond for books. He admits to being a beneficiary of Booth's often chaotic buying in his early days, picking up bargains from the Cinema and selling them on, and he went on to considerable success as a bookshop owner. Booth was unique, he says:

Hay used to be the back of beyond. I'm an enormous fan of Richard, who embodied the spirit of 'build it and people will come'. Richard was absolutely larger than life, a legend in the trade. He wasn't a bibliophile in the finest sense. You wouldn't trust him to catalogue a collection in the way that booksellers like Quaritch or Maggs would, but he was a man who loved bookselling and he made it work. He changed the economy of Hay-on-Wye by saying and doing insane, pretentious things, but he brought a huge amount to the area. The festival wouldn't have landed there had it not been for Richard.

Richard really started something, he was a true, true pioneer. I don't see being a successful entrepreneur as the highest achievement of mankind. I regard contributing to life much higher, and he did that. Of course he had a giant ego and sometimes people didn't get paid because he didn't have any money, but somehow he would scramble through. Of course it was a weakness, but he wasn't setting up a Sainsbury's. He was an inspirational maverick who brought thirty or forty booksellers to Hay, and they came because of what he had created. They would simply not have come without Richard. Was it sustainable? Well, it sustained. Hay is still a town of bookshops. It has changed, it's on the internet now, but a lot of those shops are still going. The Castle is still there. It is still a town of books. I would say his legacy is phenomenal. He was an annoying, ego-driven person, but also a star and a pioneer.

Acknowledgements

An enormous number of people have made this book possible and are owed thanks. Chief among these are Hope Booth, Richard's widow, and her daughter Lucia, who wrote her stepfather Richard's autobiography *My Kingdom of Books* with him. Both Lucia and Hope have been generous with their time and their willingness to allow me to quote from various sources, including the autobiography and Richard's diaries and pamphlets.

They have also been sympathetic, receptive and patient in listening to my tentative thoughts and in correcting some of the wilder stories which Booth's personality provoked. In reading or hearing about parts of the manuscript, they may not have agreed with everything I have written, but they were patient in putting me straight on matters of fact. Joanna Booth, Richard's only surviving sister, was unfailingly helpful in answering my questions, as well as giving me access to the diary her brother wrote when he was just out of university.

Thank you to Hugh Purcell, whose idea it was to pull together a book that stands back from Richard's own, to convey something of the atmosphere that he created. *My Kingdom of Books* was a valuable guide to his life, but it was not exhaustive and, Hugh and I felt, it called for some more detached reporting. This book does seek to be less partisan even if it, too, is not exhaustive. One could continue collecting Richard Booth stories for ever. Also, a number of figures appear as names only, and some not at all. I can think of at least a dozen people of whom it might be said: 'But you've left out so-and-so.'

Several people to whom I spoke have died in the last year or so. Two in particular should be mentioned here. Despite illness, both Val Morgans and Michael Twigge-Molecey went to great trouble and showed candour and kindness in sharing their experiences. Both are much missed in Hay.

Two longstanding friends of Booth, Lennox Money and Ivor Windsor, were extremely generous with their recollections and insights, and a great many Hay booksellers and shopkeepers past and present have contributed. Some asked not to be named. Special mention should be made of Derek Addyman, Lesley Arrowsmith, Steve Ballinger, Anne Brichto, Gerard Brookes, Reg Clark, Greg Coombes, Michael Cottrill, Barry Gibbons, Rosie Hayles, Val and Paul Haynes, Haydn Pugh and Mark Westbrook.

Countless people are entitled to much more than a name-check, but that would probably tax the reader. The contribution of some was huge, in some cases larger than they might like advertised here. In innumerable cases the mere mention of a name is no reflection of the extent of their help or of my debt.

Writing about so prominent a local figure as Booth has been a reminder of the potency of what are called – probably heretically – Chinese whispers. Many stories about him might be deemed 'too good to check' but I have done my best at corroboration. If the flawed part of the grapevine has got the better of me, I hope it is not for lack of effort.

With so much to include, gems and personal favourite anecdotes may have been overlooked – I'm grateful for all and take responsibility for all errors of fact, however generated. Almost everyone I approached was willing to talk, and most of those without stinting, though some asked for no attribution.

Special thanks are due to the ever-encouraging James Gurbutt for getting behind this project. Zoe Gullen at Little, Brown was her usual hawk-eyed and patient self, and Linda Silverman performed her customary miracles with brilliance, charm and humour. They could not have done more to make the birth of this book as painless as possible. Thanks, as ever, are due to my wife Emma and daughters Eleanor and Alice for their tolerance.

Many thanks to:

Kamma Andersen
Fiona Axe
Steve Bainbridge
Oliver Balch
Rebecca Barratt
David Batterham
Mick Baulch
Noelle Beales
Finn Beales
Sue Bell
Rachel Blake
Diana Blunt
Noel Bolingbroke Kent
Joanna Booth
Rupert Boulting
Nick Bourne
Michael Bowers
Werner Borchert
Catherine Boulton

Caroline Bowler
Stacey Bowman
John Boyle
Sally Bradshaw
Andrew Brewer
Scott Brinded
Kate Brotherton-Ratcliffe
Emma Brown
James Burmester
Rachel Buckler
Toby Buckler
William Burr
James Buxton
Anna Capaldi
Phil Capaldi
Roger Capps
Guy Carless
Horatio Clare
Kate Clarke

Lyndy Cooke
Peter Dance
Iwan ap Dafydd
Gwyn Davies
Janice Day
Martin Dearden
Camille de Selys Longchamps
Pierrette de Selys Longchamps
Georgie Downes (now Uxbridge)
Margaret Drabble
Shan Egerton
Richard Emeny
Athene English
Marianne Faithfull
Duncan Fallowell
Mary Ferris
Simon Finch
Peter Florence
Jane Flower
Mari Fforde
Peter Ford
Helen Furnell
Lesley Garner
Jess Gill
Charlie Gilmour
Derek Glashan
Jonnie Golesworthy
Rob Golesworthy
Alex Golesworthy
Mary Golesworthy
Sue Robinson Gooch
Gary Goodman

Robbie Griffiths
Kate Hadley
Marshall Hall
Christopher Hamilton
Mike Harris
Val Harris
Neffy Hensher
Paul and Val Haynes
Jennifer Hitchcox
Peter Horsbrugh
Fiona Howard
Rob Hughes
Lesley Hughes
Jane Hughes
Janet Hughes
Richard Ingrams
Charlie Janson
Sue Jenkins
Kelvyn Jenkins
David Jones
Nicholas Jones-Evans
Brian Lake
Judith Landry
Julia Lawless
Will Laywood
Naomi Levine
Michael Like
Karen Loome
Darren Lynch
Stewart Macindoe
Dawn Madigan
Nic McGegan

Fay Maschler

Peter Milicevic – Mil

Lennox Money and son

Pat Morgan

David, Val and Giles Morgans

Roger Morris

Andrew Morton

Paul Mullard

Alan Nicolls

Sean O'Donoghue

Sir Mark Palmer

Elly Parker

David Parker

Simon Pettifar

Guy Philipps (sic)

Nigel Phillips

Dawn Pitt

Oli Pitt-Booth

David Pryce-Jones

Haydn Pugh

Tim Pugh

Clare Purcell

Hugh Purcell

Sarah Putt

Bruce Robinson

Susie Robinson Gooch

Bernadette Robson

Edina Ronay

Mary Rose

Nick Russell-Pavier

Richard Sachs

Denise Salmon

Roc Sandford

Ian Sanger

Mark Seddon

Kurt Schaffhauser

Willo Shaw

Alice Sherwood

Jan Shivel

Geoff Simkins

Laura Simkins

Ingjerd Skogseid

Ron Smart

Paul and Dundy Smith

Wayne Somers

Gary Spencer

Colin Stark

David Szewczyk

Rita Tait

John Taylor

Crispin Thornton-Jones

Jeff Towns

Tom True

Michael Twigge-Molecey

Miep Van Duin

Anna Van Praagh

Jo Van Praagh

Phil Wajda

Jan Watkins

John Watkins

Christina Watson

Stephen Weeks

Martin Westlake

Evelyn Westwood

Alex Williams

Fr Richard Williams

Valmai Williams

Andrew Wilson

Ivor Windsor

Georganne Young

Michael Zinman

Rob Zohn

Michael Zubal

Image credits

Courtesy of Joanna Booth: 1

Portman Press Bureau/Courtesy of Joanna Booth: 2 (*top*)

Hay Castle: 2 (*bottom left*), 3 (*bottom*), 5 (*top*)

Chris Chapman: 2 (*bottom right*), 6 (*bottom*)

David Parker: 3 (*top*)

Courtesy of Guy Carless: 4

Author's collection: 5 (*bottom*)

Courtesy of Hope Booth/Hay Castle: 6 (*top*)

Courtesy of Hope Booth: 7 (*top*)

Wolverhampton Star: 7 (*bottom*)

Adam Tatton-Reid and Hay Festival: 8

Quotation credits

'Richard Booth Collects Honour', *Hereford Times*, 8 January 2004

'Turning a Welsh Valley into a Utopia for Bookworms', *The Times*,
    20 December 1974.

Richard Booth with Lucia Stuart, *My Kingdom of Books: An
    Autobiography* (Ceredigion: Y Lolfa, 1999)

Duncan Fallowell, *20th Century Characters* (London: Vintage, 1994)

Peter T. Kilborn, 'Richard, King of Book Dealers, Set to Proclaim
    Welsh Kingdom', *New York Times*, 9 November 1976

Ian Marchant, *A Hero for High Times* (London: Jonathan Cape, 2018)

Henrietta Moraes, *Henrietta* (London: Hamish Hamilton, 1994)

Ross Reyburn, 'The Birth of a Mini-Nation', *Birmingham Daily Post*,
    10 January 1977

L. T. C. Rolt, *The Clouded* Mirror (London: Bodley Head, 1955)

Yves St Laurent, 'Meeting with Loulou de La Falaise 1968',
    museeyslparis.com

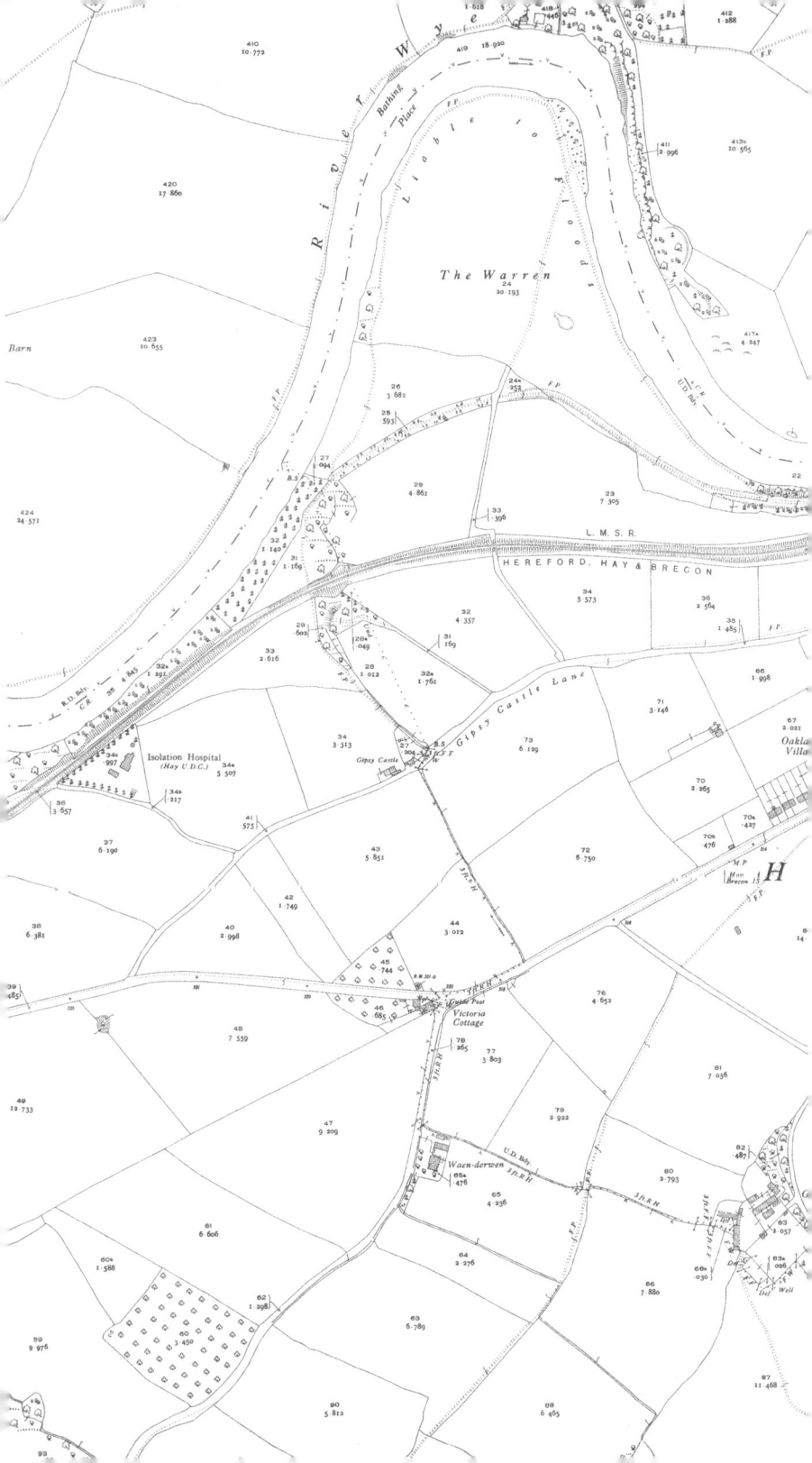